Leviticus

v.

Leviathan

Choosing Our Sovereign

By Wayne B. Holstad, J.D.

ALETHOS PRESS LLC
PO Box 600160
St. Paul, MN 55106
http://www.alethospress.com

LEVITICUS V. LEVIATHAN

ISBN 0-9702509-4-0 Hardcover

http://www.wayneholstad.com

Printed in the United States of America

10 9 8 7 6 5 4 3 2 1

TABLE OF CONTENTS

INTRODUCTION

WILL WE HAVE LAW OR UNFETTERED POWER?

BY DAVE RACER

M innesota's Constitution, like the United States Constitution, is mute as it concerns abortion. Given that, I expected the court to uphold the legislature's ban on funding of abortions. The legislature had a nearly two-decade record of forbidding such funding.

Instead, Hennepin County Attorney Michael Freeman decided to enter the case on the side of the plaintiffs, identified as Gomez. Gomez wanted the state to fund abortions.

As bad as it was for a "neutral" prosecutor to get involved in this manner, even worse was Attorney General Hubert "Skip" Humphrey's stipulation to the court that the state constitution contained a right to abortion. No such thing exists.

As I scratched my head about these matters, I received a call from Wayne Holstad, an attorney whom I had known casually because of Alan Keyes, a 1996 Republican candidate for president. I had served as Keyes' National Campaign Manager, and Wayne had grown interested in Keyes' knowledge, intellect and rhetoric concerning a wide variety of issues. As a result, in 1997 Wayne asked me to arrange a meeting between him and Alan Keyes — they, along with Julie Holstad, met Keyes for lunch in Alexandria, Virginia. As well, Wayne asked me to review a book he had begun to write.

The busyness of life interrupted my review of the book, but when Wayne called me, he also asked if I would be a plaintiff in a lawsuit he planned to bring on behalf of James Tarsney, another Minnesota attorney. Tarsney meant to overturn the Gomez decision, and Wayne offered powerful and unique insights to help him do it. But they failed. The Eighth Circuit Court ruled against them.

I know enough about law that when I read the <u>Gomez</u> decision, I could see it contained numerous fatal flaws. What I lacked in understanding the case was how decades of bad decisions by other courts effected such a tragic finding in Minnesota.

In 2002, I took a run at the Minnesota State Senate, and I also brought Alan Keyes to Minnesota to help me raise money. Wayne and Julie came that day, and brought others. After the campaign, I became curious about Wayne's book and called him. I asked for an updated copy and as I read it, I realized how vital, timely and important a book it is.

At the time, I worked on a true crime book about Andrew Cunanan, the gay spree killer. But I had days away from that work, and asked Wayne if I could help him whip his book into shape. We began slowly sifting and sorting it during April of 2003, and began to aim for completion during the late fall of the year. The more we worked on it, the more I saw how essential had become Wayne's work.

American courts have shown in recent decisions that they are very confused about religious freedom and moral issues.

During 2003, in Alabama, in <u>Glassroth v. Moore</u>, a federal court decided that displaying a Ten Commandments monument in a public building violated the constitution. During the same period of time, a Texas federal appeals court decided that the constitution does *not* bar the public display of a Ten Commandments monument. These decisions closely followed on the heels of yet another Texas case, <u>Lawrence vs. Texas</u>, in which the United States Supreme Court declared that state laws banning sodomy were unconstitutional. Then the Massachusetts Supreme Judicial Court declared in <u>Goodridge v. Department of Public Health</u> that the state must bestow marital benefits on homosexuals and lesbians.

What seems apparent in these recent decisions is that justice has almost nothing to do with our constitution or the wishes of the people, and everything to do with the power the Court has amassed for itself.

Leviticus has been replaced with Leviathan.

James Madison, universally acknowledged as the "Father" of the United States Constitution said, "We have staked the whole of all our political institutions upon the capacity of mankind for self-government, upon the capacity of each and all of us to govern ourselves, to control ourselves, to sustain ourselves according to the Ten Commandments of GOD." According to Leviathan, Madison's utterance was unconstitutional. The carvings of the Ten Commandments above the Supreme Court's bench need to be chiseled out of the wall; the etchings, statues, paintings, murals, ceramics, and mosaics that represent thousands of references to America's Christian heritage, many of them fashioned during the time of the founding fathers, must be expunged because Leviathan has declared them to be unconstitutional.

If you are like me, you sense the absurdity of it all, and ask "Why? How did this happen?" That is why Wayne's book needs to be read, to understand how the Court, conceived as the weakest of the three branches, became the strongest; how Leviathan wrestled power away from the people and turned its back on Leviticus.

Is there an antidote to Leviathan? Oh, yes. Wayne clearly identifies it. Christians, and constitutionalists who do not fear an honest evaluation of history, be ready to have your lives changed.

> — *Dave Racer is an author, columnist, publisher and political consultant.*
> *He was the founding President of The Declaration Foundation.*
> *He is the President and CEO of Alethos Press LLC, and editor of this book.*
> *See http://www.daveracer.com*
> *See http://www.alethospress.com*

To my father, who defined his own concept
of the American Dream, and acted upon it.

Wayne B. Holstad

FOREWORD

BY WAYNE B. HOLSTAD

There are many good books written by well-known legal scholars and historians that discuss the most critical legal issue of our time - the ongoing secularization of American law. Many of these books clearly support the fact that America was established as a Christian nation.

An honest review of history reveals there really is no legitimate dispute that the founding fathers were Christians who wanted to build a government based on Christian principles. Theirs' was the great political experiment that had never before been tried. Arguments to the contrary are simply without merit. The source documents are clear. Too many history teachers have misled us in an effort to convince us that America's first governments were secular in nature.

In 1992, I began leading a class at a local church with no ambition to do anything other than relay what others had already said and published about the subject. I quickly found that I had smart students who asked tough questions, and that drove me deeper into the subject. Since it became obvious to them that we had long since left behind our Christian legal moorings, they wanted to know exactly where and when we went astray. They asked about the theological and philosophical roots of particular legal issues. They wanted to know how the Court should have rendered certain decisions differently from their eventual rulings. During the next three years, I attempted to answer these questions as part of my Sunday lectures.

Much of what I relayed to the class was based on research from my own cases. I saw that those commentators whose work I reviewed as preparation for the teaching sessions were right when they showed us that things were wrong. I also saw that modern judges have a difficult time understanding how the founding fathers' beliefs are still relevant.

It became obvious that the Court's new separation of church and state doctrine is the foundational problem. But to simply criticize the Court, whose members are generally well meaning and as churchgoing as their critics, is shortsighted and simplistic. On the other hand, by simply saying America needs to acknowledge God or remember her Christian heritage also fails to answer the root question.

As an attorney, I pose the issue as a legal question: Which is the controlling factor, the First Amendment or the First Commandment? For instance, there is nothing in the Ten Commandments about diversity, not literally or in the "penumbra."

If God's law means anything, it must be supreme. The Common Law was mostly rooted in God's law. James Madison expressly stated that our constitutional law was to be based upon the Ten Commandments. Sam Adams said that our rights are based upon the New Testament.

Many of the cases in which I have been involved argue that God-given rights be respected — a First Amendment issue — and not mandated. As Christians, we see that our rights draw legitimacy only from our status as individuals created as equals; we see rights that appear contrary to God's law as political, illusory and short-lived.

I learned that the Supreme Court's current definition of separation of church and state is purely political. The rights to speech and beliefs are still fundamental and can be protected in court because of the First Amendment. It is the ability to encourage correct behavior and restrain sinful behavior that is at issue.

And so, after many lessons where I related historical facts and taught legal principles inherent in both the practice and the adjudication of law, I arrived at the conclusions that follow. I hope that you will find them useful as together, we work to preserve liberty for our posterity and ourselves.

Wayne B. Holstad practices law in St. Paul, Minnesota, specializing in title work. He received a B.A. in Economics from the University of Minnesota in 1976, and a J.D. from William Mitchell College of Law in 1980. As a litigator, Wayne has been lead counsel in more than 100 cases as well as an Appeals Attorney before the Minnesota State Supreme and Appeals Courts, and the Federal Eighth Circuit Court of Appeals.

He is a member of the Real Estate Section of the Minnesota State Bar Association, the Antitrust Section of the American Bar Association and the Litigation and Business Law Sections of the International Bar Association.

He has represented low-income criminal defendants for Ramsey County, and asylum cases for the Minnesota Advocates for Human Rights. He serves as an affiliate attorney for the American Center for Law and Justice. He is a member of the board of directors of Lawyers for Life and of the Independent Land Title Association.

CHAPTER 1

SEPARATION OF
CHURCH AND STATE

"Religion is of general and public concern, and on its support depend, in great measure, the peace and good order of government, the safety and happiness of the people.

"By our form of government, the Christian religion is the established religion; and all sects and denominations of Christians are placed upon the same equal footing, and are equally entitled to protection in their religious liberty."

Justice Samuel Chase
Kunkel v. Winemiller (1799)

Christian lawyers are winning first amendment cases. They have carved out a niche. Essentially, Christians have been able to maintain free speech rights in the marketplace of ideas—for now. Unfortunately, even though we have won some battles we are losing the war. The cornerstone principle of law that Divine Law is sovereign, which was understood as fundamental to Common Law and our founding documents, a principle that defined us as a nation, is now anathema. Instead, as lawyers, we litigate as we were taught. We have to ignore the fundamental principles of traditional law, and distance ourselves from the principle of God's sovereignty. To win, we substitute as fundamental law the ideas and politics of the Supreme Court justices who have unilaterally changed everything in law as we knew it, obligating us to follow their new principles under the doctrine of stare decisis.

1

I have litigated many First Amendment and other civil rights cases. I have seen how precarious individual rights are when granted by the court and how difficult justice is to obtain when the court decides to disregard those rights. This is not what the founding fathers believed or intended. It also is a bad idea.

Rights are God-given, not court-given. Justice is a requirement, not a privilege or the result of luck. And truth is not just an opinion limited to a kiosk in the marketplace of ideas; man's interpretation of the law is either consistent with God's law or in conflict with it. The Courts' false separation of church and state doctrine does not really respect speech or religion—nor does it allow the promotion of virtue and the restraint of evil—unless those goals are stated as secular goals and not too clearly consistent with Christianity.

I believe it is essential that Americans, and all lovers of freedom, understand that what comes from God or is contrary to God's law cannot be ignored. God's law is so important that it is nearly not possible to overstate it.

Not all constitutional issues have Biblical solutions. These issues are wide open for political discussion, debates about proper Biblical interpretation and democratic political solutions. The current constitutional problem is that the new separation of state jurisprudence has completely confused the distinction between which issues are fundamental and which issues are political, and we are left wondering what is appropriate for legislation or litigation; we wonder which Biblical issues should be interfered with at all. I believe that Christian principles must be considered—not excluded—when considering the rights of litigants and the wisdom of legislation. And the new amended constitution—created by Judicial order, which no Congressman or state legislature voted on—must be rejected, along with the case precedents that have created so much turmoil and confusion in the law with which we live today.

◆　◆　◆

A quiet revolution has occurred in America. The foundations of American government were laid upon the principles of Christianity. Christian principles in government were common in the Old World at the time of the Declaration of Independence. But no government had ever been conceived upon a set of principles intended to reflect both obedience to Old Testament law and the New Testament principles of equality as taught by Reformation theologians who attacked the principles underlying the church and state establishment in the Old World. The statements in the Declaration of Independence proclaimed, as self-evident truths, that all men are created equal and are endowed by their Creator with inalienable rights, are based on principles unique to a Christian worldview deeply rooted in New Testament theology. Not only were these principles understood and accepted by James Madison, Thomas Jefferson and the remainder of the drafters and signers of the Declaration of Independence, United States Constitution, and Bill of Rights, but it was also understood and accepted that the new government was to be built and made dependent upon these principles. Furthermore, as a republic built upon principles of government by consent of the people, a common understanding and acceptance by all of the people of these principles was a prerequisite to sustaining the American form of government.

This common understanding and acceptance of these original American principles has been lost. It has been lost despite the legal requirement set by the founding fathers that our principles, Constitution and laws must be in writing to be valid, so that they would be understood by all people. It has been lost despite the universal understanding that the Declaration of Independence, Constitution and Bill of Rights incorporated those principles into a binding contract between representatives of government institutions and the people. This social contract, as a legal contract, is a unique characteristic of American law. Modern Americans have no common understanding despite the drafters' efforts to support, justify, document and memorialize their philosophy and understanding of constitutional law keeping extensive records, recollections of the proceedings, deliberations and positions underlying their actions, during their debates and discussed in later correspondence. It has been lost so that a new constitution can be inserted in place of the original—a constitution based on sexual freedom and religious indifference—to justify a new culture.

In recent times, the United States Supreme Court, and advocates of an entirely different philosophy of law rooted in an entirely contrary worldview, have corrupted the written law by either misinterpreting or misunderstanding the principles upon which the American government is based. This corruption of the law depends upon a misinterpretation, or misapplication, of the principles of the separation of church and state. This corruption has succeeded and is currently maintained by a lack of a common understanding of the principles of Christian self-government, from which the term separation of church and state is derived, by the people for whose benefit the government was created. Without a correct understanding of the original meaning of the separation of church and state, the Declaration of Independence

3

cannot be understood and the Constitution and Bill of Rights are susceptible to misinterpretation.

CREATIVE CONFUSION

The confusion about the separation of church and state can be traced to two United States Supreme Court decisions. The first case, Everson v. Board of Education, the New Jersey Bus Law case, was decided on February 10, 1947. The second case, McCollum v. Board of Education, the Illinois Religious Education case, was decided on March 8, 1948.

Everson involved a decision upholding a New Jersey statute that allowed public school buses to be used to transport children to private Catholic schools. The decision to challenge the longstanding view of the separation of church and state in the courts was deliberate. The goal was to change the prohibition against "establishment of religion" to a prohibition against "aid to religion." In a letter dated January 28, 1948, Bishop Oxnam, one of the chief protagonists of the "separation of church and state" and a founder of "Protestants and Other Americans for Separation of Church and State," indicated his support and recommendation to religious leaders that Congress should no longer attempt to amend the Constitution to change the Establishment Clause to an Aid to Religion Clause because there was no hope that Congress could achieve that result. Bishop Oxnam admitted in his letter that he felt the chances were good that the Supreme Court would get the same result by interpreting the Constitution in accordance with the hoped for results.

To reinterpret the Establishment Clause the Supreme Court had to overcome its own history. The Court had to be convinced to not only reinterpret the First Amendment but also reinterpret past case precedents. From 1872 to 1947, there had been five cases upholding the clear meaning of the Establishment Clause. The last case was decided in 1917. Those cases were ignored in favor of directly reinterpreting the positions of Madison and Jefferson. Although the New Jersey statute was upheld in Everson, both the majority and the dissenting opinions set forth a misinterpretation of the Establishment Clause, purportedly based upon writings of Madison and Jefferson, which denied the use of public funds for any sectarian purpose. Over 300 years of legal and political history were swept aside when the Court announced, "This case forces us to determine squarely for the first time what was 'an establishment of religion...in the First Amendment conception.' " Without regard to history and tradition, new rules were announced and a new starting point for Establishment Clause cases was set.

THE BEGINNINGS OF A NEW JURISPRUDENCE

The newly constructed legal analysis of the Establishment Clause was set forth in both the majority and dissenting opinions in Everson, all of which contributed to the opinion in McCollum. In McCollum, the school board in Champaign, Illinois was prohibited by the United States Supreme Court from permitting representatives of religious institutions to enter school premises during a mandatory half-hour time period to teach religious subjects to public school students. McCollum did not include an analysis of political and legal theory. It was based entirely on the analysis set forth in Everson. The principles of Everson and McCollum led to more cases in which the pattern of resting the theory underlying the decision on Everson, rather than the old principles, continues to this day. Recent cases, such as Engel v. Vitale (1963), the school prayer case, and Lee v. Weisman (1992), the prohibition of prayer at the school commencement case, are based on Everson, rather than language of the First Amendment, and have firmly implanted in America a form of secular government. Advocates of this new interpretation of constitutional principles, instituting a totally secular government in which religious truth is not allowed, have also prevailed in the court of public opinion. Modern government officials and citizens alike, struggle with understanding their roles in managing self-government when the original principles necessary to define government have been repudiated.

REDEFINING THE TERMS

The Supreme Court's confusion and the modern misinterpretation are not difficult to understand as long as the fundamental principles of proper church and state roles are understood and addressed. Three questions underlie the debate about the separation of church and state. (1) What is a religion? (2) What is an establishment? (3) What is free exercise? That "The Founding Fathers didn't say" is the common belief held by most Christians. This belief is historically inaccurate and is inconsistent with the Declaration of Independence. The founding fathers were Christians and so were their ideas about government. Original documents and correspondence clearly explain the founding fathers' beliefs and principles. By creating ambiguity, the Supreme Court has been able to apply its own rules of construction and to interpret the terms of the First Amendment in accordance with an entirely different philosophy than that of its drafters. The result is that the rules governing our institutions have been changed. The changes did not occur by

5

amendment, but by misinterpretation.

For the moment, the majority view of the Supreme Court has defined the key terms of our church-state debate as follows: (1) "Establishment" means "aid to religion." (2) "Religion" means "any sincerely held belief." (3) "Free exercise" means "any religious activity that isn't offensive to a compelling government interest." The question of what government interest is not "compelling" is unanswered.

The First Amendment to the United States Constitution is in part as follows:

> "Congress shall make no law respecting an establishment of religion, or prohibiting the free exercise thereof;..."

The founding fathers were good lawyers and skilled draftsmen. They understood law, theology, philosophy and history, and were precise in their observations and citations. Yet, current legal historians must claim that they were vague about the meaning of the term "establishment" and that they really meant to say "aid to religion." This claim of an apparent ambiguity is indispensable to the Supreme Court's analysis of the <u>Everson</u> and <u>McCollum</u> cases in which, for the first time, the Court ruled that aid to religion was unconstitutional. Because they found that the founding fathers were unclear about the meaning of the term "establishment," they inferred the founding fathers' intent and gleaned a new meaning from passages found in James Madison's *Memorial and Remonstrances* and Thomas Jefferson's letter to the Danbury Baptist Church in 1802.

Not many people are aware any more that there is even a debate over the real meaning of the separation of church and state. What is significant is how easily the Supreme Court, and the advocates behind the changing of the old understanding, rewrote the definition of separation of church and state. The change reflected a more "modern" definition that had taken hold on the European continent and was a rejection of over 300 years of English and American history. To revise history, it was first necessary to misinterpret it. The misinterpretation began with a misunderstanding of the writings of Jefferson and Madison. But Jefferson and Madison were not the first persons to consider the issue. Jefferson and Madison wrote in response to particular issues presented in particular legal and political contexts. The <u>Everson</u> court, and most modern constitutional scholars, simply take their words out of context and begin in a new place. In truth, the separation of church and state issue arose in England, long before the <u>Everson</u> court, or even Jefferson and Madison, decided to address the issue for the first time.

SEPARATION OF CHURCH
AND STATE IN THE OLD WORLD

The First Amendment to the United States Constitution is an American political response to a tumultuous period in English history. From the time that Christianity first appeared in northern Europe and throughout the Middle Ages, the church and civil government had been unified under the leadership of the king. Different courts of justice were organized under the control of the king, including those pertaining to ecclesiastical matters.

English Common Law developed during the same time. In their decisions, judges applied principles gleaned from experience, tradition and Scriptures. The wisdom of the church contributed heavily to the development of Common Law. The judges and the kings relied on the clergy and the Scriptures in the adjudication of both secular and ecclesiastical cases.

The authority of the church was not challenged until the Sixteenth Century. In 1532, Henry VIII broke with the Roman Catholic Church and established the Anglican Church. The rejection of the authority of the Roman Catholic Church in England was a political parallel to the rejection of the Roman Catholic Church as the final authority in church doctrinal matters. Martin Luther's posting of the "Ninety-five Thesis" in 1517 and the publication of Jean Calvin's *Institutes of the Christian Religion* in 1559 triggered a re-examination of the relationship of the church both with the state and with individuals.

The chief political debate of the Sixteenth and Seventeenth Centuries centered on obedience and to which authority. The Roman Catholic Church had been civilization's only legitimate authority in western Europe after the fall of the Roman Empire. That authority of the church changed in England. According to William Tyndale, who wrote in *The Obedience of a Christian Man* (1528), obedience should be to the king and not to the church. His position was based upon an anti-Catholic belief that the Pope was not supreme in all matters. In *The Leviathan* (1651), Thomas Hobbes advocated obedience to the king without church sanction. The Puritans and the lawyers after the early 1600s would modify both positions and reject all obedience to the king that was not based on lawfully obtained consent. The first appearance of major opposition to the monarch occurred after the ascension of King James I of Scotland to the throne of England in 1601. James declared that obedience to the civil ruler by the people was based on Scripture and he proceeded to legislate and grant prerogatives and generally exercise all authority necessary to implement his will. The response of the clergy and the barristers was concerted and persistent. The clergy continued to preach and publish sermons questioning the king's authority in church matters and the barristers brought lawsuits to challenge the king's prerogative to grant monopolies and levy taxes.

The early Puritans believed God to be the absolute and final ruler of the world and all that lay therein was subject to God's sovereignty. Calvin's idea of an all-embracing divine sovereignty, similar to John Wycliffe's Fourteenth Century view, could not be divided or qualified. James' interference with Puritan sermons that preached obedience to God and Scripture over obedience to the king permeated the entire middle class and influenced, and was later aided by, the barristers and judges who similarly resisted the king's encroachments on the fundamental Common Law. Puritan and barrister opposition was intensified against King Charles I, James' son and successor, who offended the Puritans by the publication of the *Book of Common Prayer* (1625), which included prayers acknowledging the authority of the king, and the barristers were challenged by the King's claim of an unlimited authority to tax, resulting in the landmark decision known as The Ship Money Case (1637).

The Ship Money Case was not about church and state separation but about sovereignty. In England, it was the practice of the king to levy taxes and call upon ships and men, without the consent of Parliament, to resist unexpected attacks by pirates and ships of other nations. The practice was not challenged until John Hampden, a country gentleman from Buckinghamshire, challenged the judicial opinion that had already upheld the tax.

The case challenged the core principles of government that existed at that time. Hampden's challenge required an answer. Either the answer of the court would articulate a reason to maintain the status quo, on principle, or longstanding assumptions about government had to be changed. The court's answer attempted to maintain the king's prerogative. But the court's opinion would not be the final answer.

The judges issued individual opinions and English constitutional law would never be the same. A majority of the judges found in favor of the king. The reason for finding in the king's favor ranged from arguments that it was necessary to maintain the government to that it had always been done that way. The dissenting opinions ranged from opinions that the king had failed to follow procedures set forth in prior constitutional documents to an opinion that the king exceeded his power. The court, by holding in favor of the king, while providing inadequate reasoning, tried to sidestep the fundamental question raised by Hampden. Hampden then appealed to Parliament, which had appellate review under English law.

Hampden's challenge to the king's power to tax converged with other challenges being made to England's established order. The barristers of England, led by Sir Edward Coke, Chief Judge of the King's Bench, were challenging King James' assertion that the monarch's decrees were the only source of fundamental law. The legal profession maintained that the fundamental law originated from Magna Charta, tradition, and other sources that comprise what we now understand to be the Common Law. Similarly, the Puritan and Presbyterian clergy were challenging the king's authority as head of the Church of England. All challenges converged in the Long Parliament of 1640.

Parliament reversed the Court of Exchequer's decision. The judges who sided with the king were either impeached or banished. The king and his counsel were executed. The Puritans seized control of Parliament. Parliament seized control of England.

For 50 years, England suffered through civil wars and conflicting political claims with the Puritans, the Presbyterians, Catholic heirs of the Stuart kings, and Anglican and royalist supporters of the old monarchy and the established Church of England. During this period, the fundamental role of government and the fundamental relationship of citizens to church and state were being re-examined. Samuel Rutherford, a Presbyterian clergyman and professor from Edinborough, Scotland, published *Lex Rex* in 1644, which not only subordinated the king to the rule of law, as the title of the book symbolized, but stated, in theological terms, the Biblical basis for the radically new political concepts of the equality of men, and government by consent.

At the end of civil war, culminating in the Glorious Revolution of 1688 and the Bill of Rights of 1689, John Locke, counsel to William and Mary, anonymously published his *Two Treatises of Government* (1690), which finally and definitively refuted the philosophical and theological arguments that had been advanced to support the theory of absolute divine sovereignty.

Weary of civil war, England was as anxious to negotiate peace among different religious denominations as it was to limit the scope and authority of government. Locke also published his essay on religious toleration that was revolutionary in England at the end of the Seventeenth Century.

IN VIRGINIA

The English experience, culminating in Locke's essay on toleration, would be the focal point of debate in the Virginia Legislature when the serious task of governing began once independence from England had been achieved.

The main advocate for the disestablishment of the Anglican Church in

Virginia was James Madison. Madison had married a Presbyterian. He was educated at Princeton College, which at that time was an enclave of reformed, fundamentalist theology. He had appreciated the support given by Presbyterians and Baptists in Virginia during the war. He was not willing to continue to support the status quo of relegating Presbyterians and Baptists to second-class status to the established Anglican Church, which was the Church of England. Madison would be a key figure in Virginia and in the First Congress.

REDEFINING THE ESTABLISHMENT CLAUSE

The "establishment clause" language in the First Amendment was approved in 1791 by the First Congress. The adoption of the First Amendment to the Constitution was the first attempt to incorporate into law the evolving principles first presented as theory by Samuel Rutherford and John Locke and the actual practice of religious tolerance that had slowly developed in England in the Seventeenth and Eighteenth Centuries. The adoption of the Establishment Clause by America's founding fathers incorporated as binding legal principle the idea that the federal government should not impose sectarian or denominational codes upon other denominations.

The application of principles of separation of church and state to individuals and to state governments involves issues of federalism as well as theology. It was not intended that the First Congress resolve the theological issue of church and state separation by the First Amendment. That issue was for the states and had been most thoroughly and dramatically debated in Virginia. James Madison's support of the First Amendment at the national level was done to merely draw a line between national and state jurisdiction over religion. The Establishment Clause was not meant to set the boundaries of church and state jurisdiction *but to keep the federal government out of the conflict*. This was the true nature of the national debate.

The record evidence from the First Congress can be read in the library. Court cases from 1791 until 1947 are still on the books. The actions of Congress and past presidents are also in the historical record. Until 1947, the American people and all branches of government had a consistent and undebatable understanding of what the Establishment Clause meant.

While not everyone liked the founding fathers' theory, the founding fathers evidently did; and they had a clear understanding of what was meant by an establishment of religion. They were obviously aware that there were established state churches at the time of the ratification of the First Amendment. They were also most likely aware of what they were doing when they engaged in policies inconsistent with the modern, post-1947 interpretation of the Establishment Clause.

There is evidence that the American people and their elected representatives in Congress had a consistent and clear understanding of what the Establishment Clause meant. Since first ratified, numerous attempts to redefine the First Amendment had failed. All attempts to amend the Constitution by the lawful means set forth in Article V ultimately failed to pass. The last failed attempt was in 1947.

Establishment, as a legal term, had always meant "monopoly." In 1949, one year after the <u>McCollum</u> decision claimed that the term "establishment" had no clear meaning, the Encyclopedia Brittanica defined the term as, "an establishment is of the nature of a monopoly." The founding fathers understood what the word "establishment" meant because establishment of religion, as a practice, was commonplace. The "establishment" of religion referred to one, exclusive religion. In 1791, Americans belonged to many different Protestant denominations. The differences in denomination were, to a large extent, geographical. The northern states, descendants of the Puritans, were Congregational. The southern states, descended from Royalists, were Anglican. The middle colonies were mixed. States with established religions objected to the exclusivity of a different, nationally established denomination.

In 1776, at the time that the Declaration of Independence was enacted, nine states sanctioned state churches. The states of Massachusetts, Connecticut, and New Hampshire had established Congregational churches. New York, Maryland, Virginia, North Carolina, South Carolina and Georgia had sanctioned Anglican churches. Only Rhode Island, Delaware, New Jersey and Pennsylvania had no official, sanctioned, established denominations.

In 1788, following the Constitutional Convention, and during the time that state legislatures were debating the ratification of the Constitution and proposing the Bill of Rights, five states continued to sanction specific denominations. Those states endorsed the Congregational churches in Massachusetts, Connecticut, New Hampshire, and the Anglican churches of Maryland and South Carolina. Supporters of established denominations in those states refused to adopt the Constitution without a legal guarantee that the other states could not erect a national religion superseding the existing established state churches. This issue was especially important to the New England Puritans. New Englanders remembered the Puritan-Anglican battles of the 1600s from which they had fled. Bostonians especially remembered the attempt by Parliament to impose Anglican doctrine on New England that sparked hostilities in Massachusetts. New England Congregation-alists were wary of the Anglicans from the southern colonies. They refused to ratify the new Constitution without legal protection for their state's denominational choice from federal domination.

Then came 1947 and <u>Everson</u> and the historical context was forgotten. In <u>Everson</u>, the Supreme Court claimed that it had to interpret "establish-ment" for the first time because the First Amendment was unclear about its meaning. To some extent, the <u>Everson</u> and <u>McCollum</u> decisions were made with reference to selected historical references, woefully incomplete, that misrepresent what the founding fathers attempted to accomplish in the First Amendment. To a larger extent, supporters of the court's "new, improved" separation of state definition have revised history.

By ignoring what happened, by ignoring the written record, and by completely mischaracterizing the historical context from which the First Amendment arose, supporters of a "secular" separation of church and state doctrine have been able to confuse most people today and leave them defenseless to the new interpretation, unaware that there is another side to the argument: the original side. Historical revisionism is based upon four common misrepresentations: (1) we don't know what the founding fathers discussed because the debates were private; (2) the founding fathers were deists, not Christians, who were afraid of religion in government; (3) Jeffer-son was an ardent opponent of Christianity and its effect on government; (4) Madison opposed taxation for churches because he didn't want Christianity to interfere with government. The opposite is true in all four cases. Unfor-tunately, the Supreme Court in <u>McCollum</u> and <u>Everson</u> accepted all four untruths as truths and the confusion and misinterpretation persist today.

The first historical inaccuracy, advanced to support the Supreme Court's constitutional noninterpretivism by modern supporters of the separation of civil institutions from religious principles, is that we cannot understand the founding fathers' intention of the meaning of "establishment." They cite as their reason that the Constitutional Convention was conducted secretly in Philadelphia in 1787. That argument is partly correct but misleading. The Constitutional Convention of 1787 *was* held secretly in Philadelphia in 1787. The misleading aspect of this understanding is that the Establishment Clause and the Bill of Rights *were not drafted at the Constitutional Conven-tion of 1787*. The Bill of Rights resulted from the inability and resistance of some of the states to ratify the Constitution without a Bill of Rights.

It appeared that the Constitution was doomed to failure because of the lack of ratifying states until Samuel Adams, a member of the Massachusetts ratifying convention, proposed that the Massachusetts Legislature ratify the

Constitution contingent upon the First Congress approving and passing certain amendments. Massachusetts, then, agreed to ratify the Constitution provided the Bill of Rights would be enacted at the First Congress. Otherwise, the ratification of the Constitution would not have occurred. This maneuver was followed rapidly by enough states, including Virginia, to allow the ratification of the Constitution and enable the First Congress to meet. It was at the First Congress, of which all the proceedings were recorded (still maintained in the *Annals of Congress*) where the Bill of Rights was debated and adopted. Accordingly, the assertion that we don't know what was discussed is patently false.

The historical record of public debate was not just at the congressional level. Records from the state ratifying conventions, at which the conditional acceptance of the Constitution occurred, also shed light on what was meant by an "establishment of religion." Several states, including Massachusetts, South Carolina, New York, New Hampshire, Virginia, North Carolina and Rhode Island, still maintain their records. The dialogue and debates over specific interpretations of the words used provide ample guidance and precedent for the Supreme Court to properly decide the issues missed by the Court in <u>Everson</u> and <u>McCollum</u>. A well-known example of a publicly recorded statement of the separation issue is James Madison's address to the Virginia Convention, in which he stated:

> ...for when there is such a variety of sects, there cannot be a majority of any one sect to oppress and persecute the rest...a majority of the people are against any exclusivist establishment ...it is a strong security against religious persecution...no one sect will ever be able to outnumber or depress the rest.

Madison's statement made no mention of taxation, aid to religion or education; neither of those issues were discussed in any of the other debates. The reason he never addressed those topics is because aid to religion was never a national issue with respect to establishment of religion. The representatives of the states wanted a specific, limited theory and they expressed it, to use the words of Madison, "as well...as the nature of language would admit."

The debates regarding the exact wording of the First Amendment were recorded in the *Annals of Congress*. Numerous questions from the floor were addressed to Madison, the presiding officer of Congress' first session, regarding the meaning of the Establishment Clause. Both the New York and Connecticut delegations expressed concern that the Amendment would prohibit aid to religion and they wanted specific assurance that the Amendment would not apply to the states. The states specifically wanted to maintain their own established religion. The states were concerned that the federal government would establish as an official religion, a denomination different from the states' own official choice, given the diversity of denominations. Madison assured the members that, (1) aid to religion was not an issue and that (2) each state was free to maintain its own established religion without federal interference.

After sidestepping the historical record and other usual means of determining the drafters' intent to define "establishment," the Supreme Court in 1947 and 1948 cited Jefferson and Madison as the sole authority for its new definition of the word "establishment" in the McCollum and Everson cases. Their writings, quoted out of context, may have lent some support to the new view, but their actions do not.

In contract law, subsequent actions, or course of conduct are evidence of intent. Did Jefferson's and Madison's actions as president support the Supreme Court's Everson and McCollum decisions? The records of Madison and Jefferson as president have been maintained in their correspondence and in the legislation they proposed and signed. The record refutes the Court's conclusion that either Jefferson or Madison considered aid to religion as an unconstitutional establishment of religion.

For the Everson and McCollum Court to be correct, then Jefferson must be viewed to be a clear and consistent violator of the Establishment Clause. Jefferson proposed specific legislation and funds for the establishment and maintenance of Catholic clergy to evangelize the Indians in the Northwest Territories. He also supported public funds for the establishment of seminaries and universities that taught religion. Jefferson, noted as the "Father" of the University of Virginia at Charlottesville, has never been given adequate credit for his main mission in establishing the University of Virginia, which was to prepare clergymen for the teaching of religion. In his many letters of correspondence, Jefferson consistently maintained that the teaching of the Christian religion was essential to the maintenance of a civil and moral society.

Madison cannot be accused of violating the McCollum and Everson Establishment Clause definition as frequently as Jefferson did. In fact, Madison's actions might indicate to some that he disapproved of government aid to religion; however, his reasoning is not commonly understood.

Madison has been characterized today as an Enlightenment thinker because of his training at Princeton College, allegedly a freethinking, Enlightenment institution. But Princeton's and Madison's sympathy and support for Presbyterians and dissenting religions intended to separate the

Anglican Church from the state, not all churches from all of government.

James Madison's mentor was the President of Princeton College, the Reverend John Witherspoon. Witherspoon was a delegate to the 1776 Continental Congress in Philadelphia and a signer of the Declaration of Independence. His view about the separation of church and state does not represent Enlightenment thinking in a form that would be acceptable to modern constitutional experts. In a sermon Witherspoon presented at Princeton on May 17, 1776, shortly before signing the Declaration of Independence, he stated:

> While we give praise to God, the Supreme disposer of all events, for His interposition on our behalf, let us guard against the dangerous error of trusting in, or boasting of, an arm of flesh ...I look upon ostentation and confidence to be a sort of outrage upon providence, and when it becomes general, and infuses itself into the spirit of the people, it is a forerunner of destruction . . . but observe that if your cause is just, if your principles are pure, and if your conduct is prudent you need not fear the multitude of opposing hosts.
>
> What follows from this? That he is the best friend to American liberty, who is most sincere and active in promoting true and undefiled religion, and who sets himself with the greatest firmness to bear down on profanity and immorality of every kind. Whoever is an avowed enemy of God, I scruple not to call him an enemy in this country.

Princeton College, that supposed center of Enlightenment thinking in America, had as its first president the Reverend Jonathan Edwards, the preacher and theologian whose most famous sermon, "Sinners in the Hands of an Angry God," sparked the great awakening of the mid-1700s which played a major role in the theological and philosophical training of the founding fathers. Reverend Edwards' theology represented orthodox Calvinism. This factually different view of Princeton College, and its effect on Madison's training and philosophy, gives a different interpretation of Madison's actions as president and a different understanding of his "Memorial and Remonstrance Against Aid to Religion" published in opposition to Patrick Henry's bill in support of a tax directly payable to Virginia's religious institutions, and Madison's support for the Virginia Statute of Religious Freedom of 1786. Madison's personal belief was that religion and civil government should not be mixed because of the negative effect on religion. It was his belief that mingling religion and politics, especially that which occurred from taxation for religious purposes, corrupted true religion. Madison's opposition to the Anglican Church was not based on Enlightenment philosophy. His opposition was based upon orthodox Presbyterianism. This view of Madison is entirely contradictory to that discussed by the Supreme Court in Everson and McCollum.

Justice Joseph Story, often cited as America's greatest legal scholar, whose *Commentaries on the Constitutional Law* was written only 50 years after the passage of the Constitution, stated, "Christianity ought to receive encouragement from the state." The object of the Establishment Clause was "to exclude all rivalry among Christian sects, and to prevent any national ecclesiastical establishment which should give to a hierarchy the exclusive patronage of the national government." He further stated, "It is impossible for those who believe in the truth of Christianity as a divine revelation to doubt that it is the especial duty of government to foster and encourage it among all the citizens and subjects." It is interesting that rather than taking a position of government neutrality, as the modern Supreme Court has expressed as the essential tenet of the First Amendment, or even hostility, which is apparent from many of the recent decisions, Justice Story clearly articulates a positivist, Christian perspective. Christianity should be promoted, not ignored or opposed.

THE ESTABLISHMENT OF EDUCATION

The Supreme Court interpretation of the Establishment Clause in McCollum and Everson is historically and legally unsupportable. The decision may have reflected a longstanding popular bias, not limited to the Supreme Court, against private Catholic education. But the direct result of this attitude against private Catholic schools has been the demise of public schools in general due to the restriction on providing assistance to any institution teaching religious truth, and the prevention of discussing any subject matter that may appear to be religiously based.

There is a significant and historical disagreement regarding the relationship of church and state and separation of public education that first arose in the state of Virginia during the debate over the Statute of Religious Freedom. The disagreement had Patrick Henry and his supporters proposing a tax for the support of all religions. The support was not biased against any denomination but was also not limited as to the use of funds. It was Henry's intent to support churches, in general, by taxation. Henry was successfully opposed by Jefferson and Madison and their supporters. Madison, who was tutored at home, opposed all forms of taxation for religious institutions as government interference that would corrupt the teaching of religious truth. That position was the point of his *Memorial and Remonstrance*. Jefferson, who opposed Henry's proposal as too broad, supported public religious education as necessary for the continued support of self-government. The conflict in principle between Madison and Jefferson has never been resolved. Madison wanted education to be private so the Christian religion could be taught and promoted aggressively. Jefferson was less strident in his personal beliefs, so he was more open to the promotion of "cultural" Christianity. But contrary to the assertion by the Supreme Court in <u>Everson</u> and <u>McCollum</u>, the conflict in principles of the role of government in public education never presented an Establishment Clause issue that was the business of the court until 1947.

REDEFINING THE FREE EXERCISE CLAUSE

The redefinition of words is essential to the reinterpretation of both First Amendment religion clauses. "Establishment" was redefined to mean "aid to religion" when it had always meant "monopoly." Similarly, the Free Exercise Clause could only be reinterpreted by redefining the word "religion."

The word "religion" had a precise definition in 1776. Jefferson defined it and put it in the Virginia Statute of Religious Freedom. Jefferson's definition did not allow for the reinterpretation of the First Amendment necessary for the secular theory adopted in 1947.

AN ENGLISH LESSON

The word "religion" appears once in the First Amendment:

> "Congress shall make no law respecting an establishment of religion, or prohibiting the free exercise thereof..."

The construction of the command is obvious. Because the word "religion" is used once, the word "religion" is applied to both the Establishment Clause and the Free Exercise Clause. The Free Exercise Clause is a dependent clause, not a sentence. The term "free exercise" refers to the word "religion." The connection of "free exercise" to "religion" is to the same word "religion" as the word relates to "establishment." Some modern constitutional scholars and judges have attempted to define "religion" differently for each clause, but such an interpretation is intellectually and grammatically dishonest. The use of the word "thereof" after "free exercise" binds each clause to the same word "religion." Even Laurence Tribe, Harvard Law

School professor and eminent constitutional law expert, while arguing in favor of the dual definition approach, concedes that the approach is "dubious." The proper construction, as originally understood, is that whatever can be established as a religion, should be entirely protected. So the question becomes, "What is "religion?" Similar to the word "establishment," the common belief is that the founding fathers failed to define the word "religion."

MULTIPLE THEORIES

Modern scholars have attempted to provide new definitions and interpretations of the word "religion." Neither the Supreme Court nor theologians are clear on what they want "religion" to mean. Justice John Paul Stevens, in a concurring opinion in the recent case of Wolman v. Walter (1977), defined religion by stating that "the realm of religion is where knowledge leaves off, and where faith begins." Where did Justice Stevens find his definition? It appears that he attributed a Clarence Darrow quote from the infamous Scopes trial when Darrow attempted to separate science from religion.

The Supreme Court had already established its own new concept of religion in United States v. Seeger (1965), a case involving a conscientious objection claim from a Vietnam War opponent. It essentially adopted the new theology of Paul Tillich that rejected all religious tradition that conflicted with a person's own subjective viewpoint of God. In Torcaso v. Watkins (1961), the Court placed all religions, not just Christian denominations, on an equal footing. The Court specifically brought under First Amendment protection, Buddhism, Hinduism and even "secular humanism." A new non-Christian, even Godless definition of religion needed to be redrafted. Tillich's argument that any matter of sincere and ultimate concern should qualify as "religion" was adopted by the Supreme Court in Seeger. The philosophical conflict between Justice Stevens' definition and the Seeger decision was hardly noticed, however, because the Court now had to address a new concern. These new definitions of religion could be dangerous. The "compelling government interest" test, specifically rejected by the founding fathers at the first Congress, had to be reinserted by the Supreme Court.

More recently, Justice Harry Blackmun, in his concurring opinion in Lee v. Weisman, secularized John Locke's religious toleration argument by asserting that:

> When the government appropriates religious truth, it trans-

forms rational debate into theological decree, those who disagree
are no longer questioning the policy judgment of the elected but
the rules of a larger authority who is beyond approach.

None of these definitions are supported by basic theological principles.
Nor are any of these definitions consistent with the religious toleration principles advocated by Locke and Madison.

The problem with Justice Stevens' definition is that he overly restricts
religion to whatever is not science. Under Stevens' definition, faith is the
same as religion, and science is the same as knowledge. Religion, then, is
limited to what is mystical and unknowable, and cannot, by definition, be
based upon reason or evidence. Justice Stevens' definition, as philosophy,
makes a distinction between supernatural and natural philosophies, and
restricts faith to matters that cannot be known. His narrow definition of faith
ignores the relationship between faith and reason, discussed and written
about by philosophers and theologians for centuries. Justice Stevens' theory, as law, extends "religion" to the limits of creativity and imagination.
Thus, "religion" is both restricted and expansive. Religion cannot be
extended to what is knowable. But what is not knowable cannot be verified
or proven. Religious practices, consequently, could consist of almost any
acts reflecting the sincere beliefs or creative imagination of the believer.
From this viewpoint, the "compelling interest" test was formed. Drug use,
immorality, theft, murder, and almost any other crime existing since the
beginning of Common Law could be part of a religious practice. The Court
had to give the government the power to restrict crime, if crime was part of
the free exercise of a believer's religion.

Just as Stevens' definition of religion is too restrictive, Tillich's definition is too broad. Similar to the practical effect of the modern philosophical
views of determinism and materialistic naturalism, Tillich's definition leaves
nothing for lawyers or judges to do. If science governs our actions, no individual can be accountable under the law. If religion is protected, and religion is any matter of ultimate concern, then all actions are allowed, as long
as they are sincere. If a subjective religious viewpoint exempts all of our
actions, there is no jurisdiction under the law to restrict conduct as there can
be no judgment of any actions resulting from the subjective good faith belief
of the actor. So, the only allowable limitations are those identified as a compelling government interest.

Justice Blackmun's view simply misses the point and purpose of 200
years of theological and legal debate regarding the entire church-state issue.
The Reformers, in resisting the authority of the church on doctrinal matters,

and the Puritans, in opposing the Stuart kings, separated religious truth that is knowable by all individuals from theological decree that supposedly rested with a higher, larger human authority. Blackmun is merely restating the issue from a secular point of view. But the exercise of authority in ecclesiastical matters is not the same thing as conceding the existence of self-evident truths, even if those truths are Biblical.

Consistent with postmodernist thought, Blackmun assumes that religious truth is not knowable. Blackmun's solution is to separate the functions of government from all questions of religious truth. This is a radical change from 1776. To the Reformers, the Puritans and the founding fathers, the institutions of government derived from religious truth. As evidenced by the statement, "We hold these truths to be self-evident, that all men are created equal and endowed by their Creator with certain inalienable rights..." American government institutions are also dependent upon religious truth. These views are unacceptable to Blackmun. Blackmun, and his modern counterparts who fear theocracy, fail to account that the reason for the Protestant Reformation was the same objection.

It was the Protestants who suffered from the religious inquisitions of the established churches. Blackmun is correct that theological interpretations were centralized and decreed out of dark chambers. One of the most important characteristics of the Protestant Reformation was that scriptural interpretation was not limited to decrees issued from dark chambers; the basic understanding of Scriptures was knowable by all. In the same manner, basic understanding of law and its origin as a by-product of creation is also knowable and understandable by all. Coke and Blackstone, when referring to general and special revelation, were not referring to decrees issued from dark chambers. General and special revelations are legal understandings that were either self-evident or so embodied in tradition that these principles were no longer subject to being questioned. Blackmun rejected all of these basic understandings in principle that are knowable and understandable by all, and replaced them with a new set of decrees issued from the dark chambers inhabited by Supreme Court Justices.

ORIGINAL INTENT AS THEORY

It is necessary to understand the difference between the "free exercise of religion" in Virginia's Bill of Rights and the compelling government interest test that existed in other original constitutions. The other states allowed freedom of worship and tolerated religious conduct or acts that did not violate the public safety or welfare. That standard is the same as the current compelling government interest test that is the state of the law today. Virginia rejected the compelling government interest test. The Virginia language was incorporated into the Bill of Rights adopted by the First Congress.

The first draft in the Virginia Bill of Rights guaranteed religious freedom "unless under color of religion any man disturb the peace, happiness, or safety of society." The final draft in the Virginia Bill of Rights changed the language of toleration to "free exercise" and the limiting language was dropped. The final draft, adopted as Article I, Section 16 of the 1776 Virginia Constitution:

> That Religion, or the duty we owe to our Creator, and the manner of discharging it can be directed only by reason or conviction, not by force or violence, and therefore all men are equally entitled to the free exercise of religion, according to the dictates of conscience.

The choice of the drafters to use "free exercise" without limitation replaced the tolerance standard that could be overruled by the threat to public peace.

The 1786 Statute for Religious Freedom adopted by the Virginia legislature also contained no language of limitation in Jefferson's preamble:

> [T]hat the impious presumption of legislature and ruler...have assumed dominion over the faith of others and...hath established and maintained false religions over the greatest part of the world and through all time: that to compel a man to furnish contributions of money for the propagation of opinions which he disbelieves is sinful and tyrannical.

Madison stated the same principle in his *Memorial and Remonstrance* in 1785, written to oppose a general tax for the benefit of religion under consideration by the Virginia legislature:

> [T]hat religion, or the duty which we owe to our Creator, and the manner of discharging it, can be directed only by reason and conviction, not by force or violence...[R]eligion, then...must be left to the conviction and conscience of everyman...and...is wholly exempt from [the]...cognizance [of civil society].

The Virginia definition accomplishes a number of objectives. Most important, it defines "religion." Those who claim that the founding fathers never defined religion must have never read the definition in Article I, Section 16 of the 1776 Virginia Constitution or Madison's full argument in his *Memorial and Remonstrance*. It is perplexing from Justice Reed's dissent in McCollum that not only does it look like the Supreme Court read these authorities, but they claimed to endorse and adopt them as precedent. They cited the source but ignored the text and its meaning.

The Virginia practice of tolerance was a legislative adoption of Locke's view. Locke did not endorse full tolerance. He made an exception for Islam, Catholicism and atheism. Locke wanted tolerance for sectarian differences because non-biblical squabbles had led to a century of war. Neither the legislature nor civil ruler could adopt the particular religious sect or denomination's position and impose such practices on other religions under Locke's proposal. England practiced Locke's version of tolerance unofficially and continues to do so to this day.

Jefferson followed Calvin's theory that separated the roles of church and the government but left both accountable to God and limited both to specific purposes. The Reformers preached that each individual was accountable to God. The church and state both had limited jurisdictions. What remained after accounting for the duties of the church and state were rights left with each individual. Coke was the first to apply Calvin's concept of separate, independent institutions to church and state and to the legal profession, the realms of education and employment. Each jurisdictional function was independent from the other, related in that each was subject to the ultimate sovereignty of God. Jefferson was the first to attempt to guarantee the Reformers' belief that Christianity was ultimately personal, but he never tried to separate religion from government any more than he tried to separate religion from the church.

It is upon this framework of separating institutions, which includes not only the church and state, but also education, employment, the family and the individual, that Jefferson's definition can be understood. The Reformers redefined the vertical relationship between individuals and God. The human intermediaries, the papal authorities for ecclesiastical matters and the kings in civil matters, were removed as intermediaries and made subject to the same laws as everyone else. What remained was the question of what duties were due to God and what duties were due to other individuals. The jurisdiction of the civil law could only apply to horizontal duties to other persons.

ORIGINAL INTENT AS PRACTICED

The colonists had to address the freedom of religion issue twice in a matter of a few years. Each colony addressed the free exercise issue upon drafting the constitution for each new state. The record of what each new state did is available to us. The free exercise issue had to be debated again when considering the Bill of Rights and its application to the federal government. The records of those debates and proposals are also available to us.

Prior to the Bill of Rights debate, different states had adopted religious freedom provisions that included clauses permitting the limitation of religious practices that conflicted with the peace and safety of the community. Members of the first Congress proposed similar language for the new First Amendment but those proposals were rejected. The free exercise principle in the First Amendment was eventually based upon the Virginia theory but the language was not the same. The Virginians deleted references to protecting the peace and safety of the community. The compelling interest test was rejected. The free exercise language in the First Amendment is not limited. The language is absolute.

The absolute prohibition of infringement of the free exercise of religion cannot be allowed under the modern view of separation of church and state. Justice Hugo Black wrote the <u>Everson</u> opinion. Black was an absolutist when it applied to free speech. He was a balancer when it came to freedom of religion. To Black, and the judges who have followed him, the compelling interest test is necessary because they changed the original meaning and definitions. The proposals rejected as unnecessary by the First Congress have to be put back into the First Amendment by interpretation. Jefferson is acknowledged as the reason for the change but his reasoning has been rejected.

FREE EXERCISE FOR WHAT IS TRUE

The Free Exercise Clause has no valid purpose if religious belief is untrue. If we know that a religious belief is false, without any basis in fact, or advanced in bad faith for other motives, there is no reason to tolerate the practices that result from the false belief. On the other hand, the entire purpose of the Virginia Statute of Religious Freedom was to protect what was known to be true. Stevens' definition protects all beliefs that cannot be proven. Tillich's definition protects all beliefs. Blackmun merely assumes that religious beliefs are made up and announced by religious authorities. None of these viewpoints allow for the possibility that religious beliefs are based upon facts and theories which are true and knowable.

The problem that the Free Exercise Clause jurisprudence presents to modern Christians is not whether Christians can practice their religions.

23

Mainstream and evangelical Christians have nothing to fear for the moment. It is highly possible, maybe probable, that "compelling government interests" will eventually force all denominations to tolerate and even accept beliefs otherwise repugnant to them. Those trends need to be confronted openly and resisted.

The deeper problem for modern Christians is the premise of modern constitutional law, that core beliefs of modern Christians and the founding fathers are presumed untrue. The effect of substituting secular philosophy for reformation theology is fundamental and all pervasive. The nature of law has to be changed. The role of government institutions has to be changed. Because Christians have not insisted upon or supported Reformation principles that formed the basis for the establishment of this nation and its institutions, the nature of law and the role of government institutions have been changed. All that remains for Christians is to ask the new revolutionaries, "Changed to what?" And what exactly is the basis for the new secular theory upon which our new system of government is based? Unfortunately, Christians have for so long abandoned the law and stopped questioning the modern theories, that they no longer understand how American government was supposed to work in the first place. For Christians, a good place to begin is by reviewing and understanding the Declaration of Independence.

CHAPTER 2

PHILOSOPHY, FAITH, SCIENCE AND REASON

"The human understanding is like a false mirror, which, receiving rays irregularly, distorts and discolors the nature of things by mingling its own nature with it."

Francis Bacon (1620)

"It is our preference that decides against Christianity, not arguments."

Friederich Nietsche

Recently, a Minnesota school board removed a high school biology teacher from the classroom because he privately questioned some of the teachings of Darwinian evolution. When called before the administration to explain his private beliefs, the teacher pointed out that some of the evidence for evolution presented in the textbook contained factual inaccuracies which had already been admitted to be fraudulent. He thought he should be able to tell his students about the errors, but had not yet done so.

I assisted the American Center for Law and Justice in an attempt to have the teacher reinstated to his classroom. We were unsuccessful. Eventually, the Minnesota Court of Appeals ruled that because of his religious beliefs, the Court did not believe that he could teach the curriculum. Neither the Minnesota Supreme Court nor the United States Supreme Court heard our appeal. We alleged that the reassignment of the teacher, based on the administration's fear of what he might say, violated the teachers "academic freedom" and his right to hold private religious beliefs.

What intrigued me was that the administration did not fear the teacher because he was a Christian—but because he was a certain type of Christian, the type that might interpret the Bible literally. But the teacher never talked

25

about the Bible. He only wanted to discuss the scientific evidence. Times have changed since we older Americans went to school.

It is now 75 years since the Scopes trial. It is obvious that evolutionists do not just fear religion; they fear new evidence scientists discover each year that contradicts the science that students are still taught as "fact." The theory of evolution has become faith-based and no more grounded in science than is mythology.

◆ ◆ ◆

THE ASSAULT ON SELF-EVIDENT TRUTHS

W e hold these truths to be self-evident" is the beginning point of the political philosophy of the Declaration of Independence and the legal philosophy of American law. Self-evident truths lay the foundation for the institutions necessary for government.

Self-evident truths, as religious truth, form the foundation for the institution of the church. Self-evident truths, as legal philosophy, form the foundation for the institutions of the state: the legislative, executive and judicial branches of American government. Basic definitions and assumptions that set the standards for the concept of "rights" that are to be protected and the "justice" to be administered—without self-evident truths—would continuously need to redefine their purposes and standards. Constantly evolving standards and purposes would necessarily find their origin with the new rulemaking authorities who would write the rules as a product of their own will, not the people's will. Such a situation defines "tyranny." In many ways, this situation describes current American law and government.

The term self-evident truths was well-accepted and commonly used at the time of the Declaration of Independence. The term derives from the Latin *per se notum* meaning that which is known through the instrumentality or agency of one's own efforts. St. John of Damascus, the first theological encyclopedist, used and defined the term as one of the first principles. Thomas Aquinas, in the *Summa Theologica*, his comprehensive exposition on theology and knowledge, acknowledges God as the source of "self-evident" knowledge. Aquinas' proposition still survives as the foundation of natural law theory. St. John of Damascus attributed "self-evident truths" to Augustine. The concept of self-evident truths is described by the Apostle Paul.

The whole idea of truth is best illustrated by the verbal exchange between Jesus and Pontius Pilate. The most vigorous offense against Chris-

26

tianity and orthodox doctrine is the allegation that there is no definable truth. The question, "What is truth?" is often used to definitively exclude the possibility that truth actually exists, that it is a philosophical impossibility. Pilate asked Jesus the question, "What is truth?" but Pilate did not wait for the answer. Either he assumed there was no answer or he did not understand Jesus' answer. Unfortunately, most people never ask the question. Yet, the answer is as critically important in the attempt to establish a foundation for law and government as it is in establishing a personal worldview based on a rational, recognizable theory.

Christianity is premised upon knowable truth. Christians believe that scriptures, as a written expression of God's will and truth, and the life of Jesus, as a demonstration of God's will and truth, have been intentionally communicated by an omniscient God to humans who lack, but need understanding. Humans gain understanding by reason and revelation, and understanding consists of truth, both understood intuitively and accepted as fact demonstrably.

John Locke, in his *Essay Concerning Human Understanding* (1704), attempted to define knowledge and demonstrate the process of obtaining knowledge and understanding. His definition of knowledge is intertwined with truth and reason. Locke classifies knowledge as being of three kinds. One, he defines intuitive knowledge as the connection of ideas which are immediately and necessarily perceived. Two, he defines demonstrative knowledge as where the connection of ideas is certain, but is perceived indirectly by means of an intermediate idea. Locke called the process of putting ideas together "reason." The result of combining ideas in agreement he called "proofs." Three, sensitive knowledge is defined as being the assurance or perfect conviction that some object extrinsic to the mind actually exists because at a time past, our senses experienced that object. He believed we have an intuitive knowledge of our own existence, demonstrative knowledge of God, and a sensitive knowledge only of the objects present to our senses.

According to Locke, there are only two sources of knowledge: "sensation," which is perceived externally, and "reflection," which is perceived internally. He defines "reason" as "the faculty of deducing unknown truths from principles or propositions that are already known." He elevated the process of reason as a means to understand self-evident truth and to understand the process of obtaining evidence to prove or disprove a proposition. Locke never rejected the divinity of God or Jesus. For Locke, faith and belief were natural and based upon reason.

Locke's influence on natural law theory and the Declaration of Indepen-

dence are unquestioned. Jean-Jacques Burlemaqui (1694-1748) applied natural law theory to government, arguing that all government powers should
be stipulated in definite terms and their limitations written in a constitution
based upon natural law, as ordained by God, and known to all by "the sole
light of reason." Locke's principles and theories were advanced to advocate
modifications in England's constitutional law, which contained written documents with oral tradition. America rejected the English oral tradition but
incorporated English principles in its written documents.

Similarly, Locke's theories provided the substantive basis for William
Blackstone's *Commentaries on the Law of England*, published in 1765.
Blackstone's summary of law served as the basic text for all English and
American lawyers for over a century (new Americans had no need for
Blackstone's guidance about English constitutional law, since America
rejected the monarchy). But American lawyers followed and cited as
authoritative Blackstone's principles of Common Law; modern lawyers who
hold to the natural law tradition still do. Blackstone defined the origin of all
law, both scientific and moral, as rooted in and subject to the immutable
laws of good and evil established by God which are superior to all manmade
laws. Blackstone said that all law was known through reason and revelation.

Explaining and expanding upon Locke's definitions of how knowledge
and truth were perceived, Blackstone incorporated Calvin's explanations
that man obtained knowledge by general and special revelation. Calvin
defined general revelation as that which remained through creation and after
Adam's fall. Scriptures provided special revelation available to all through
study and meditation. Blackstone's complete definition described the English Common Law tradition that had developed throughout England's civilized history and was unquestioned in England and America at the time of
America's founding.

THE END OF REASON

By 1776, a contrary secular philosophy was emerging. The Reformation and the Renaissance occurred at approximately the same time in history. They were not necessarily in conflict and even were somewhat allied in
their opposition to established Catholic teaching. The Reformation was primarily theological but its teaching profoundly affected law and politics. The
Renaissance was primarily related to art and science and its short-term influence was cultural. The perspective of the two movements was, however,
entirely different.

The Reformation leaders' perspective was heavenward. The reformers and their followers worked to remove earthly intermediaries that interfered with each person's proper relationship with God. The Renaissance leaders concerned themselves only with man's liberation. Renaissance leaders' opposition to church authority led to the philosophy of the Enlightenment that taught that each man exists as an end in himself, not merely as a means to be arbitrarily used by another's will. When that other will referred to intervening civil and ecclesiastic authority, the Renaissance and Enlightenment thinkers had a common cause with Christian reformers. When that other intervening will referred to God, the Renaissance leaders were rebelling against God and Christianity, and the path to a distinctly separate worldview was laid.

The two vehicles used to follow the new path to what is now known as "humanism" were "science" and "reason." The separation of the humanists from Christian liberalism onto a different path occurred during the Eighteenth Century. In the Seventeenth Century, the principles and lessons of science and reason were not only consistent with Christianity, but they flourished among Christians and provided the basis for the scientific advancement and modernization of legal and political theory. The most visible changes occurred in England, the most evangelical Protestant nation of the Seventeenth Century.

The Age of Reason, also known as the Enlightenment, predated the Age of Science. Modern secular humanists trace their origin to Enlightenment philosophy and attempt to characterize American Eighteenth Century liberalism as Enlightenment-based. Both premises are wrong. Eighteenth Century American liberalism was based on the Reformation principle of equality that rejected claims of the monarchy and the papacy as divine intermediaries in the lives of individuals. American liberalism also advocated religious freedom, based on Locke's principles of toleration. But Locke's religious toleration argument was specifically antithetical to atheism and his viewpoint was continued in America by Madison. In early America, religious toleration did not extend to atheism, religions that believed in another god, or Catholic teachings that subjected the civil authorities to papal authority.

The Age of Reason had scant to no impact in America, and none by 1776. The leaders of the Age of Reason were continental philosophers, such as Rousseau, Spinoza and Kant. But the Age of Reason was short-lived. Deism, which avoided the teleological argument by acknowledging God as Creator and then assuming the remaining tenets of secular philosophy, based on Hume's epistemology, shortly collapsed from its own weaknesses. Evolutionary theories never adequately address "intelligent design" theories and it never made much sense that a creator god would abandon the world and not continue to act as "divine providence" or as a "supreme judge." Culturally, the rejection of God by individuals led to the rejection of God's will as a general moral standard. Rousseau's vague general will and Kant's moral imperatives were substituted in place of what William Ames, the English Puritan leader of the early 1600s, called "that Law of God, which is naturally written in the heart of all men." Rousseau's general will was symbolically represented by the guillotine, as the Reign of Terror brought to a climactic end the Age of Enlightenment. The Concordat of 1801, whereby Napoleon Bonaparte agreed to re-establish the Roman Catholic Church in France, wrote the Age of Enlightenment's last chapter.

As the modern American philosopher Francis Schaeffer clearly demonstrated, the Age of Reason, as philosophy, led to an irrational conclusion. Through reason alone, man could not, by his own initiative, perceive the supernatural. Secular philosophy had traveled its own path and reached a dead end. To transcend existence discernible by reason alone to what Kant defined as "the phenomenal realm" required a leap of faith into an absurd world that could only be limited by the imagination. No matter how irrational, however, to remain secular the philosophy steadfastly had to deny the continuous existence and intervention of God.

THE END OF SCIENCE

A new faith in science arose to rescue secular philosophy from the demise of the Age of Reason. In the mid-Nineteenth Century, Darwin's theory of evolution overcame the deists' uncomfortable compromise as they tried to balance their belief in God as a creator while rejecting belief in the existence of a God who could, but would not intervene in the universe which He created. Secular philosophers had found their hope to provide the answer to their teleological argument dilemma even though, at the time of Darwin, the premise of the Age of Reason had been discredited and abandoned. But scientific inquiry has not fulfilled the hope of those philosophers; that science would stand alone without God.

A major change in scientific thought began with Francis Bacon (1561-1621) and it provides the starting point for understanding the modern view of science. Bacon was by profession a lawyer who served as chief legal counsel to the King of England. His legal training, which required an understanding of the relationship of fact and proof in the law of evidence, led to a broader change in the philosophy of thought. Bacon denounced false doctrines proceeding from certain assumed first principles and redirected the method of inquiry. He argued that investigation should lead to factual observations, confirmed by experimentation, in order to form generalizations. Bacon's principles were not dissimilar to the modern law of evidence. Knowledge resulted from independent investigation, not from the decree of established authorities. Bacon's theory actually had more long term impact on the field of science than the practice of law.

Meanwhile, the field of philosophy developed separately, but concurrently, from the advancement of science. The philosophical movement grew as man's understanding of the role played by human reason increased. Rene' Descartes (1596-1650) provided the starting point for understanding the modern role of reason with his assertion, "I think, therefore I am." This provided the basis for Locke's theory of intuitive knowledge. Descartes introduced the philosophical process of "methodical doubt," the denial of everything not wholly certain, in order to begin a rational inquiry without prejudice. Descartes argued that knowledge was obtained through abstract, rational thought, best expressed and understood through mathematics.

Descartes' view of man and the mind was dualistic. His process began in the understanding and assumption that there were clear and self-evident premises *and* a Supreme Being. Descartes rejected the idea that objective truth, based only on supernatural experience, could be knowable by the reasoning process such that the truth could then be applied to others. His analysis, like Thomas Hobbes who came later, opposed an excessive belief in supernatural experience, expressed in the rampant superstitions of medieval times.

After Bacon and Descartes came Sir Isaac Newton and John Locke. Locke's influence and objectives were political and his study focused on the role of reason in the field of philosophy. Newton's name is synonymous with science. He represents the understanding that the world is orderly and susceptible to discovery through scientific inquiry. The teleological philosophic argument that God is the Creator of the universe is based upon scientific observation that the physical universe is ordered. Newton's principles of science were based upon a philosophical belief in a created and orderly universe that could be tested and shown to be true.

The divergence between Christianity and humanism in the fields of science and philosophy did not result from new discoveries but rather because the humanists changed the rules. The humanists' denial of long accepted self-evident truths did not result from new persuasive arguments or scientific discoveries, but because they closed certain paths to obtaining knowledge of the truth. The source for this divergence is David Hume, a Seventeenth Century English philosopher, who advocated a new theory of epistemology from his self-imposed exile in France. Epistemology is the theory of the origin, nature and boundaries of knowledge. Hume changed the definition and reoriented the process. Epistemology, for a Christian, includes all knowledge obtained through personal experience, history, science and divine revelation. Secular epistemology is limited to knowledge obtained through empirically validated and regular recurring events. To a secular philosopher, if man cannot find God, then God cannot exist.

Shouldn't it be true that if the objective of knowledge is to find truth, then any evidence that tends to determine truth should be considered? Secular philosophy rejects all objectivity when it assumes that the existence of God and all belief in the supernatural cannot be proven scientifically and is, therefore, not susceptible to proof. All evidence of miracles, which are the result of divine supernatural intervention, must be rejected. All testimony of personal experience with the supernatural must be rejected. All belief in creation must be rejected. All of Christian truth, based on scripture, testimony of witnesses to miracles and to the divinity of Jesus Christ, must be rejected. Secular philosophy does not reject belief in the supernatural because it cannot be proven, but because no evidence that would establish the existence of the supernatural is allowed. At the same time, however, secular philosophy places absolute trust and blind faith in the belief that science will establish its own theories even though no scientific evidence or scientific proof has ever been shown to contradict the Christian worldview.

Secular philosophy, based on science only, has had to abandon all of its Newtonian roots as it shifts its objective from explaining how the world works to explaining its worldview. The philosophers abandoned methodical doubt, which rejected the prejudice advanced by the medieval church authorities, and replaced it with their own prejudice of vindicating Darwin's premise that the world evolved. They replaced the flat earth prejudice with the Big Bang dilemma. Newton's belief that the world was orderly because God, as cosmic designer/architect/creator, ordered a physical universe, had to be sidestepped.

Just as the deists could not overcome the teleological argument, neither have those with faith in science alone been able to overcome the Second Law of Thermodynamics. In recent times, scientists have even abandoned the basic premise of science, that science is based on empirical evidence leading to factual observations. A recent scientist exclaimed, "No one looks at the thing itself anymore. We look at what the thing does, at the traces it leaves behind." The scientific method has become as faith-based as the believer's faith in God. But believers in science alone are not as objective in seeking ultimate truth.

Darwin's theory of evolution, incorporated into a comprehensive philosophy of naturalism, forces its believers to overcome their own lack of evidence and to reject all contrary evidence obtained by scientific inquiry. The evolutionist's faith in no God renders evidence discrediting evolution as no evidence at all. They must abandon the objectives of scientific inquiry to determine scientific truth, to sustain their faith that the world simply happened. Their faith requires that evolutionary science will somehow be proven if the existence of the supernatural evidence is ignored.

This irony is unmatched. Secular philosophy had hoped to disprove the existence of God, but in the process of denying that self-evident truths exist, secular philosophers, relying on naturalist philosophy, have had to reject truths observed through scientific inquiry in order to sustain their faith in the basic premise of evolution.

THE END OF DEBATE

Science teachers have not been very scientific about allowing discussion about evolution or evidence contrary to evolution to be taught. They have been neither open-minded nor thoughtful. They do not confront the evidence contradicting evolution on the merits. Rather they attack any person who asserts a non-evolutionary viewpoint, no matter how impressive the credentials. The lack of evidence for evolution is overlooked. They continue to teach as fact, fraudulent evidence for evolution even after the fraud has been discussed and openly acknowledged by the scientific community to be unreliable and without merit. The case for evolution is a cover-up.

A recent case illustrates the rather amazing extent to which the scientific education establishment goes to perpetuate fraud and silence their opponents. In LeVake v. Independent School District No. 656, et al. (Minnesota 2001), a high school biology teacher was not allowed to continue to teach biology after a colleague informed the curriculum director that LeVake may not believe in evolution. After the teacher was asked to put his views on evolution in writing, in which LeVake questioned some aspects of Darwinian evolution, LeVake was reassigned. The Minnesota Court of Appeals upheld the actions of the school administration on the basis that LeVake's Christian beliefs were an obstacle to teaching the subject matter, notwithstanding LeVake's scientific approach to the subject.

The United States Supreme Court in Epperson v. Arkansas (1988), had already immersed itself in the creation-evolution debate by not allowing schools to exclude discussions about evolution. Even though the teacher Scopes lost the "monkey trial," the trend had been, when Genesis is presented to oppose science, that scientific evidence should also be presented. After Epperson, local school districts and state governments could not mandate the teaching of "creation science" or restrict an individual teacher's "academic freedom" to present an open discussion or debate about evolution. This dictate applies only to evolution, however. For critics of Darwinian evolution, there is no "academic freedom." And there is no freedom of thought. LeVake taught us that if the school administrator suspects that a teacher may not believe in evolution because of Christian beliefs, the teacher can't teach biology.

THE END OF SELF-EVIDENT TRUTHS

The drafters of the Declaration of Independence were neither deists nor evolutionists. They believed in truth knowable by reason and science as well as in Scripture. They forcefully stated their convictions when they established the first principles of America's civil institutions declaring, "We hold these truths to be self-evident." This central holding of the Declaration of Independence has never been overruled or refuted. Rather, the premise of self-evident truths has been ignored. In the place of self-evident truths, the courts, legislatures and American people have substituted either false philosophies or have simply acquiesced as courts and legislatures substitute their own will. The principles of the Declaration of Independence have not been proven false; they have simply been discarded as irrelevant and no longer discussed.

From the beginning, the courts have attempted to define the law as based on tradition and precedent without considering and acknowledging the core first principles and legal philosophy that form the foundation for all law and the foundation for the Declaration of Independence. From Calder v. Bull (1797), that rejected Justice Chase's attempt to incorporate natural law as fundamental law, to Ogden v. Saunders (1827), when the majority rejected Justice Marshall's view that the sanctity of contract was immune from legislative interference, to Dred Scott v. Sandford (1853), that elevated states' rights over individual liberty, to The Slaughter-House Cases (1870), that refused to hold that the privileges and immunities required to be protected under the Fourteenth Amendment would apply to protection from government granted monopoly and preferences, to Nebbia v. New York (1934), that subordinated individual economic freedom to government discretion, to Roe v. Wade (1973), which rejected the right to life of one group in favor of personal freedom for another group, the courts have decided cases in the name of fundamental law. But the fundamental law the courts tried to find expressed as "truth" was discovered without any reference to the self-evident truths in the central holding of the Declaration of Independence. For what purpose is this truth if, like Pilate, we fail to be diligent in understanding the truth or its source, or if we don't even bother to look for or understand the answer? The objective of the establishment of legal institutions is to find the truth and then apply it. The rules of the process exist to aid in discovering the truth. If there is no self-evident truth, there can be no justice, and the institutions that we have established to administer justice will fail to achieve their essential purpose.

CHAPTER 3
THE MULTI-CULTURAL MYTH

"The Freedom then of Man and Liberty of acting according to his own Will, is grounded on his having Reason, which is able to instruct him in that Law he is to govern himself by, and make him know how far he is left to the freedom of his own will. To turn him loose to an unrestrained liberty, before he has Reason to guide him, is not the allowing him the privilege of his Nature, to be free; but to thrust him out amongst Brutes, and abandon him to a state of wretched, and as much beneath that of a Man, as theirs."

John Locke, *Second Treatise on Government*,
Chapter VI, Section 63

"The real object of the First Amendment was not to countenance, much less to advance Mohammedanism, or Judaism, or infidelity, by prostrating Christianity, but to exclude all rivalry among Christian sects and to prevent any national ecclesiastical patronage of the national government."

Justice Joseph Story

I served as local counsel to the American Center for Law and Justice in a Minnesota federal court case involving three employees of the Minnesota Department of Corrections. They had been reprimanded for their conduct at a mandatory diversity training session entitled, "Gays and Lesbians in the Workplace." The state alleged disruptive conduct such as silent prayers and Bible reading during the session. Other employees at the session who were napping and reading magazines were not sanctioned. Our plaintiffs conceded that theirs was a Christian-based protest as they were offended by the subject matter. The state, by virtue of mandating their attendance at these training sessions found their behavior so offensive that they needed to be punished.

  The trial judge ruled that the jury verdict in favor of the plaintiffs, which included punitive damages against the State of Minnesota, would stand. The judge ruled that government officials should have known that selective discrimination against Christians is unconstitutional.

  From the perspective of the government officials, as they purposely promoted diversity, Christianity could not be tolerated. The Christians, on the other hand, were viewed as intolerant because they disagreed. We won this one, but the other side still believes we are wrong.

◆ ◆ ◆

THE MARKETPLACE OF IDEAS

It is commonly believed that the importance of the First Amendment is to "preserve the debate of ideas in the 'marketplace of ideas.'" The term "marketplace of ideas" does not exist in any of the writings or correspondence of the Eighteenth Century. The term is attributed to John Stuart Mill, an English utilitarian thinker in the mid-Nineteenth Century, and not to any of the authors or supporters of the original Bill of Rights. The concept of the "marketplace of ideas" was not a First Amendment concept until used by Justice Oliver Wendell Holmes in the <u>Abrams</u> case in 1919.

  This belief in a "marketplace of ideas" echoes the sentiments of Justice Douglas expressed in <u>Gillette v. U.S.</u> (1971). He stated, "At the core of the First Amendment's protection of individual expression, is the recognition that such expression represents the oral or written manifestation of conscience" within the "sphere of intellect and spirit" as the domain of the First Amendment was described in <u>West Virginia State Board of Education v. Barnette</u>. The core principle governing contemporary America is the belief in the debate. This idea that such a debate in the marketplace of all ideas is guaranteed by the First Amendment's protection of free expression provides the cornerstone of modern constitutional law, rather than that there is one true idea.

  What happens when the marketplace of ideas sits in a naked public square where nothing is sacred and ultimate truth is rejected? The modern idea that Judeo-Christian theology cannot be relied on as singular truth results from the belief that epistemology is limited to scientific experimentation. Truth can never be claimed if one believes that ultimate reality can only be realized through the process of dialectic reasoning.

Differences in viewpoint, however, arise not only from the field of philosophy, but also from theology. Numerous religions are rooted in pantheism, not Biblical theism. And some religions are simply cults that exist outside of Christian orthodoxy, based on different interpretations of Scripture and new revelations rejected by orthodox Christians. Can these different philosophies and religions with their unique cultures coexist? More importantly, from a Christian perspective, should the Christian response be tolerance, evangelization or separation?

THE LIMITS OF TOLERATION

The issue of toleration was addressed by John Locke following 50 years of civil war between the Puritans, Anglicans and Catholics in Seventeenth Century England. Locke's *Two Treatises of Government* was contemporaneous with the passage of the English Bill of Rights that formed the basis of free speech in England. It provided a starting point for the broader expansion of freedom of speech and religion in America. But before assuming that Locke's ideas must be expanded to include toleration of all religions and all philosophies, it is important to distinguish between toleration of Christian sects—differing primarily in structure or minor doctrinal matters—as opposed to tolerating religions and philosophies that reject the existence of the one true God and the authority of the Bible, that ultimately reject the Christian idea of truth.

Christians believe that some ideas and facts can be known absolutely. A core belief of Christians is that God's existence can be demonstrated through evidence discernible by reason and that the life, death and resurrection of Jesus Christ was proven as historical fact by evidence of written and oral eyewitness testimonies. Such a viewpoint contrasts directly with the basic premises of modern philosophy that God's existence cannot be determined scientifically and that Jesus' resurrection was simply another myth created by religionists.

The discussion of religious tolerance pertains to two entirely different areas of disagreement. The first pertains to issues of church doctrine and ecclesiastical organization that were often exaggerated into conflict, particularly in the Seventeenth Century, because of the infusion of political and ethnic factors. The second area of disagreement pertains to disagreements over fundamental beliefs, such as the existence and nature of God and the deity of Jesus Christ. Locke advocated toleration for ecclesiastical and church doctrinal differences, and it was this advocacy that was eventually incorporated into the First Amendment to the United States Constitution and the various state constitutions. In contrast, modern multiculturalism attempts to demand tolerance for disagreements over fundamental beliefs. That was never intended by the founding fathers and never tried until recently.

Modern multiculturalism conflicts with America's Declaration of Independence. The Declaration establishes America's political identity, legally and philosophically. Prior to the Declaration, the colonists were Englishmen, subject to English laws and the sovereign powers of the English monarchs, limited by the jurisdictional restraints imposed by the many documents which comprise English constitutional law. The Declaration of Independence, as an act of an association of persons representing a political body, was both a separation from the jurisdiction of the English government and laws, and a formation of a separate political institution. It was a formation document that identified a specific political beginning. The Declaration laid the groundwork necessary to form a new and separate nation with new and separate principles to unite and govern its inhabitants. Legally, nothing has changed from the time of that beginning, 1776, to today.

From the standpoint of international law, the formation of a separate nation has two major consequences. All citizens and aliens residing within its territorial limits are subject and entitled to the protections of the laws under which the nation operates. Secondly, the nation, as an entity with a separate identity, is identifiable by characteristics and a purpose that are distinctive from all other nations. Unless a nation's sovereignty has been voluntarily surrendered to another nation or an international body, or if sovereignty has been involuntarily appropriated by another nation, the people retain the ability to define the laws under which their government and the people are bound. The people as a whole will determine the purpose and characteristics of the nation.

MULTICULTURALISM IS NO FIRST PRINCIPLE

The first flaw of multiculturalism is that the principle of tolerance has been elevated to a first principle of philosophy without regard to the considerations of a national identity and the right of people to define their own characteristics. Modern tolerance is refuted as a principle in Israel in Numbers 33; it denounced the idea that the Israelites could live alongside Canaanites that practiced the pagan Canaanite religion. If Israel remained faithful to God, Israel would be blessed as a nation. If Israel tolerated the

Canaanites' religion, Israel would be destroyed. This Biblical instruction supports the principle of national sovereignty and identity. No scriptural or legal principle supports the position that a sovereign nation relinquishes its identity as subordinate to a greater principle comparable or similar to modern multiculturalism.

Scripture further addresses the issue of divine sovereignty from the duty of the individual and of the nation. The Great Commission, "Go therefore and make disciples of all nations," commanded all believers to express one, specific, identifiable idea to all persons, without regard to political or language or cultural barriers. The Great Commission transcends national sovereignty. America was founded on the principle that this new nation, free from the burdens, restrictions and historical baggage that dominated the Old World, would be built on the principle of the Great Commission. The founders subsequently incorporated the principle of the Great Commission into America's national identity. They recognized it in the Charters of Virginia and Massachusetts; John Winthrop declared it in his famous "City on the Hill" message in 1630. The relationship of divine sovereignty to national sovereignty was similarly addressed by Samuel Adams immediately after the vote to declare independence was recorded. Adams said, "On this day we have restored the Sovereign..."

Ultimately, the issue of divine sovereignty is intertwined with the establishment of truth. When Pontius Pilate asked Jesus, "What is truth?" and Jesus said, "I am the Truth," Christ claimed jurisdiction to establish truth; God did not leave that issue to the state. When truth is established as an act of divine sovereignty, it is mankind's responsibility to act in accordance with it. When commanded to engage an enemy in battle the Old Testament judges and lawyers were obliged to act in accordance with divine command. When commanded to begin the Great Commission, the New Testament apostles and missionaries were undeterred by any civil command.

God's command to submit to His divine truth is irreconcilable with modern multiculturalism. Multiculturalism proponents advance a false premise that religion is the same as truth. The establishment of religion—any religion—in their view refers to ideology and not just the establishment of a monopolistic institution. Contrary to the intentions of its drafters, the modern reinterpretation of the First Amendment Establishment Clause combines God and truth within the same prohibition against the establishment of a nationally recognized Church. The drafters were not guilty of such confusion; they knew the difference between philosophy and corporate organization.

Historically, religion referred to organized religious sects and not to a set of beliefs. Historically, establishment referred to a monopolistic institution. An establishment of religion, therefore, is an institution with monopoly power over matters of religion enjoyed by one religious sect. An establishment of religion has nothing to do with advocating beliefs that are religious.

Although Jefferson broadened the definition of religion in the Virginia Statute of Religious Freedom—to protect religious beliefs—he did not make the error that the modern Courts have made; equating religion with all truth. Truth about God encompasses more than an individual's duty to God. Truth, as it relates to God and His impact on the universe, also includes the nature and existence of God, and history as impacted by Divine Providence. Truth also includes the nature of the created universe, which includes all immutable physical and moral laws, among other things. To broaden the definition of religion to include all truth as it relates to God is simplistic and misleading.

Jefferson's definition was intended to protect from government interference each person's individual relationship with God. Jefferson's definition did not affect God's role as Divine Providence in history. Jefferson's definition did not affect God's role as Creator. All persons may be entitled to their own opinion about God but they are not entitled to make up their own facts. In America, just because we permit individuals to worship and believe in false gods, it does not follow that those who do so can tell falsehoods about the one true God. Nor does such limited tolerance require America, as a nation, to deny the existence of the one true Biblical God, His nature, His role in history as Divine Providence, and His role as Creator. The modern misunderstanding of what is "religious" has nothing to do with Jefferson's definition of "religion." To exclude religious truth, that is, things that are true even though derived from and related to religion, by equating "religious truth" with "religion," is to exclude the very basis upon which all of our government institutions are based. Essentially, all of our government institutions, and the Constitution itself, would then be considered unconstitutional under the new definition of "establishment of religion."

Ultimately, broadening the definition of "religion" to include all of what is true that is connected with religion, suppresses truth in the name of separation. Worse, the "new" First Amendment conflicts with the First Commandment and it eliminates the Declaration of Independence as the foundation of the nation. The "new" First Amendment and the "new" Constitution look like the old models, but they are similar in external appearance only. The guiding principles are gone—replaced by false ideas perpetuated by false religions. The flawed logic behind modern multiculturalism is demonstrated by the failures experienced by those seeking refuge from their Old World or Third World misery in our "New World" land of promise. Logic and experience alone, without reference to clear Biblical guidance to keep God first, should be enough to warn all of us of the dangers of unrestrained multiculturalism.

THE MULTICULTURAL MYTH AND THE DISINTEGRATION OF TRUTH

The second flaw of multiculturalism flows from the contrast between a perception of the world as a "marketplace of ideas" as opposed to a battleground between forces of good and evil. Rather than considering truth as a comparison of ideas in which some ideas dominate, in the context of good versus evil, truth has consequences whether accepted or rejected. These consequences are clearly defined in the Bible. While obeying truth is an individual choice, it is also a cultural, societal, or national choice.

The Old Testament provides a clear, historically verifiable chronology of the results of Israel's national choices. Obedience to the Lord brought blessings. Disobedience to the commands of the Lord brought suffering and exile. Israel's example and the Bible's historical record are consistent with the historical record of modern and ancient civilizations.

Historians can manipulate man's story by what is included or excluded, and the perspective from which they tell their story. History is also complex. Events occur as a result of a combination of people's actions, both good and evil, and a multitude of circumstances existing at any time and place. The history of modern western civilization cannot be viewed as the events of a single, monolithic culture different from and irrelevant to the development of eastern or other cultures.

Modern multiculturalism oversimplifies history and contrasts western civilization with the rest of the world. Western civilization is portrayed as rigidly Christian, warlike and patriarchal. The reality of most other cultures is ignored so as not to offend by revealing the backwardness and barbarianism of non-Christian cultures.

The portrayal of western civilization as a monolithic, Christian culture is unfortunate. More can be learned from reviewing and comparing Christian cultures with each other than comparing western civilization as a whole with the Third World.

Even though the major western powers are all Christian, the approach to church and state by the nations is different. The effect of the different

43

choices made regarding separation of church and state is dramatic. Private Christianity that tolerates public evil suffers consequences as serious today as it did for Old Testament Israel.

To best understand the current religious and political situation in America today, the religious and political history of England, France, Germany and America from 1600-1800 should be a basic requirement. The Reformation affected all four nations and each responded differently in applying Reformation theology to these legal and political institutions.

AMERICANS LEARNED FROM THE ENGLISH

Although Calvin was French and Luther a German, Reformation theology had its first significant impact on culture in England. Calvin's *Institutes of the Christian Religion* was first translated into English in 1570. Its influence in England was almost immediate. By 1570, England had already separated from the Roman Catholic Church, as the Anglican Church was established under Henry VIII. The Anglican Church, however, was not formed to advance a theological principle. The Anglican Church was formed solely to accommodate the personal preferences of Henry VIII.

The Puritans, on the other hand, arose as an identifiable group in England, and grew into a political force because of Reformation theology. The Puritans first began to develop and grow as a predominant cultural dissenting class during the reign of Elizabeth I, shortly after the publication in England of Calvin's *Institutes*. In a very short period of time, the Puritans had become a prominent political force by their opposition to the Stuart kings at the beginning of the Seventeenth Century.

Great champions of individual rights marked this period in England, men such as Sir Edward Coke in the early 1600s, Samuel Rutherford and John Milton during the years when Cromwell and the Puritans assumed power, and John Bunyan and John Locke at the close of the century. Furthermore, the Wesleys led a great spiritual awakening in the first half of the Eighteenth Century. The Biblically based new covenant theology of Luther and Calvin invigorated politics and law, leading to political ideas of freedom and liberty. Because the Puritans' religion was also fiercely evangelical in practice, the Reformation was ingrained into the social culture and the political institutions.

The evangelical commitment of the Puritans in England became an experiment in applied New Testament theology in New England. The Puritans and Royalists both settled in North America, but were divided geographically and politically. New England never experienced or tolerated the class structure that existed in France and England. Privilege and preroga-tives violated the Biblical view of equality. The conflict between the aristo-cratic South and the middle class North would be a growing problem and factored into the many conflicts leading to the American Civil War. In 1776, however, class struggles were nonexistent in America as a political issue.

The southern opposition to England's attack on Massachusetts in 1775 was led by southern aristocrats. Patrick Henry, Thomas Jefferson, George Washington, George Mason and James Madison, among others, opposed religious intolerance, supporting and accepting the Biblically-based princi-ples of equality and rights of John Locke in unity with the New England colonies. Culturally, the Europeans considered the Americans as frontiers-men and backwoodsmen. But the Great Awakening had an even greater impact in America with the efforts of the Wesleys, George Whitefield, Jonathan Edwards and others.

Culturally, America was Calvinist in principle both spiritually and polit-ically. The condescension of the French towards America was met by an even greater revulsion of the French by the Americans. Rousseau and Voltaire were not widely read in America. Even Jefferson, America's most visible and tolerant Francophile, had not read Rousseau until after the War for Independence. Tolerance and diversity in Eighteenth Century America meant something entirely different than it did in Eighteenth Century France.

A LESSON FROM THE GERMANS

The Reformation began in Germany but never had the overall effect there that it did in England and America. At the time of Luther, Germany was not a unified nation, but rather, dozens of autonomous local city-states. Political battles between the small principalities were injected with religion, as military alliances were often based on the leader's Catholic or Lutheran beliefs. Eventually, the conflicts escalated, resulting in the Thirty Years War (1618-1648) that included all of the major powers of continental Europe and Scandinavia. Germany was the battleground, and the long struggle left the war-torn Germans cynical and culturally depleted.

Unlike the English, Germany and its rulers were influenced by French philosophy, the anti-philosophies and freemasonry. Although German rulers later attempted to renounce freemasonry and its influence, German culture was impacted and led by its dark and pessimistic philosophy and literature from Kant and Goethe in the late 1700s; Von Kleist, Schopenhauer and Hegel in the early 1800s; Nietzsche in the mid-1800s. German political leaders rejected intellectuals. Karl Marx wrote from his exile in England.

Other Germans fled to America and introduced principles that seeded modern socialism into American politics in the mid-1800s.

German Christians responded to the intellectual hostility to Christianity by withdrawing into a pious spiritualism. The theology of Soren Kierkegaard and Karl Barth lacked the intellectual base and moral authority of American and English Christians and, consequently, German Christians lacked the evangelical commitment to engage the culture and become politically involved. The consequences of vertical pietism, without a horizontal commitment, would be manifested in the Twentieth Century. How German Christians responded to Adolph Hitler in the 1930s, with the exception of the dissenting Confessional Church led by Martin Niemoeller and Dietrich Bonhoeffer, provides us with one of modern history's best examples of the consequences of Christian toleration of evil.

Interestingly, the Germans may understand the implications of the legal principles that laid the groundwork for the Holocaust better than most Americans. In a 1975 decision of the German Constitutional Court, the German judges reflected upon the last quarter century's most controversial issue, abortion, with the mid-Twentieth Century's most notorious human tragedy, the Holocaust. In contrast to America's equivocation in <u>Roe v. Wade</u> on the question of when life begins, in a decision made two years before the Germans' landmark case, the German court matter-of-factly stated, "the interruption of pregnancy irrevocably destroys an existing human life." The German court acknowledged that it had departed from the abortion laws and decisions of other countries. But it eloquently justified its departure because of Germany's unfortunate experience:

> Underlying the Basic Law are principles for the structuring of the state that may be understood only in light of the historical experience and the spiritual-moral confrontation with the previous system of National Socialism. In opposition to the omnipotence of the totalitarian state which claimed for itself limitless dominion over all areas of social life and which, in the prosecution of its goals of state, consideration for the life of the individual fundamentally meant nothing, the Basic Law of the Federal Republic of Germany has erected an order bound together by values which places the individual human being and his dignity at the focal point of all of its ordinances.

A fundamental law based upon a self-evident truth that the law protects life had been disregarded by the German courts and legislature in the 1930s. In 1975, the German court refused to follow the cultural trend and the international precedents that threatened to lead them down the same path.

A LESSON FROM THE FRENCH

Religion in Eighteenth Century France may have been weaker in influence than in Twentieth Century Germany. Whatever influence the Reformation may have had in Catholic France, the persecution of the Protestant Huguenots expunged it. By the middle of the Seventeenth Century, while the Puritans controlled Parliament and England, the remaining Huguenots who were able to escape were settling in America.

Culturally, the Huguenots in America may have been as significant as the Puritans. The *Vindiciae Contra Tyrannos* was as significant a work as *Lex Rex* and Locke's *Two Treatises of Government*. Politically, however, the Huguenots were a minority in America.

Back in France, the Jansenists and Jesuits fought for institutional control of the Catholic Church. The political battle weakened the spiritual emphasis of the clergy. At the same time, a developing class animosity pulled the clergy and the church into the middle of the struggle between the aristocracy and the common people. The French monarchy was absolutist but managed to manipulate the people against the aristocracy. The "divine right" theory that led to the demise of the Stuart kings in England had prevailed in France, partly because France's King Lewis XIII, had shown political shrewdness as he refused to align himself with the aristocracy. An English-style Puritan middle class was nonexistent in France.

The spiritual void in French culture was filled by the Enlightenment philosophers and anti-philosophies such as Jean Jacques Rousseau and Voltaire. Rousseau was pantheistic in philosophy and popularized a set of democratic principles in France that were a corruption of Locke's themes of equality and human rights. In France, equality became a class and egalitarian concept; rights were stated in terms indistinguishable from the modern description of secular humanism. Voltaire was atheistic and fiercely anti-Christian. Voltaire's lifestyle and philosophy reflected a belief in an individualistic, personal autonomy unrestrained by any law of nature or political limits. French philosophy grounded that country in class hatred, anti-Christian cynicism and personal decadence. It was indeed the tale of two cultures. The English and Americans reviled French culture.

In France, the spiritual void left by the failure of Christianity was filled by an evil corruption of Christian principles. A small, secret society known as Illuminism, led by Adam Weishaupt, had formally united with the freemasonry movement in July 1782, at the Masonic Convention of Wilhelmsbad.

It united more than three million members of secret societies in a common cause not fully understood even by the vast majority of its members. At the lower levels of freemasonry, the aims appeared to be consistent with and more committed to human improvement than organized religion.

In July 1785, a courier enroute from Frankfurt to Paris was struck dead by lightning. Secret Illuminati plans for revolution in France that he carried were discovered. The Elector of Bavaria began an investigation and raided Weishaupt's home and those of many other conspirators. The authorities believed they had broken up the Illuminati, and subsequently the popularity of freemasonry plummeted. But the secret plans of the clandestine occult organization survived in the French district of Orleans and ignited the French Revolution.

The theological content of the worldview of the followers of the Duke of Orleans, a leading early figure of the French Revolution, was clearly presented in this statement by Adam Weishaupt:

> Man is fallen from the condition of Liberty and Equality, the state of pure nature. He is under subordination and civil bondage, arising from the vices of man. This is the Fall, and Original Sin. The Kingdom of Grace is that restoration that may be brought about by Illumination and a just Morality. This is the New Birth. When man lives under government, he is fallen, his worth is gone, and his nature tarnished. By subduing our passions, or limiting their cravings, we may recover a great deal of our original worth, and live in a state of grace. This is the redemption of men—this is accomplished by Morality, and when this is spread over the world, we have the Kingdom of the Just.

The statement symbolizes the corruption of the fundamental theological principles that had prevailed as Christian orthodoxy for centuries. These demonic counterfeits energized the disillusioned with a false hope when the church on the continent was weak and inward looking. The occult made little headway in England and America but thrived in France and elsewhere on the Continent.

WHAT MADE AMERICA DIFFERENT

The comparison between America's War for Independence and the French Revolution presents a stark contrast and study into the effect of good versus evil. They were different revolutions. They were caused by different principles. The rhetoric, however, seems similar.

Americans were different from the French. They lived differently and they thought differently. In *Democracy in America*, Alexis De Tocqueville compared the French and American experiences, determining that the difference was not in superior American principles or institutions. Rather, the difference was in the moral viewpoint and moral behavior of the American people in contrast to the corrupt viewpoint and the decadent, hypocritical lifestyle of the French aristocracy, as well as the ignorance and disillusionment of the Parisian lower class.

The battle between good and evil is complex in all of its facets but simple at the core. The Biblical metaphor that a "tree is known by its fruit" applies to the aggregate as well as the individual. The danger, which underlies the importance of Christian education, is that truth understood, as opposed to corrupted truth, can be explained in rhetorical and similar sounding themes that can be easily misunderstood by an uninformed and disillusioned public.

Like the Twentieth Century Germans, the Nineteenth Century French made changes to their legal system that serve as a reminder to a bloody moment in its history. The French passed laws to restrain judges from interpreting legislative acts counter to the legislative intent. Those laws are still in effect today. Judges must apply the law, rather than interpret the law. The penalty for violating this law is a misdemeanor. In response to the secular and occult hostility to Christianity that characterized the French Revolution, the Catholic Church was re-established as the official church in 1801.

The Germans, after experiencing a culture of private Christianity co-existing with a purely secular state, elevated the protection of life to a fundamental self-evident truth beyond legislative reach. After experiencing a secular revolution, the French re-established the Catholic Church in what remains a largely secular culture. To the east, the invigoration of politics by the church tore down the "iron curtain" and the American principles set forth in the Declaration of Independence were that revolution's ideal.

It's not the organized church, but the knowable and well understood principles about God and Christianity that form the basis of the Christian church, and Christianity itself, that give us the self-evident truths that provided the groundwork for our laws. It's not the institution of any particular Christian church, but well-informed Christians, that is necessary to form a democratic government that protects individuals from the state and leads the people as a bulwark against bloody revolutions. For a Christian to be weak is to submit to slavery after being liberated. For a Christian to be ignorant results in being misled, aiding those who sanction evil by using Christians appearing to be good.

OUT OF MANY, ONE

The multicultural myth is based upon a misconstruction of the term *e pluribus unum*. The correct definition is not "out of one, many," but "out of many, one."

America's strength has been our uniform adherence to a written set of rules that transcends race, Christian sectarian beliefs, and ethnic origin. The truths that form the rules tolerate, but do not incorporate non-Christian religions. The beliefs of non-Christian religions cannot be reconciled with the written set of truths that form the basis for our government. It is not "out of one set of laws, all laws" or "out of one set of laws, different meanings." Multiculturalism can include many different kinds of people with different beliefs and customs, but multiculturalism does not accommodate all different kinds of beliefs and laws with many different meanings. There can be only one set of laws with one accepted meaning.

The danger in America from modern multiculturalism is not limited to entirely distinct religions, such as Islam and Hinduism, which are repugnant to America's legal system and America's core values and principles. Rather, America is threatened by its own corruption of Christianity as practiced in this country that parallels the practices existing in pre-Holocaust Germany and pre-French Revolution France.

America is overwhelmingly Christian, but modern American constitutional law has become overwhelmingly secular—even anti-Christian. The change from a legal system that defended Christianity to one that attempts to ban it happened as American Christianity grew to resemble Eighteenth Century France and Twentieth Century Germany. The propagation of the corruption of Christian idealism in modern America has been well received by the same uninformed and disillusioned elements in mainstream Christianity that existed in Eighteenth Century France and Twentieth Century Germany. If America has an advantage, it is that self-evident truths are historically grounded in the Declaration of Independence and in our institutions. The secret, occult societies that infected continental Europe have never been historically grounded in America and are repugnant to our cultural tradition; our great advantage in America's war of good versus evil. Today's danger is that Americans no longer see good and evil as a choice with consequences.

To accept the myth of multiculturalism while ignoring the reality that history is a study of the battle between good and evil, is to be blinded while traversing a course that leads to the slow and steady dismantling of the institutions and principles upon which America's uniqueness and greatness was built.

Chapter 4

"RIGHTS"

"That we are endowed by our Creator with certain inalienable rights."

Declaration of Independence, 1776

"The sacred rights of mankind are not to be rummaged for among old parchments or musty records. They are written as with a sunbeam in the whole volume of human nature by the hand of the Divinity itself and can never be erased or obscured by immortal power."

Alexander Hamilton

"Show me that age and country where the rights and liberties of the people were placed on the sole chance of their rulers being good men, without a subsequent loss of liberty."

Patrick Henry

Trial lawyers understand something about rights that most other people don't. Talking about rights is just talk unless there is a judge that recognizes those rights in court. Judges have a lot of direct control over what "rights" are because the "rights" that a plaintiff alleges mean nothing if the judge dismisses the case for lack of standing—a judicial limitation. The judge, then, identifies which rights will be protected and which will not.

From 1993 until 1995, I represented a plaintiff in two separate federal court actions in which I alleged that RESPA, a federal statute regulating certain activities in the real estate, financial, and title insurance industries, unfairly discriminated against independent competitors in favor of vertically-integrated real estate brokers—an esoteric issue interesting to some antitrust lawyers and economists. I filed briefs, met with Congressmen from both political parties, testified before Congress, and lost. One court held that only the government and class action lawyers, acting on behalf of consumers, had standing to litigate the issue. The judge in the second case disregarded the statute granting standing to competitors, and substituted his own five-part test. He considered his own factors and decided who could bring a suit. According to the judges, my client had no "rights" as it regarded this case. For liberals, the government would decide. For conservatives, the market would decide.

More disturbing to me was the result in a more recent case. In a 1995 case brought by fictitious, non-existent plaintiffs, the Minnesota Supreme Court decided that the Minnesota constitution required taxpayers to fund abortions, striking down a 1978 statute that prohibited taxpayer-funded abortions. In February 1999 I filed suit in federal court on behalf of 47 Christian taxpayers, Catholics and Protestants, alleging that paying for abortions violated their religious convictions. The court never decided the issue; the religious "rights" of Christians were not sufficient to give them standing under the Civil Rights Act; even as taxpayers they had no standing. So the court refused even to address the merits of the claims. On appeal, the Eighth Circuit Court of Appeals decided that the First Amendment granted standing to oppose government acts that offended because they were religious, but did not give standing to oppose government acts which offended Christians.

I appealed to the United States Supreme Court and asked if it was now to be the law that atheists are protected whenever they are offended, but that Christians have no rights when they are offended. The Supreme Court declined to take the case.

◆ ◆ ◆

Ironically, the vacuum created by the denial of truth has resulted in the arrival of a multitude of new "rights." The new ideas and definitions of rights did not appear spontaneously. New definitions of "rights" result from each new philosophy that leases space in the "marketplace of ideas." "Rights" was originally a Christian concept. The modern conflict and confusion regarding the specific "rights" that are entitled to legal protection result from the refusal to define the origin and nature of "rights" in the same way that Jefferson stated them in the Declaration of Independence.

When rights are adequately defined, an individual whose rights have been infringed can protect them by appealing for justice to the courts of law. When the courts of law misdefine rights or refuse to enforce justice by not protecting individual rights, individuals will inevitably seek redress and justice outside of the courts of law. It is a historical fact that the major civil wars, in England in the 1600s and America in the 1860s, followed erroneous court cases.

The American Revolution, in contrast with the French Revolution, was not rebellion from legitimate authority, but rebellion from illegitimate authority exercised by the King of England and Parliament. The American revolutionaries did not spontaneously reject English law; rather, they tried long and hard to win justice. "But when a long train of abuses and usurpations, pursuing invariably the same object evinces a design to reduce them under absolute despotism, it is their right, it is their duty, to throw off such government," they stated in the Declaration. They declared, via a long list of refusals by the King and Parliament to hear their petitions, that they had to resort to rebellion to secure their natural rights as Englishmen. As a consequence, the colonists sought protection of their natural individual rights from the Supreme Judge of the Universe, rather than from King George III.

The various usages of the term "rights" is analogous to the imprecision in the usages of the terms "liberty" and "freedom." All three terms relate to the same subject, and vary depending upon philosophy and worldview.

Essentially, modern conflicts over the correct meaning of "rights" are traceable to three, separate and distinct worldviews: (1) Christianity, (2) humanism, and (3) libertarianism. These three distinctive worldviews have been in conflict in different forms for 2,000 years.

Christian orthodoxy has often been in conflict with humanism and sometimes been corrupted by humanist philosophy. Christianity and humanists both emphasize the need to have compassion for and provide assistance to fellow humans. Christians do so because God has commanded them to do so. Humanists do so because mutual assistance, absent divine protection, is the only way to elevate mankind above tribalism and the law of the jungle.

Superficially, the philosophies of Rousseau and of Locke appear consistent with each other. At the roots of their philosophies, however, their assumptions about God and man are entirely different. The law of nature and of nature's God in the Declaration of Independence was Biblically-based. Discussions about the law of nature can also be traced to the Greek philosophy of Plato and Aristotle. The true nature of a pure law of nature, absent Divine Providence, was represented by the symbol of Leviathan, and was eloquently identified by Thomas Hobbes. Hobbes' view was rejected by John Locke and was not relevant to the Declaration of Independence.

THE AMERICAN INNOVATION

The American experience is unique in world history because, (1) the rights of Americans are based upon a democratic system, and (2) the rights of Americans are in writing. In America, the people are the political sovereign. No Old World nation recognized the sovereignty of the people.

In England, Parliament was the political sovereign. Parliament derived its sovereignty from a number of documents that slowly pried rights away from the monarchs: the Magna Charta of 1215, The Petition of Rights in 1628, the Bill of Rights of 1689. Nowhere else in the Old World had rights been as well-defined and the political sovereignty removed as distant from the monarch as in England. Still, England's constitutional government only in a small way resembled the new American model.

The United States Constitution defines the nature of America's form of democracy. This nature is evidenced by the insistence of many founding fathers of a written and binding statement of rights, followed by ratification of the Bill of Rights. Later, the people, through their representatives, demanded additional amendments, and rejected others.

John Marshall, who had served in the Virginia House of Burgesses and as Chief Justice of the United States Supreme Court, understood the radical significance of a written constitution. He saw that the Constitution bound the federal government, but that other Common Law rights had been retained by the people. While referring to the right to contract, Marshall wrote in his dissenting opinion in <u>Ogden v. Saunders</u>:

> "[I]ndividuals do not derive from government their right to contract, but bring that right with them into society. That obligation is not conferred on contracts by positive law, but is intrinsic and is conferred by the act of the parties. This results from the right which every man retains to acquire property, to dispose of that property according to his own judgment, and to pledge himself for a future act."

Despite Marshall's rigid adherence to the written constitutional text, he rejected the legislature's attempt to write laws in contravention of the Common Law. Marshall paid the written Constitution proper deference, and understood its limitations as it regards Common Law. The modern Court ignores Marshall's deference to the written Constitution, creating, instead, a completely new set of rights.

THE COLONIAL DEFINITION OF RIGHTS

The rights of American citizens, as a matter of law, are secured by the Declaration of Independence. The Constitution defines the powers of the government and imposes limitations on it. The Bill of Rights, as a written response to delegates' doubts about the limits of government power, further restricted government power. The Bill of Rights guaranteed specific individual rights, held to be particularly important to the delegates, but it never limited other individual rights, not specifically envisioned, which were retained by the people. The Declaration of Independence was a corporate document. It expressed the corporate status of the American colonists in opposition to the assertion of the King's authority over them.

At a minimum, the rights of citizens defined in these formative legal documents bind the government to respect the rights of citizens. The federal government contracted with each citizen whose will was expressed through their elected representative. The parties to the contract, that is, the people and their government, were limited by the terms of the contract, i.e., the Constitution. The federal government is viewed in this contract as a perpetual institution to be legally evaluated as it existed at the time of the ratification; it is indisputable that the federal government is still bound as one of the parties to the contract.

The government cannot unilaterally change the precise definition of rights of its citizens. Nowhere is it stipulated by the citizens that the government could act independently of them as it regards the Constitution and the Declaration. Yet, despite being denied this authority, the federal government has progressively increased its power, the result of which is to reduce the rights retained by the citizens, and promulgate a unilateral redefinition of those rights.

The colonists clearly understood their rights prior to the Declaration of Independence. This is evident in their clear articulation of those rights in public documents and in their private correspondence and discussion. The Declaration of Rights in the "Resolutions of the Stamp Act Congress" dated October 19, 1765 firmly asserted the colonists' right to be free from taxation without their consent, and stipulated that consent could only be granted by elected representatives of colonial governments.

Time, distance and communications made it impossible for the colonists to have direct representation in Parliament. In response, the colonists established their own legislative bodies and began to redefine the terms and conditions of their governing authorities. To the extent that they had control over their local governing franchise, they had achieved a limited form of government by the consent of the governed.

Two committees produced The Declaration and Resolves of the First Continental Congress of 1774. One committee prepared a "bill of rights" and the other produced a list of infringements of those rights. During the First Continental Congress, delegates from Suffolk County, Massachusetts, presented the Suffolk Resolves. These resolves related to England's repressive measures aimed directly at the Massachusetts colony, and it defined its authority for the source of colonial rights and individual liberty as the "law of nature," laying the foundation for the Declaration of Independence.

The colonies united in their support of the "Massachusetts Circular Letter," which had been first approved by the Massachusetts colonial legislature in 1768. The circular letter advocated a new legal theory that the Constitution is fixed, that the legislature derives its limited authority from the Constitution, and cannot exceed that authority. The Massachusetts delegation maintained, "it is an essential, unalterable Right, in nature, engrafted into the British Constitution, as a fundamental Law & ever held sacred & irrevocable by the Subjects within the Realm, that what a man has honestly acquired is absolutely his own, which he may freely give, but cannot be taken from him without his consent." The colonists further asserted that, notwithstanding any limitation in the colonial charters, the right "of free men" existed as a "natural and constitutional Right."

The circular letter achieved its purpose, and each colony passed resolutions supporting its objectives. The Declaration and Resolves then adopted the authority of the law of nature, while also enumerating additional rights to appear later in the Bill of Rights. The drafters of the Declaration of Independence incorporated these rights, demonstrating that the King and Parliament had violated the law of nature and natural rights, thus providing the legal grounds for the separation.

THE FOUNDATIONS OF AMERICA'S CREED

The Declaration of Independence concluded the colonists' development and application of the new rights theory and was stated in the form of a creed.

> We hold these truths to be self-evident, that all men are created equal, and are endowed by their Creator with inalienable rights, among them life, liberty and the pursuit of happiness.

The reference in the Declaration of Independence to "all men are created equal," and rights as "endowed by their Creator," and that these rights were "inalienable," and specified life, liberty and the pursuit of happiness were specific and identifiable as Christian and Protestant. The ideas were not new. These ideas were advocated and discussed in numerous pamphlets and speeches promoted throughout the colonies and were based upon principles clearly defined by Locke, Rutherford, and England's Puritan clergy during the early 1600s. These were the same ideas traceable ultimately to the Protestant Reformation.

The reference to "life, liberty and the pursuit of happiness" were directly based on John Locke's proposition of life, liberty and property as inalienable rights in his *Two Treatises of Government*. Locke's treatise had been widely read and supported by the colonists after its first appearance in the colonies in the 1730s.

Locke's political theories are based on principles derived from the Old Testament. Locke attended Oxford a short time after Samuel Rutherford's tenure at the University of Edinburgh, Scotland was ended by the controversy over the publication of *Lex Rex*. Locke accepted Rutherford's Biblical principles of equality, but his primary contribution came from his reliance on the law of property, as a basis for liberty, later seen in the writings of James Madison. Madison then expanded the property right to include the rights of conscience and religious freedom as a liberty attached to the ownership of one's own ideas.

Combining Locke's views of life, liberty and property with Jefferson's definition of religious freedom, a clear picture develops of a worldview based on teachings originating with the Protestant Reformation. Luther's rejection of religious intermediaries is parallel to Locke's rejection of political intermediaries. For the first time in history, America wrote both principles into law. Both principles rest upon the conviction that man's relationship to God cannot be interfered with by another human. For one man to place himself between another person and God is idolatry.

The founding fathers knew that the rights of man derive from his unique nature as a created being. Man's character is a result of his having been created in God's own image. This separates man from the rest of creation. The "Creation Mandate," expressed in Genesis 1:28-30, gave man dominion over the earth and its resources.

> And God blessed them: and God said unto them, Be fruitful, and multiply, and replenish the earth, and subdue it; and have dominion over the fish of the sea, and over the birds of the heavens, and over every living thing that moveth upon the earth.
> And God said, Behold, I have given you every herb yielding seed, which is upon the face of all the earth, and every tree,

in which is the fruit of a tree yielding seed; to you it shall be for
food: and to every beast of the earth, and to every bird of the
heavens, and to everything that creepeth upon the earth, where-
in there is life, I have given every green herb for food: and it was
so.

God created man as a rational being, with the ability to reason, to distinguish right from wrong. Man can choose to do good or evil, but has both
the duty and the authority to live for God, though he can also reject Him.
The duty and the authority to live for God establish the rights that existed
between men. So long as man pursues a vertical relationship with God, no
horizontally situated man can interfere. To the extent that a society or individual chooses to reject the vertical relationship of men to God, the rights
theory established in the Declaration of Independence becomes irrelevant
and inapplicable.

Historians generally attribute the rights of individual religious freedom
to Luther's "priesthood of all believers," but it is more accurately attributable to the Protestant Reformation in general. Property rights derived from
mankind's status as stewards with dominion over creation, are attributable to
the medieval Catholic church. The English word "dominion" in Genesis
1:28 is a translation of the Hebrew word "rahdah," which means to reign or
rule. The English word is derived from the Vulgate-Latin "dominammi,"
meaning dominate, derived from "dominus," meaning lord or ruler, and
"dominium."

The church did not promote the inalienable rights theory, though present in the Scriptures, until the Gregorian Reform in the Eleventh Century.
The early church had avoided the inalienable rights theory because it was
too easily identified with the mysticism of Greek and Roman philosophy.
The medieval church, however, embraced the dominion mandate as a principle ordained by God as evidenced by the division of property among the
twelve tribes of Israel.

The Dominicans, led by Thomas Aquinas, engaged in a long dispute
with the Franciscans over whether property was an individual right or a
community right. Eventually, the Dominican position became the official
position of the Roman Catholic Church. Locke, influenced by the Dominican position on property and Rutherford's principle of equality, advocated
that property rights, including the whole product of an individual's labor,
were inalienable.

THE GREEKS AND THE UNENLIGHTENMENT

The definition of rights held by the colonists stood in stark contrast to the view of rights held by the Greeks and the Enlightenment. The French view of the "rights of man" was a corruption of the English and American view. The French Enlightenment/humanist view sounds similar to the Christian view of rights, but it is rooted in two fundamental principles traceable to the Renaissance and the Greeks that sharply and irreconcilably conflict with the Declaration of Independence.

First, the humanists believe that rights emanate from a vague pantheistic philosophy rooted in man's humanity. God does not endow rights, man does. The humanist denies that rights are inalienable because they, like the Greeks, practice pantheism, though they appear atheistic. They posit that because law does not originate from the law of nature or nature's God, it must originate from the *polis*, or state. Rousseau spoke of a "general will," adopted by a democratic majority. The Greeks disdained the law of nature and viewed the state, and the political process, as an escape from natural law.

Second, the Greeks and the Renaissance rejected the idea of equality. As evolutionists, Greek and Renaissance thinkers, like their modern counterparts, believe that all men are unequal. The Greeks differed from modern evolutionists only in the reason inequality exists. The Greeks believed that some men possessed more divinity than other men, a pantheistic view. The hierarchy of divinity seen in the polytheistic Greek and Roman religions extended to the hierarchy of men. Aristotle supported slavery as a natural result of the higher nature of some men over other men.

Modern evolutionist humanism necessarily sees inequality because of the varying degrees and stages of evolution. National Socialism, with its emphasis on eugenics, easily classified different ethnic groups as unequal, and accordingly, some groups had protectable rights. They could do so because individuals were evolved beings rather than created beings. French Enlightenment humanists followed a different road to the same end. Because the French did believe in equality, nonconformists to the general will had to be made to conform to the general will. As with modern America's "political correctness," freedom for the individual is a philosophical fiction. Robespierre and the "Reign of Terror" showed how the French saw individual freedom as a philosophical fiction; they could not reconcile individual rights and equality in their pantheistic world.

The humanist solution, whether of the ancient Greeks or modern humanists, is pure positivism. Positivism is the rule of law as proclaimed by the state. The Greeks were unabashed positivists, elevating the *polis* to the

61

position of ultimate authority and source of law, with the thinkers and states-men as the natural rulers set over the subordinate classes.

AMERICA'S DIFFERENT VIEW

The conflict between the Dominican/Reformation tradition of rights and the Aristotelian/Renaissance/Enlightenment position is very much alive in modern America. The judicial branch of government provides the arena for its modern skirmishes. This philosophical conflict is one of both definition and appropriate actions, just as it was when the colonists settled it in 1774. In the Declaration and Resolves and the Declaration of Independence, the colonists defined rights and explained their origin. The natural rights defined by self-evident truths were set forth in writing and are unchanging. It is the duty of the legislature to provide the definition. It is the duty of the courts to protect those rights, by adhering to that definition, and then to con-tinually and diligently protect individual rights as other individuals and insti-tutions attempt to infringe upon those rights. The protection of rights requires an appropriate action. It is an unmistakable sign of the change in the Court's philosophy that the modern Supreme Court has reversed both functions. The modern Supreme Court neither adheres to the unchanging definition of rights and self-evident truths, nor protects individuals from infringements of those inalienable rights. The Supreme Court of the Twen-tieth Century has it backwards on both grounds. The Supreme Court took action to change the legislation and withholds its judicial authority when rights are infringed.

Chief Justice Marshall, in his landmark decision of Marbury v. Madison (1803), stated that it was the province and duty of the court to say what the law is. He was correct. The court must accurately state the law and apply it in administering justice when the interests of two parties collide. This fun-damental principle is ancient, seen in Moses' deliberations as judge, and it still defines the role of the judiciary. But Marshall did not say that it was the province and duty of the court to *make the law*. Divine law was supreme. And the natural rights of man were superior to the power of the legislature to make law. To argue otherwise meant that the legislature could make law defying both divine law and the natural rights of man. The Court's function was supposed to be limited. It could only apply the law in an adversarial proceeding.

Proper application of law is not always certain. At times, the intent of the legislature is unclear. The court has a definite role in interpreting law and in assisting in the just enforcement of the laws.

Justice James Wilson, an original signer of the Declaration of Independence and Constitution and a member of the First Supreme Court, articulated the necessity that the judiciary be clear and consistent in the enforcement
of law. Justice Wilson first quoted Bracton, England's first great legal scholar, who said, "It would be superfluous to make laws, unless those laws, when
made, were to be enforced." Justice Wilson distinguished between the executive and judicial authority in our early constitutional history. Justice Wilson stated, "When the laws are plain and the application of them is uncon-
troverted, they are enforced immediately by the executive authority of government." However, "...when the application of them is doubtful or intri-
cate, the interposition of the judicial authority becomes necessary." In that
case, Chisholm v. Georgia (1792), the United States Supreme Court said that
anyone subject to the law had a right to have the law interpreted correctly
and applied fairly.

DEVIATING TOWARD THE UNENLIGHTENMENT

Sadly, and worse yet, dangerously, the Court has deviated from Justice
Marshall's and Justice Wilson's correct interpretation of the Court's role.
The modern Court has found rights where none previously existed and then
refused to enforce traditional rights unless those rights earn favor with the
courts. Today's Court only enforces civil rights it chooses to validate, while
rejecting natural rights it deems archaic.

Some rights, especially those found by the Court as the "right to privacy," have been defined as fundamental. For centuries, especially since the
publication of Thomas Hobbes' *Leviathan,* legal and political scholars have
debated the question of authority. If the individual is the subject of the political authority, the individual's rights exist at the whim of the political authority. For the founding fathers, the legislature had some authority to make the
rules and the court had the authority to enforce the rules. But the rights of
man were God-given and could not be taken away by the legislature or the
court. Today, the court declares what is fundamental, and therefore, what are
rights. These new rights are fundamental only because the court says so, and
they will remain fundamental only so long as the court interprets them to be
fundamental. Rights are no longer set in stone, inalienable and predictable,
but are set in a confusing and volatile mixture of mud and straw, subject to
removal by the will of a future court.

The modern American view is pure legal positivism with roots in Aristotelian elitism. God's law has been rejected because of fear of violating the
new contrived definition of separation of church and state. In its place has

been substituted a new, evolving pantheistic concept of liberty. This new liberty concept can be found both in the rights of conscience decisions of Justice William O. Douglas and in the joint opinion of Justices Souter, Kennedy and O'Connor in <u>Casey v. Planned Parenthood of Southeastern Pennsylvania</u> (1992). The modern concept of liberty is a combination of libertarian philosophy and pantheistic theology balanced with utilitarian considerations, provided that the considerations are secular.

The new most fundamental of all modern rights is the freedom of conscience. The roots of the modern jurist's freedom of conscience are found in Jefferson's and Madison's appeal for protection of the freedom of the mind and conscience. Jefferson and Madison referred to the duties owed by each person to the Creator. So Jefferson and Madison saw it as improper for governments to regulate or coerce individual conscience. But Jefferson and Madison did not limit their concept of liberty to conscience; they extended it to all blessings and obligations derived from an individual's relationship to God.

Jefferson's and Madison's view has been discarded by the modern Supreme Court. In <u>Casey v. Planned Parenthood of Southeastern Pennsylvania</u>, the Supreme Court acknowledged, "although the abortion decision may originate within the zone of conscience and belief," the act of abortion must be protected as a product of the exercise of an individual's own determination "of meaning, of the universe, and of the mystery of human life." The Court cited a previous case for its authority that "the liberty guarantee" is a "rational continuum which, broadly speaking, includes a freedom from all substantial arbitrary impositions and purposeless restraints." The Court thereby removed the definition of liberty from its original understanding, placing it within the exclusive realm of judicial opinion. The Court declared that liberty is no longer the result of a commonly understood acknowledgment of an immutable truth. It is, instead, a conditional grant or license from the exclusive jurisdiction of judicial opinion.

All members of the modern Supreme Court agree that rights are "alienable," rather than "inalienable," but disagree as to whom the decision of what constitutes alienability has been entrusted. The disagreement ranges from whether the Court should apply a "strict scrutiny" test or a "rational basis" test, and whether the determination as to alienability rests with the legislative or judicial branch of government. Ironically, as the modern Supreme Court has reserved to itself the role of defining rights, the Court has convinced both liberals and conservatives that it has expanded the definition of liberty. The Court accomplished this, however, by only recognizing a limited number of secular rights as fundamental while simultaneously liberty is curtailed, excluding religious or moral considerations. Locke has been dismissed and the positions of Jefferson and Madison have been narrowed to refer only to selective passages that support our modern secular definition of liberty.

SURRENDERING RIGHTS

American Christians fail to consider that their rights are God-given and specifically secured by the Declaration of Independence, Constitution and the Bill of Rights. The colonists, steeped in a tradition of covenant theology, saw all rights as God-given, assisted by Divine Providence. The colonists established inalienable rights to life, liberty and the pursuit of happiness as a matter of law. For modern Americans to abandon this unique American gift, by passively and ignorantly acquiescing to the usurpation of those rights by proponents of a new philosophy, is to submit to the yoke of slavery in violation of the command given in Galatians 5:1-3; "For freedom did Christ set us free; stand fast therefore, and be not entangled again in the yoke of bondage."

The colonists refused to allow the King of England or Parliament to usurp their rights because they believed them to be natural rights due all men; God's creative act deemed it to be so. For modern Christians to submit to an illegitimate authority whose usurpations have far exceeded those of the King of England evidences Americans' decline in understanding of law and theology, and their lack of commitment to the declaration of religious truth.

CHAPTER 5
LAW AND INSTITUTIONS

"But the Right of Nature, that is, the naturall Liberty of man, may by the Civill Law be abridged, and restrained; nay, the end of making Lawes, is no other, but such Restraint, without the which there cannot possibly be any Peace. And Law was brought into the world for nothing else, but to limit the naturall liberty of particular men, in such manner, as they may not hurt, but assist one another, and joyn together against a common Enemy."

Thomas Hobbes, *Leviathan* (1651)

"Nothing distinguishes more clearly conditions in a free country from those in a country under arbitrary government than the observance in the former of the great principles known as the Rule of Law. Stripped of all technicalities, this means that government in all its actions is bound by rules fixed and announced beforehand—rules which make it possible to foresee with fair certainty how the authority will use its coercive powers in given circumstances and to plan one's individual affairs on the basis of that knowledge."

F. A. Hayek, *Road to Serfdom*

An issue that the courts have not really yet settled has to do with the limits of the "Full Faith and Credit Clause" of the Constitution and how it affects the laws of different states. Citizens and politicians are very concerned about the legislative response to the possibility that a ruling from one state on the issue of "gay marriage" can somehow be enforced on the rest of the states. Recently, more Americans have also become concerned at how, during recent Supreme Court cases, American justices consulted the law of other countries rather than applying "original intent" from our American Constitution.

Years ago, I addressed these issues in a case where I asked a Minneso-

ta court to ignore a ruling from a South Dakota court which had misapplied the requirement of finding "minimal contacts" to establish jurisdiction over my client. My client, a Minnesota resident, had never been to South Dakota. Judgment was entered against him in South Dakota because that is where the bank attempting to collect money from my client was located. I argued that South Dakota courts had no jurisdiction over my Minnesota client, and because the jurisdiction requirement of the Fourteenth Amendment had not been met, the Full Faith and Credit Clause did not apply.

State court judges are used to being overruled by federal judges, though they never like it; it is easy to understand their reluctance and hesitation to invalidate a ruling of another judge by recognizing the rights of an ordinary citizen who owed someone some money. The predicament of Roy Moore, Chief Justice of the Alabama Supreme Court, who was removed from the bench because he refused to recognize the validity of a ruling of a federal judge, is another example. The federal judge in deciding that case likely violated Alabama's own constitution. Moore's predicament shows why any judge who wants to stay out of trouble would often look the other way.

Let me say it bluntly. Judges have shown that they are very capable of making up The Rule of Law. It would be far better if the Law was rooted in something more predictable than a judge's will. While I contend in this book that the Rule of Law must be rooted in historical Biblical and theological truth, it should not be that hard for judges to require that another judge's rulings at least be rooted in the Constitution, as it was commonly understood for centuries.

◆ ◆ ◆

By July 4, 1776, the colonists had agreed to a common understanding of the meaning of "the laws of nature and of nature's God." They adopted this terminology as part of their legal argument in the Declaration of Independence. American law would rest upon this principle.

The law of nature and of nature's God was understood to be God's eternal moral law, or divine law, and was based on the same law of God described in the Old and New Testaments. The founding fathers' understanding of the "law of nature and of nature's God" does not even closely resemble the "law of nature" described by Hobbes. Hobbes saw the need for law to counter the uncivilized and barbaric existence of the beasts and the brutes. Hobbes' law of nature needed to be restrained. The founding fathers' definition of the "law of nature and of nature's God" also stands in sharp contrast to the modern view of natural selection and the law of the jungle. The evolutionist view of the law of nature resembles Hobbes but presents a negative view of man, needing protection by a greater power to protect it from itself, rather than the positive portrayal of the aspirations of man as used in the Declaration of Independence. From John Locke to Sir William Blackstone, the rights of Englishmen were tied to the natural law of man found in God's general revelation through creation and God's special revelation given through Scripture. Locke and Blackstone were basic texts of political and legal philosophy in the colonies, read and followed by all political leaders and the courts.

LEGAL RIGHTS AS ENGLISHMEN

The colonists appealed to the British authorities for protection of their rights as Englishmen. Though they lived in the colonies, they were still British citizens. The Resolution of the Stamp Act Congress in 1765 rested upon the colonists' entitlement to "all the inherent rights and privileges of his natural born subjects within the kingdom of Great Britain." The colonists declared allegiance "to the crown of Great Britain...and all due subordination to that august body, the Parliament of Great Britain." Despite the repeal of the Stamp Act, Parliament imposed numerous other oppressive measures.

At the First Continental Congress in 1774, the delegates considered and adopted the law of nature, as well as the British Constitution, and the American Colonial Charters, as the source of colonial rights. The Declaration of Rights in the Resolves of the First Continental Congress specifically referred to "the immutable laws of nature." Later, when the Declaration of Independence was written, there was no mention of the rights of Englishmen, as it was their purpose to sever all ties to the British Constitution.

The colonists' view of law was linked to their view on ultimate authority. The colonists believed that resistance to authority could not be justified if the lawmaker acted with proper constitutional authority. The colonists objected to the legitimacy of the laws passed by Parliament from 1763 to 1776 because their understanding of the English constitutional law did not allow Parliament to usurp authority previously granted to the colonial legislatures. The basis for their objections stems from three sources: (1) John Locke's *Two Treatises of Government*; (2) the anonymous Huguenot publication *Vindiciae Contra Tyrrannos*; and (3) Samuel Rutherford's *Lex Rex*. Relying upon the Old Testament account of Jephtha appealing to God to deliver the Jews, Locke wrote that in a dispute with an unjust ruler, people must appeal to God, "where there is no jury or if there is no judge on earth."

Rutherford wrote to refute those who defended divine right monarchy. Rutherford's theology rejected the nature-grace humanist dichotomy which included some of the Anglican clergy of his day; he argued that God's grace is inseparable from nature. Rutherford advocated that the king was subject to nature, and could not rule contrary to it. Divine law and the law of nature were inseparable.

The *Vindiciae Contra Tyrannos* (Defense of Liberty Against Tyrants) was possibly more influential in the colonies than any other source. Huguenots wrote the *Vindiciae* after the St. Bartholomew's Day Massacre in 1572. The author wrote that the laws of God and nature bind the government. The theory and analysis of the *Vindiciae* is almost identical to that later used by Rutherford and Locke. All three documents were published in response to tyranny. They all relied upon the fact that the law of God transcends the law of nature, binding the sovereign and making him submit to a higher law than himself.

THE LAW OF NATURE AND NATURE'S GOD AND THE COMMON LAW

The reference to the law of God and the law of nature did not originate in political theories. They were a simple extension of the well-accepted use of the law of God and the law of nature as legal theory. The political argument was a legal argument used against the actions of the sovereign. Constitutional law in English history was nothing more than the application of the Common Law to the king.

The three primary sources of constitutional and Common Law theory in English history are: (1) Bracton; (2) Sir Edward Coke; and (3) William Henry Blackstone. All three can be cited as absolute authority for the proposition that the source of the Common Law is the same law of God/law of nature theory cited in the Declaration of Independence. John Marshall continued the tradition in American constitutional law in his historic opinions in the first years of the American Supreme Court.

Bracton and Blackstone both defined the term "law of nature" as the moral law established through creation. Blackstone's definition of the "law of nature" was given in his *Commentaries on the Law of England* (1765):

> Man, considered as a creature, must necessarily be subject
> to the laws of his Creator, for he is entirely a dependent being
> ...And, consequently, as man depends absolutely upon his Maker
> for every thing, it is necessary that he should in all points con-

form to his Maker's will. This will of his Maker is called the law of Nature...This law of nature being coeval with mankind, and dictated by God himself, is of course superior in obligation to any other. It is binding over all the globe, in all countries, and at all times: No human laws are of any validity if contrary to this; and such of them as are valid derive all their force and all their authority, mediately or immediately, from this original.

Blackstone's *Commentaries* sold as well in America as in England, providing the basis of John Marshall's legal study, as well as that of other leading lawyers of the late Eighteenth Century and early Nineteenth Century. Blackstone drew his definitions from Scripture, Locke's legal philosophy, and the canon law and philosophy of Aquinas and the medieval Catholic Church.

Blackstone's definition of the "law of nature" grew out of the unified system of law and theology present in the medieval Catholic Church. English Puritan theology and Common Law in the Seventeenth Century and the worldview of the drafters of the Declaration of Independence never deviated from early Catholic teaching about Common Law and the law of nature. Thomas Aquinas summarized the Catholic principles in the *Summa Theologica*. Richard Hooker, a Sixteenth Century Anglican theologian, also endorsed those same Catholic principles. Hooker wrote that all law derived from God. He believed that social progress could be achieved if man learned and studied all natural laws, human and supernatural laws. Hooker emphasized balancing reason, Scripture and tradition as the foundations of truth. Shortly thereafter, the Puritans adopted these same principles.

William Ames, the leading Puritan theologian during the first Stuart regime referred to, "That law of God, which is naturally written in the heart of all men." The Puritans held absolutist views on the issue of divine sovereignty, and so, would necessarily believe that all law came directly from God. Orthodox Christianity never deviated from the fundamental principle that the field of law derived its theory and legitimacy from the field of theology.

The unified theory of law and theology has always had support from lawyers even though they do not necessarily acknowledge that legal theory has its roots in theology. The most significant early example of such lawyers whom later movements of lawyers could look to as a model, were the Common Law lawyers who opposed the absolutist policies of the Stuart Kings of England in the 1600s. The intellectual leader of the movement and most feared by the Stuart Kings was Sir Edward Coke (1552-1634). In 1606, he was appointed as Chief Justice of the Common Pleas. In 1613, the King appointed him Chief Justice of the King's Bench. Coke was dismissed from judicial office by King James I in 1616 because of Coke's consistent opposition to the royal prerogative. Then Coke led the fight against the monarchy in Parliament, later publishing the *Institutes of the Laws of England*, which came to be regarded as saving the medieval Common Law. Edward Coke seized upon and popularized the term "fundamental law" and appropriated it to his view of constitutional law.

Judges and barristers like Coke believed that fundamental law was found in the customs, Common Law precedents and statutes which comprise "the law of the land." They used the term "fundamental law" interchangeably with "Common Law" or "the Common Law tradition." The lawyers believed that the fundamental law either originated with the law of God or was closely connected and parallel to it.

John Marshall's American Contribution to Constitutional Law

The major advancement in American constitutional law occurred through the judicial opinions of Chief Justice John Marshall. Marshall never rejected the law of nature and nature's God as superior over all man-made law, as so many modern jurists appear to believe. Marshall retained Bracton's and Coke's reliance on Common Law as superior to constitutional law. But Marshall elevated constitutional law over the ordinary legislative acts, using Coke's principle of supremacy of fundamental law as the tool.

Marshall recognized that the defining characteristic of American law is that the basic governing principles were reduced to writing. No other government had successfully accomplished the task achieved by the members of the First and Second Continental Congress and Constitutional Convention in adopting a comprehensive body of organizational documents that outlined the nature and theory of individual rights and government responsibility. The task was accomplished under the authority and with the consent of the corporate body, comprised of the American people.

Marshall defined the organizational documents as fundamental in Marbury v. Madison (1803):

> The principles...are deemed fundamental...they are designed to be permanent...The powers of the legislative are defined and limited; and that those limits may not be mistaken, or forgotten, the Constitution is written...The constitution is either a superior, paramount law, unchangeable by ordinary means, or it is on a level with ordinary legislative acts, and like

other acts, is alterable when the legislature shall to please to alter
it.

In implementing and interpreting the documents, Marshall consistently
and rigorously applied a set methodology in ascertaining the intent of the
document and, accordingly, the binding effect of the document's contractual scope. In Ogden v. Saunders (1827), he wrote in his dissenting opinion:

> To say that the intention of the instrument must prevail; that
> this intention must be collected from its words; that its words are
> to be understood in that sense in which they are generally used
> by those for whom the instrument was intended; that its provi-
> sions are neither to be restricted into insignificance, nor extend-
> ed to objects not comprehended in them nor contemplated by its
> framers, is to repeat what has been already said more at large,
> and is all that can be necessary.

Marshall believed that the Constitution, by its delegation of power to
the judicial branch, required adherence to the written text. He stated in Marbury v. Madison (1803):

> Certainly all those who have framed written constitutions
> contemplate them as forming the fundamental and paramount
> law of the nation...Those then who contradict the
> principle...would subvert the very foundation of all written con-
> stitutions. It would declare that an act, which, according to the
> principles and theory of our government, is entirely void; is yet,
> in practice, completely obligatory...[I]t thus reduces to nothing
> what we have deemed to be the greatest improvement in politi-
> cal institutions—a written constitution.

But the judicial power was limited by a fixed understanding of law. The
court's function was to apply law rather than make law. In Osborne v. Bank
of the United States (1821), Marshall wrote:

> Judicial power as contradistinguished from the power of the
> laws has no existence. Courts are mere instruments of the law
> and can will nothing. Judicial power is never exercised for the
> purpose of giving effect to the will of the judge; always for the
> purpose of giving effect to the will of the law.

There was, to Marshall, no basis for the court to roam beyond fixed
understandings of law and jurisdiction as established by the written Consti-

tution and the Common Law. In <u>Gibbons v. Ogden</u> (1824), Marshall wrote:

> [W]e know of no rule for construing the extent of such powers, other than is given by language of the instrument which confers them, taken in connection with the purposes for which they were conferred.

The courts had no rulemaking authority and any such attempt to usurp the legislature's rulemaking authority was not law. Marshall made that clear in <u>Marbury v. Madison</u> (1803):

> [W]here the law is not prohibited, and is really calculated to effect any of its objects entrusted to the government, to undertake here to inquire into the degree of its necessity, would be to pass the line which circumscribes the judicial department, and to tread on legislative ground. This court disclaims all pretensions to such a power.

Marshall's view on the judicial role is the same as the role defined by Sir Edward Coke. Coke incorporated the law of nature into Common Law. In <u>Calvin's Case</u>, Coke wrote that:

> 'The law of nature is part of the law of England' and 'the law of nature was before any judicial or municipal law' and 'the law of nature is immutable.'
> 'The law of nature is that which God at the time of creation of the nature of man infused into his heart, for his preservation and direction; and this is *lex eterna*, the moral law, called also the law of nature. And by this law written with the finger of God in the heart of man, were the people of God a long time governed, before the law was written by Moses, who was the first reporter or writer of law in the world.'

Coke had not deviated from Bracton who wrote:

> The king himself ought not to be under man, but under God and under the law, because the law makes the king. Therefore, let the king render back to the law what the law gives him, namely dominion and power, for there is no king where will and not law wields dominion.

For Coke, constitutional law was subject to Common Law, and the court had authority to hold an act of Parliament void if repugnant to Common Law. In <u>Dr. Bonham's Case</u>, Coke wrote:

And it appears in our books, that in many cases, the Common Law will control Acts of Parliament, and sometimes adjudge them to be utterly void. For when an Act of Parliament is against common right and reason, or repugnant, or impossible to be performed, the Common Law will controul it, and adjudge such an act to be void.

Marshall's constitutional adjudications established the precedent for the Supreme Court's continuing role in interpreting the Constitution with respect to the constitutionality of legislation. But the Supreme Court's assumption of authority to interpret the Constitution is neither exclusive nor supreme.

Andrew Jackson battled both Congress and the Supreme Court in his opposition to the Second National Bank. Censored temporarily by the United States Senate, Jackson defiantly upheld the Executive's role in interpreting the Constitution:

It is maintained by the advocates of the bank that its constitutionality in all its features ought to be considered as settled by precedent and by the decision of the Supreme Court. To this conclusion I cannot assent...The Congress, the Executive, and the Court must each for itself be guided by its own opinion of the Constitution. Each public officer who takes an oath to support the Constitution swears that he will support it as he understands it, and not as it is understood by others. It is as much the duty of the House of Representatives, of the Senate, and of the President to decide upon the constitutionality of any bill...as it is of the supreme judges when it may be brought before them for judicial decision.

Jackson's precedent was followed by Lincoln. Lincoln openly opposed and refused to be bound by the Supreme Court's infamous <u>Dred Scott</u> decision. Lincoln argued that the Court's opinion bound only the parties to the case. In his first inaugural address, he maintained:

If the policy of the Government upon vital questions affecting the whole people is to be irrevocably fixed by decisions of the Supreme Court...the people will have ceased to be their own rulers, having to that extent practically resigned their Government into the hands of that eminent tribunal.

The principle that Lincoln addressed, that the principles of the Declaration of Independence must be incorporated into the Constitution to reach a

75

correct understanding of the fundamental law, remains as a necessary component to understanding the nature of law and the supremacy of the "reign and rule of law" over arbitrary and incorrect interpretations of law as imposed by the judiciary and the legislative branches.

THE NEW JUDICIAL ORDER

The modern view is that law is the result of the efficacy of command, rather than a studied observation of a created order. Twentieth Century theory is posited by Oliver Wendell Holmes, who distinctively changed the way the court looked at law during the first part of the Twentieth Century. Holmes once wrote, in 1899, in *Law in Science and Science in Law*: "Inasmuch as the real justification of a rule of law, if there be one, is that it helps to bring about a social end which we desire . . . ."

Holmes' viewpoint has been most significantly adopted by Justice William Brennan, representative of a bevy of modern judges, who undertook in the 1960s to enact social change through judicial order, by what legal scholar Eugene Rostow called in 1962 in his book, *The Sovereign Prerogative: The Supreme Court and the Quest for Law*, as "normal the fact that judges have a limited but inescapable duty to make some of the decisions through which law develops, in response to changing notions of policy."

The modern conception of the Rule of Law is ambiguous. As can easily be perceived by the modern jurists' viewpoint that the Court should play an active role in enacting social change evolving the rule of law by the fancy of the judge who hears a case, the modern rule of law can be arbitrary and despotic. Contrary to Marshall's cautious and restrictive approach to judicial decision-making, the modern court covets the responsibility to establish the Rule of Law.

THE REIGN AND RULE OF LAW

Contrasting with the modern misinterpretation of the Rule of Law is the traditional principle of what has been described as the Reign and Rule of Law. The Rule of Law can be tyrannical and arbitrary because the source of law is the assumption of ultimate rulemaking authority by men.

On the other hand, the Reign and Rule of Law requires that all men be subject to the law. The law reigned over the kings and even over the judges. It was the operative legal principle in America throughout the Nineteenth Century. The Reign and Rule of Law presupposes the existence of a fundamental law that transcends constitutional law and lesser regarded legislative and executive enactments. Only an adherence to the Reign and Rule of Law and principles of fundamental law guarantees that inalienable rights and limited government will continue. Any attempt to presume that rights cannot be changed and that government cannot be limited is illusory, unless institutions and all men are subject to some fundamental principles of law which are both objectively understood and unchangeable by any human authority. Fundamental law and the Reign and Rule of Law are the only bulwarks against tyrannical rule. References to "rational continuums" and evolving standards of morality are assertions made without any basis in rational philosophical or theological principle.

The Supreme Court's modern directive that an individual's liberty interest can only be limited for secular purposes reveals the inherent flaw and precarious standing of liberty. Ironically, it prevents the consideration of the only principled opposition to the Court's power.

The only effective, long-term principled opposition to tyranny in recent history has been Christianity. Secularists and separationists who oppose Christian influence on government confuse the role Christianity played in establishing their rights while opposing tyranny. The confusion originates when they fail to consider the impact of Reformation theology and its relationship to legal philosophy. Justice Blackmun's fear of church edict ending all political debate ignores 300 years of history and learning that led to the Declaration of Independence and the Bill of Rights. That history and learning refers to the role of reason in ascertaining the true moral law upon which all institutions are based, and is based on philosophy. But the roots of America's legal philosophy are dug deeply into Christian theology.

THE CONVERGENCE OF LAW AND THEOLOGY

An instructive reconciliation of law and theology with philosophy that helps to understand the founding fathers' view of the nature and purpose of law was accomplished by Philip Melancthon. Melancthon had been a follower of Luther. Because of Luther's absence, Melancthon represented the Reformation at the Diet of Augsburg (1530). Melancthon prepared the "Augsburg Confession" and wrote most of the public documents of the German Reformation. Melancthon attempted, and almost accomplished, reconciliation between Luther and the Catholic Church. Despite Luther's influence on the German Reformation, it was Melancthon's views that primarily influenced the Lutheran Church.

Melancthon rejected his earlier views on Aristotelian philosophy but he also did not accept Luther's rigid determinism and views on predestination.

77

In his *Ethicae Doltrinae Elementa* (1550), Melancthon laid out his ethical framework and views on law and free will and these directly influenced and provided the framework for succeeding generations of theologians and legal philosophers.

Melancthon began with the proposition that all men possess an innate consciousness of God's existence and that man has a relationship with God to represent or pattern His image and likeness. Melancthon saw man as distinct from other creatures in that man's primary goal is "ethical knowledge" of God. Melancthon asserted that because of man's unclear perception of God resulting from the fall of Adam and original sin, man needed "moral philosophy" to supplement Christian doctrine. So, Melancthon posited that man possessed the light of reason and an innate sense of ethical conduct, both necessary for a moral life.

Melancthon's departure from rigid determinism and predestination was based on his empirical observation and scriptural references to man's ability to make choices. Melancthon correctly observed that law would be useless and meaningless if there was no free will. Because God holds man responsible to observe the moral law, free will is a philosophical necessity.

The different understanding of secular natural law and Christian ethics existed throughout the Reformation. Melancthon, like Rutherford and Locke who followed him, was careful to differentiate natural law, unrestrained by any superior law, and the law of nature established through Creation, but, accordingly, subject to the divine law. Christian ethics never depart from the assumption that divine law, established through Creation and Scriptures, is ideally to be the same as natural law. Because of man's fallen nature, however, reconciliation of the natural will and God's will is only possible through the Word of God, the Gospel of Jesus Christ, and the Holy Spirit working to regenerate the human will. The human will determines whether to accept or reject the work of grace. The curse of the law is to attempt to abide by the law without grace. Knowledge of the law, though incomplete, was possible through reason. Reason, as a means to understand the moral law, established the basis for Common Law and fundamental law theories developed throughout the centuries.

Fundamental law, derived from reason and evidence, is based on general revelation through observance of Creation, and special revelation, understood through diligent study and understanding of Scriptures. Christian moral law should not be understood or redefined in any other way. America's founding fathers knew and embraced this truth in a practical way as they laid out our governing documents.

Although man's moral and scientific understanding has always been incomplete, evidence and observation, leading to further experience, contribute to a changing understanding of law. But the changes in the law are based upon a more complete understanding of man's moral nature. These flow from a better understanding of Scripture, not new personal revelations unique to individuals who attempt to define their own existence void of God's. Nor do lawmakers' personal revelations of evolving human nature and understanding hold sway against revealed, ancient Scriptural truth. The moral law, like physical laws, is discovered rather than invented.

If law is like science, as Holmes contended, principles must be confirmed by evidence. As Chesterton observed, "The Christian ideal has not been tried and found wanting, [it] has been found difficult and left untried."

In American law, the founding fathers discovered the ideal, but subsequent generations have found the ideal difficult and abandoned it. History vindicates the Christian principle of law as the only system of law, based on reason, that maintains an inherent opposition to tyranny and the arbitrary Rule of Law. The drafters of the Declaration of Independence had to depart from principles of English constitutional law and rest the right of the colonists to seek independence on the laws of nature and of Nature's God. Likewise, to restore the Reign and Rule of Law in modern America, our basic understanding of law cannot rest solely on the written Constitution, and on the Supreme Court's interpretation of the Constitution, but must also be grounded in that same legal philosophy, rooted in Christian theology, relied upon by the opponents of tyranny for centuries.

CHAPTER 6
JUSTICE

"I can sum up my judgment of Hobbes in a single statement. He cared more about peace than about justice. This a dangerous doctrine in any age. It is a fatal doctrine in the age in
which we live."

Lyman Windolph,
Leviathan and Natural Law

"[Justice is] based on God's written Law, back through the
New Testament to Moses' written Law; and the content and
authority of that written Law is rooted back to Him who is the
final reality. Thus, neither church nor state were equal to, let
alone above, that Law. The base for law is not divided, and no
one has the right to place anything, including king, state or
church, above the contents of God's Law."

Francis Schaeffer
A Church Manifesto

*In 1997, for the first time in 40 years, Bulgaria elected a democratic
parliament. The Communist defeat, in large part, resulted from a grassroots
effort led by a friend of mine from Minnesota. After the election, he took a
group of us from Minnesota to Bulgaria where we met with business and
political leaders to discuss the political transition. We also meant to explore
business opportunities for us, and offer our help.*

*The night before we left Sofia, at a secluded mountaintop restaurant, we
celebrated the birthday of one of the leaders of the new Bulgarian majority.
I sat next to the guest of honor and during dinner asked him if he thought
that Bulgarian judges would ever have the courage to take on the rampant
corruption in that country. The Communists had transferred many of the
state-owned assets to themselves—and with a Mafia-like organization, they*

controlled many of the businesses. Americans, I told him, would not be interested in investing in Bulgaria unless corruption was brought under control. He assured me that I need not worry because, "They are our judges now."

I was not assured. I pondered whether it would be wise to invest in Bulgaria or even if the people would long support this new government.

Justice may not be the first great interest of the populace as Daniel Webster once said, but it is the great interest of lawyers and the primary function of government. The Declaration of Independence, in speaking of human rights, states "that to secure these rights, governments are instituted among men," thereby laying the cornerstone of American justice.

The structure of the American system of justice is delineated in the United States Constitution. Chief Justice John Marshall then refined the role of the judicial branch when explaining the appropriate exercise of judicial power in the early cases of the Supreme Court. The primary function of government under the original American system was to administer justice.

Rights and justice are related terms. "Rights" are possessed by individual American citizens. "Justice" is the process, with enforcement actions, necessary to secure individual rights, and to conform individual actions and will to the law.

The Biblical translation of "justice" comes from the Hebrew word "tzedek," meaning justice and righteousness, and is related to the Hebrew word "mishpat," meaning rights. "Justice" simply describes man's attempt to do that which is right. God's standard of justice is a benchmark that binds everyone, believers and unbelievers, whether living in obedience or in rebellion, and no man can change that fact. Biblical justice is the essence of God's nature and being. In the Scripture, God clearly explained His principles of justice to man, using understandable terms and setting achievable standards. Biblical justice employs fairness and equity, to which all human standards, ordinances and judicial sentences must conform.

THE LEGAL STANDARD

Aristotle classified standards of justice into two categories: commutative justice and distributive justice. These two basic definitions usefully illustrate the distinction between justice as a principle of fairness, and justice as a principle of punishment.

Commutative justice governs the law of contracts and is based upon the principle of equality. Each person is entitled to be governed by the same set of rules. Discrimination based on status, class or any other factor is prohibited. This standard is consistent with Biblical justice and American constitutional tradition.

Distributive justice assigns to each person the rewards which result from personal merit and service, or the proper punishment for crimes. Men are not all equally blameworthy or deserving. Discrimination is not only permissible, but required to maintain a comparison with the standard and the proportionate deviation from the standard. This principle of applying a measurement of deviation from a standard of equality, rather than requiring that outcomes show no deviation, directly contradicts egalitarian and collectivist theories. The artificial maintenance of class distinctions, such as in an aristocracy or oligarchy, and artificial creation of benefits based on membership in a class, such as in affirmative action or any wealth distribution reform program, violates the principle of distributive justice.

JUSTICE AND THEOLOGY

The question of whether justice is naturally resident in our hearts is a theological question. Yet, the question of whether people in general want to be just and to do justice is demonstrable and appears to have been validated over time. The democratic principle, incorporated into our political institutions through representatives chosen by the free election process, and our legal institutions through the jury process, appears to produce a majority that attempts to apply principles of fairness in their judgments. The larger disagreement among those who want to be just and to do justice is over the question of what is right.

Thomas Aquinas wrote that a man cannot see clearly enough to know how to be just. To find justice, a man must look at the Scriptures. If Scripture is unclear, Aquinus said to look to tradition for guidance. Common Law courts adjudicated conflicts in this manner. They developed their own standards and traditions by the accumulation of case precedents and judicial opinions that guided subsequent adjudications. These traditions and precedents formed the basis of "the law of the land." Over time, the right to justice as administered by the judiciary was not abstract, conceived of by judges effecting their own will, but was according to law. Judges administered it in conformity to careful consideration of precedents, and understood that they were limited to operate within the law and apply it to each situation accordingly.

DUE PROCESS

The guarantee of justice is known as due process. The term originated with Sir Edward Coke, who used it interchangeably with the phrase "law of the land," or *in terroram lex legae*, which Coke took from the Magna Charta of 1215. Coke's connection of due process to the Magna Charta has never been questioned and is the logical extension of his application of legal principle to representatives of the government.

Coke also connected due process and "the law of the land" to Common Law. Many Common Law traditions extended to a time period far earlier than the Magna Charta. Prior to the Norman Conquest of 1066, the Teutonic tribes had established democratic forms of justice that predate and resemble our modern jury system and council forms of government. The practices of Teutonic tribes were well established in northern Europe and in England by the time of the Magna Charta. Christian principles of government were also evident in the early days of Christianity in England under Alfred the Great. Coke did not base Common Law on the Magna Charta. Rather, Common Law justified using the Magna Charta as the foundation of English constitutional law.

The purpose of due process is to secure the rule of law in the administration of justice. Under American law, the rules of due process bind both the federal government under the Fifth Amendment and state governments by application of the due process guarantee of the Fourteenth Amendment.

The courts have subsequently classified due process into two categories. *Procedural* due process refers to constitutional guarantees that the rules governing the administration of justice will be applied, and will be applied fairly. *Substantive* due process guarantees that the administration of justice, or the application of lawmaking and the rule of law, cannot be used to deprive any person of their life, liberty or property unless that person is guilty of a criminal or civil wrongdoing. Procedural due process refers to the rules regarding the securing of rights. Substantive due process refers to the identification and nature of the rights to be secured.

PROCEDURAL DUE PROCESS

Procedural due process recognizes that a decision must be made in every case or conflict. In order to make a just decision, the decider must find the "truth" forming the basis of the decision. The "truth" may be a finding of fact or a legal conclusion. A just decision requires that both the facts and law of a case are accurately determined. Americans are guaranteed a predictable and certain level of justice because of due process guarantees in the Bill of Rights.

The guarantee of procedural due process consists of both evidentiary rules and procedural rules. The evidentiary rules followed by trial attorneys and enforced by judges are primarily based upon rules developed under Common Law. The purpose of evidentiary rules is to ascertain the truth. Accordingly, evidence that is unreliable, irrelevant, or produced to distort and confuse is not allowed. In addition, parties in a conflict have a right to compel testimony and the production of documents to provide necessary information leading to the truth. Despite the Biblical mandate that individuals testify willingly and truthfully to prevent injustice, witnesses are notoriously reluctant to come forward or even speak truthfully and completely when compelled to do so.

Courts have developed other rules to exclude evidence produced overzealously or illegally. For example, courts have always considered perjury to be a serious offense. In addition to perjury, the United States Supreme Court has combined its authority under Common Law to fashion evidentiary rules with the Bill of Rights to exclude all evidence which the courts consider illegally obtained. Mapp v. Ohio (1959) first established the "exclusionary rule" under which illegally obtained evidence could not be used by prosecutors in a criminal trial. In Wong Sun v. U.S. (1968), the Supreme Court expanded the "exclusionary rule" to further exclude all evidence obtained as a result of an illegal search or seizure. The "fruit of the poisonous tree" doctrine meant that if an investigation was faulty, the criminal would not be convicted. The focus of the inquiry may have, accordingly, been transferred from the alleged wrongdoer to the investigator under the modern concept of constitutional criminal justice. The justification for this rationale is that there can be no justice in convicting someone for violating the law if another violation of the law was committed in order to convict.

Modern constitutional theory also encompasses the guarantee of certain rules of procedure. These were developed to prevent arbitrary decision-making, sometimes in cases involving disputes between private citizens, but more often in cases brought by the government. The most notable guarantee is the right to be tried by a jury of one's peers.

The right to a jury trial is generally regarded as a product of the Magna Charta. But jury trials, as a common practice and right, were developing prior to Magna Charta. Jury trials were used extensively by the Germanic tribes as early as the Eighth Century. Juries were also commonplace in medieval England. Because each manorial estate wielded exclusive authority over the manor under English feudal law, the different classes in English feudal society maintained their right to be tried by their peers.

The application of the Magna Charta was often ignored by English authorities. Coke reinvigorated the Magna Charta and its application to the government.

Constitutional principles and theory, to be meaningful, should be applied in every case. The drive for justice, as a constitutional principle, emanates from each individual's unwillingness to compromise or surrender to arbitrary justice.

The fundamental principle of procedural due process in the Magna Charta is the jury trial. The right to a jury trial in England was, appropriately enough, secured by one of America's founding fathers, William Penn. In 1670, Penn was charged with disturbing the peace in London for distributing religious literature that the civil authorities found offensive. Penn demanded a jury of his peers and resisted the magistrate's efforts to coerce the jury. Penn believed an enlightened public served as the remedy for legislative and judicial violations of the due process of law. This belief led to his undertaking the task of educating Americans and Englishmen of the rights of men. His efforts resulted in an unquestioned right to trial by a jury that lasted to modern times, until the Court and Legislatures decided to limit this fundamental right.

SUBSTANTIVE DUE PROCESS

In recent years, the concept of substantive due process has been essentially repudiated. Despite the early importance of substantive due process by Coke and our founders, substantive due process no longer exists in its original form. The courts have not been able to reconcile the idea of protecting inalienable rights when confronted by the assertion of the government's "police power" by democratically elected legislatures. Except when the courts create new fundamental rights, such as the right to an abortion, the conflict between the will of the democratic majority and the fundamental rights of individuals is almost always won by the government.

Then, the courts balanced individual rights with legislative power. At first, fundamental, inalienable rights were protected. Eventually, the Supreme Court announced in <u>Ferguson v. Skrupa</u> (1963), that the Court would not recognize the substantive due process rights of individuals when opposed by any enactment of the legislative branch.

The Court's separation of "procedural due process" from "substantive due process" allows the courts to give the impression that they are still functioning to protect due process rights under the Fifth and Fourteenth Amendments to the Constitution. But procedural due process rules exist only for the purpose of guaranteeing the aspect of due process of law that was originally related to the rules of procedure. The substantive due process definition that protects life, liberty and property as set forth in the Declaration of Independence is now treated differently. Substantive due process encompasses the institutional framework and process guaranteeing inalienable rights that are essential to what was defined as the law of the land. Inalienable rights, due process of law, and the law of the land are all part of the same thing. The abandonment of substantive due process is an obvious manifestation of the Supreme Court's more subtle abandonment of "inalienable" rights and its substitution of a new "law of the land." The Court's new "law of the land" abandoned Coke's principles and those of the Declaration of Independence.

LAW FROM THE PENUMBRA

The new "law of the land" is entirely subordinate to the authority of the United States Supreme Court and is, for the most part, the result of the enactment of the Supreme Court's own will. The Court first voluntarily relinquished its duty to protect rights under the "old" substantive due process standard. Then, a new concept of substantive due process arose almost as soon as the old definition was abandoned. But the new "substantive due process" was a corruption of the old "substantive due process."

Rather than apply the old rules, the Supreme Court made up its own new "law of the land." The new substantive due process, the right to privacy, arose from the "penumbra" of the rights guaranteed by the Bill of Rights. This new "penumbra" was first discussed in <u>Griswold v. Connecticut</u> (1965). As a practical result, because the new substantive due process rights were found in the "penumbra" of rights originating in the Constitution, rather than the Common Law where they had always been before, the Constitution had become the new fundamental law.

In direct opposition to the principles of constitutional law of Coke and Marshall, the Common Law was rejected as the source of fundamental rights in favor of the Constitution. In <u>Roe v. Wade</u> (1973), Common Law was discarded by a new interpretation of fundamental rights found in the "penumbra."

Fundamental law was rediscovered in the penumbras of the constitution itself, called the "new law of the land," and fundamental rights were dispensed by judicial edict in accordance with the Supreme Court's discernment of the people's evolving will. As indicated in the dissenting opinions of both <u>Griswold</u> and <u>Roe</u>, the Supreme Court had suddenly rediscovered and revived substantive due process. Mysteriously, the court was no longer influenced by the assumption that legislation was the product of majority rule. When the Court's own opinions about the nature of fundamental law were at stake, it substituted lectures to the legislature about the Court's view of constitutional law in place of the deference to the will and authority of the legislature as the founding fathers intended.

There is a big difference between letting a court define an evolving "law of the land" as found in an evolving constitution from that of Coke and Marshall who knew and understood what the "law of the land" was because it had been the same for centuries. Modern liberals may understand the difference but they stay silent so they can substitute their own new "law of the land" in place of a Biblically-based, Common Law tradition. Conservatives apparently do not understand the distinction. Modern conservatives have responded to the new substantive due process cases, primarily abortion, by rejecting substantive due process as a concept entirely. Essentially, to defensively slow down a runaway Court, conservatives are willing to abandon all Biblically-based Common Law tradition and defer all judgments to the legislature. By historical analogy, conservatives look for their precedent in the French Revolution, rejecting their only true firm legal basis; that the "laws of nature and of Nature's God" trump the right of Parliament and the king, to limit inalienable rights, established as the "law of the land," and preserved by the courts as substantive due process rights. Liberals want all power in the courts. Conservatives want all power with the legislature. Neither really trust "We the People."

THE SEPARATION OF POWERS REINVENTED

The modern American government juxtaposes the roles of the three branches of government and nearly tosses aside constitutional checks and balances. This is a direct result of the decline of Common Law and the rise of the new constitutionalism, and it has redefined justice. The modern judiciary, by refusing to consider principles of substantive due process when reviewing legislation, has abdicated its responsibility to adjudicate in matters where the rights of individuals conflict with a legislative enactment. Judicial deference, posing as judicial restraint, assumes that the government's police power is absolute and its rights are inalienable, while the rights of individuals are qualified. Modern judicial restraint conflicts with the principles of the Declaration of Independence and Common Law.

Rather than adjudicate conflicts, the modern Supreme Court has become a constitutional law review board, determining principles of consti-tutional law without regard to justice in a case and the rights of the litigants. While deferring to the legislature in principle, the Supreme Court has reserved to itself veto power over legislation, the constitutional prerogative granted by the Constitution only to the executive branch. The practical result finds legislatures deferring to the judiciary, and passing on to the courts all questions of the constitutionality of legislation. At the same time, despite conflicts in lower court cases and obvious injustices that need to be corrected, the United States Supreme Court reduces its caseload each year, selecting cases based on its intention to make and reshape constitutional law in accordance with each justice's personal political views. It ignores its own constitutional responsibility so it can help make the laws.

A more recent development regarding the separation of powers further confuses and compounds the frustration of litigants who seek justice. The nature of recent lawmaking has led to the decline of two traditional proce-dural guarantees of justice: the right to a jury trial and the private right of action.

The right to a jury trial is guaranteed by the Bill of Rights. Yet, much of modern legislation does not provide for a jury trial. The Supreme Court has ruled that the right to a jury only exists if the right was fixed under Com-mon Law at the time of the adoption of the Constitution and the Bill of Rights. The principle underlying the necessity of a jury has not been changed. But the Court, under its implied authority to set the rules of its own proceedings, an authority that existed because of the development of Common Law, allows the legislative branch to eliminate the guaranteed right to a trial by jury.

Similarly, Common Law held as a self-evident truth that if a law exist-ed it must be enforced to be valid. The reality of modern law enforcement is far different. Modern lawmakers often grant enforcement authority only to the executive branch. If the executive decides not to enforce a law or it lacks the resources to enforce a law, or enforce a law narrowly or selective-ly, the executive decision is upheld by the courts as discretionary. If the application of a law is doubtful, the doubt cannot be resolved by the individ-ual, but only when the executive determines to prosecute the individual. Judicial restraint is an invitation to corruption by the executive and bureau-cratic branch. To the individual, justice has become uncertain and expen-sive.

JUSTICE REDEFINED

At the core of the changing constitutional view of due process are the changing and conflicting principles that define the nature of justice. Just as "rights" are often defined differently depending on a person's worldview, so has "justice" been redefined. <u>Casey</u> symbolizes the conflict between "natural justice" and "utilitarian justice" while specifically excluding the Christian worldview that had always formed the basis of America's principles of justice. "Natural justice" now reflects a libertarian philosophy exemplified by the Biblical criticism of those who did "what was right in their own eyes." (Judges 17:6, 21:25) For a libertarian, all standards of justice are subjective and personal.

Unlike the libertarian view, freedom of conscience as protected by the Virginia Statute of Religious Freedom defers ultimate justice to God. But in <u>Casey</u>, the Court extended freedom of conscience to the act of abortion and not just to the belief. Common Law courts administered justice if there was *actus reus*. Culpability required that justice be rendered upon the act of infringement of another's life, liberty or property. In <u>Casey</u>, justice was withheld for one side so that the other side could act upon their belief.

By creating a conflict between competing individual positions about justice, the justice for one causes an absence of justice for another. Inevitably, the Court has left open the possibility that individual liberty rights, as the Court defines them, must be curtailed. In the Court's discretion, the Court can assert that liberty be restrained if it serves a valid government interest. The Court's exception creates a never-ending conflict between "natural justice" and "utilitarian justice."

Under utilitarian justice, no rights can exist if they are in conflict with a paramount majority interest. This tyranny of the majority inevitably results in a collectivist mentality, where the interest of the individual is sacrificed and made subordinate to the interest of the whole. The end justifies the means under utilitarian theory, and ultimately the balancing of libertarian interests will give way to utilitarian interests. The holder of the balance, whether it be Napoleon, the Politburo, a ruling political party, or even the Supreme Court, becomes solely responsible for lawmaking, law enforcement and the administration of justice. As these distinct functions become resident within one individual, or group of individuals, by definition tyranny results. Tyranny by a presumed benevolent Court is still tyranny.

The absence of justice, for whatever reason, creates a stronger desire for justice. The lack of justice, under extreme libertarian rules, also creates a need for more order. The desire for peace easily overcomes a parallel desire for justice when the paucity of objective rules leaves citizens confused, living in a society immersed in chaos and anarchy. When the law allows each individual to define his own existence and work out his own concept of law, that individual will also develop his own system of justice. Peace and security inevitably become nonexistent. That is why, in order to secure rights, governments were instituted among men by their mutual consent in the first place.

Utilitarian justice, although more predictable, can also be more devastating. Modern Christians have often unwittingly succumbed to false utilitarian doctrines failing to safeguard individual rights as they see strong leaders promoting a form of peace in place of chaos. The Christian response to tyrannical rulers has often been an outbreak of apathy, highlighting the failure of modern Christian leaders to point out that Christian ethics and utilitarian philosophy are an alien fatality, the philosopher Santayana's term describing two philosophies that cannot coexist because of inherent conflicts in fundamental principles and objectives. The traditional wisdom behind the Virginia definition of freedom of religion and the First Amendment is the judgment that the expression of speech and ideas is not harmful to those who disagree. The courts always upheld the distinction between speech and ideas with conduct. For that reason, the language in Casey that extended the freedom of conscience to the right to act on one's own concept of self-existence is startling and completely contrary to legal tradition. Casey's libertarian viewpoint, perhaps only limited to abortion, extends complete freedom to one individual and a withholding of justice to another whose infringement of life, liberty and property is considered irrelevant. Secular critics of Christianity have no trouble understanding that Christian principles cannot coexist with a purely secular theory. Christians are dull to this truth. Secularists understand that the rights of Christians will inevitably be challenged in a purely secular state. John Dewey, a secular spokesman, once stated, "the demand for liberty is the demand for power." Secular justice is based upon control and coercion, and those who oppose its power become its victims.

When the path to justice is closed, Christians have only one solution: appeal to God for justice. The colonists did this, as they were repeatedly thwarted in their attempts to obtain justice.

JUSTICE ACCORDING TO THE SUPREME JUDGE

Hostilities had already begun in May of 1775 when the Second Continental Congress gathered in Philadelphia. Defeating the British seemed hopeless as the colonists drafted the "Olive Branch Petition." They dispatched a group led by Benjamin Franklin to England to personally deliver the American request for peace to the king. The king refused even to see the Americans. Instead, on January 1, 1776, the British attacked and destroyed Norfolk, Virginia. As a response to this, the signers of the Declaration wrote, in its last paragraph, of their appeal to God, "in General Congress assembled, appealing to the Supreme Judge" to adjudicate their actions and intentions. They borrowed from Locke's theory of revolution described in his *Two Treatises of Government*.

Locke, like Rutherford, was a student of the Old Testament. He based his principle of appealing to God on Judges 11:27. "Wherefore I have not sinned against thee, but thou doest me wrong to war against me: the LORD the Judge be judge this day between the children of Israel and the children of Ammon."

Like Jeptha, who appealed to God to choose between the sons of Israel and of Ammon, the colonists appealed to God to judge their choice of liberty and independence against continued subordination to England. Locke knew, and the founding fathers agreed, that the absence of justice is most profound when denied by formal edict of the ruling authority. The English ruling authorities had slammed shut the door to the colonists' attempt to obtain justice.

The door the colonists opened with their victory over the British, however, was denied to some Americans. America's newly elected leaders, for a time, ignored the purist principle of justice in the Declaration of Independence as they wrote and interpreted their new Constitution. It remained for John Quincy Adams, the abolitionists, and President Abraham Lincoln in the manner of Old Testament prophets to raise again the principles of justice for all in the hearts and minds of Americans.

It remains, likewise, in the hearts and minds of modern New Testament Christians to raise again the self-evident truth that justice can only exist in a society that respects God's truth, that appeals to the Supreme Judge of the universe. As it pertains to true justice, Christian apathy grows into servitude no less onerous than that of the American slaves.

CHAPTER 7
THE SLAVERY HERESY

"Indeed I tremble for my Country when I reflect that God is just, and his justice cannot sleep forever."

Thomas Jefferson

"I will not obey it, by God."

Ralph Waldo Emerson, commenting on the Fugitive Slave Act

"A day of grace is yet held out to us. Both North and South have been guilty before God, and the Christian church has a heavy account to answer. Not by combining together, to protect injustice and cruelty, and making a common capital of sin, is this Union to be saved, but by repentance, justice and mercy."

Harriet Beecher Stowe (1851)

At no time in American history has the absence of justice been more visible than when her citizens tolerated slavery.

Modern Americans regard the historical tolerance of slavery as a gross, national error. Seldom do they explore the reasons for its development as an institution, or why it continued as long as it did.

Modern Americans condemn slavery as wrong and unthinkable. They often condemn earlier generations for not opposing the evil institution, but a cursory review of the history of slavery indicates that most early Americans, in fact, thought it was wrong. Many people may be surprised to learn that the Supreme Court, in an opinion by John Marshall regarding the ship "The Antelope," slavery was condemned as a violation of natural law and the law of nations.

In a striking resemblance to modern day cultural and political debate, many early American citizens thought that, even though slavery was morally wrong, they had no business interfering with other people's problems.

The issue became sectional. The South suffered from a failing economy and a backward, anachronistic aristocratic culture. Yet, attempts by the North to restrict slavery in any way were fiercely resisted.

Churches provided little help in clearing up the moral confusion about the issue. Most Christians shied away from taking a public stand, preferring instead the peace offered by a silent acquiescence to the status quo.

By the 1850s, the laws protecting slavery as an institution had become rigid. Within a decade, the country was shattered by a bloody Civil War. Only then did America finally conquer slavery.

The slavery question is too troubling to simplistically dismiss the issue as an error committed by people from another time. The errors in moral judgment that created and perpetuated slavery were the result of a departure from fundamental principles of law and theology. These principles are universal, applicable to all cultures. These errors have been repeated in history up to our present day. They encompass doctrinal and theological misinterpretations and serious misapplications of well-known principles of fundamental law. A theological toleration of slavery meant accepting heresy. Legally, slavery was unjust and a violation of natural law and the principles of the Declaration of Independence.

DIFFERENT CULTURES, DIFFERENT VIEWS

To understand slavery in the 1850s in America it is necessary to start at the beginning. American slavery started in colonial Virginia in the early 1600s. At that time, the law of nations recognized slavery as a humane alternative to torture and execution at the hands of warring tribal enemies in Africa.

The disagreement about the acceptance of slavery evolved during the Seventeenth to Nineteenth Centuries because of a different viewpoint of man. The newer view recognized the inalienable right to liberty as a natural right of *all* men and can be traced to England during the same time period—the early 1600s.

The new, bustling middle class in England consisted primarily of Puritans. The Puritans took seriously the Reformation principle of equality. They had educated themselves, worked hard, and lifted themselves from the lower class to a new middle class consisting of merchants and professionals.

The autocratic Stuart kings viewed the rise of the middle class as a threat. Likewise, King James I and King Charles I sparred with the obstinate Puritan clergy who insisted upon preaching sermons not approved by the monarchs and/or the established Anglican church. The Puritans' fealty to evangelism and democracy worried the Stuarts. Weary of the tense, bitter struggle building in England, many Puritans decided to establish true Christianity in America.

The Puritans left England and settled in Boston. The Puritan character and principles remained dominant throughout all of New England well into the Nineteenth Century.

In sharp contrast to Puritan New England, Virginia's early history more closely mirrored the class conflicts of England. Bishop Hunt at Jamestown tried his best to carry out the terms of the Great Commission, set forth in The First Charter of Virginia of 1606, for the "...propagating of Christian Religion to...People [who]...live in Darkness and miserable Ignorance of the true Knowledge and Worship of God." But secular and economic motivations predominated among the early inhabitants of Virginia.

Virginia's early settlers consisted of both gentlemen of the upper class and commoners of the lower class. Both classes sought wealth and status greater than that available to them in England. The early Virginians remained loyal to the Stuart kings and quickly emulated the class structure of England.

Sectional differences in America were established from the beginning. The stage was set for a philosophical, theological and economic conflict. New England was fiercely fundamentalist and democratic. The South was traditional and aristocratic.

WRONG TURN DOWN A SLIPPERY SLOPE

Fate tempted those early Virginians to engage in slavery when a storm blew a stolen Dutch merchant ship off course in 1619, and it landed at Jamestown, loaded with slaves. The Virginians thought it morally wrong to send the slaves out to sea—they let the slaves stay.

The Virginians hired those first slaves and gave them written contracts of employment for a set term. There was a shortage of labor to clear land for tobacco fields. Immigrants from the upper class disdained physical labor. Immigrants from the lower class disdained working for the upper class and quickly moved west to work their own land. The original settlers had a labor shortage.

The written contracts with the Africans were originally the same as for English immigrants. The first contracts required service for a period of years before freedom was granted. Over time, the landowners amended the contracts. The term of employment became "servants for life" or "perpetual servants." The African immigrants could not appeal to their rights as Englishmen as could the immigrants from England's lower class. Virginia had, through evolution, recognized slavery.

Within a century, there were 120,000 blacks in the South as compared to 173,000 whites. The southern economy had become dependent on slave labor.

The economy of the North also prospered as Yankee slave traders sparked the building and growth of the seaport towns of Boston, Newport and Greenwich. The institution of slavery had become entrenched in the southern economy and an evil necessity for the northern elite.

The institution of slavery was always unpopular with serious Christians. George Whitefield, one of the great evangelists during the Great Awakening of the early Eighteenth Century, wrote an open letter to slave owners in Maryland, Virginia, the Carolinas and Georgia in 1739. In the letter he stated, "The blood of them, spilt for these many years in your respective provinces, will ascend up to heaven against you."

The North had no legal authority to challenge slavery in the Southern colonies. But northerners, especially in New England, despite the existence of the wealthy slave merchants in their own colonies, would never tolerate or accept the existence of slavery.

THE FOUNDING FATHERS WERE MISUNDERSTOOD

Americans are usually taught the inaccurate assertion that the Declaration of Independence was written by hypocritical men. Americans generally think that the founding fathers did not really believe what they wrote because they tolerated and practiced slavery. This assertion is overly simplistic and historically incorrect.

Five men, known as the Committee of Five, actually wrote the Declaration of Independence: (1) Benjamin Franklin of Pennsylvania, (2) Roger Sherman of Connecticut, (3) Robert Livingston of New York, (4) John Adams of Massachusetts, and (5) Thomas Jefferson of Virginia. All five men disapproved of slavery. Only Jefferson owned slaves. America's first president, George Washington, emancipated his slaves in 1776. Jefferson did the same in his will, though his executor sold the slaves to pay his debts.

The Declaration of Independence states, "We hold these truths to be self-evident, that all men are created equal." The authors of the Declaration knew "Equality" as a Biblical principle. "He created them male and female, and He blessed them and made them Man in the day when they were created." (Gen. 5:2). The founding fathers believed that all humans, regardless of race or manmade conditions of servitude, descended from Adam and Eve, and, as such, were entitled to legal equality.

William Blackstone wrote that slavery in England violated Common Law because to hold absolute power over another's life and fortune was "repugnant to reason and principles of natural law."

In the first draft of the Declaration, among the list of claims against King George, Jefferson had written:

> He has waged cruel war against human nature itself, violating its most sacred rights of life and liberty in the persons of a distant people who never offended him, captivating and carrying them into slavery into another hemisphere . . .

Southern delegates to the Continental Congress demanded that this statement be deleted from the Declaration. To leave it in jeopardized the unanimity required for independence imposed by rules of Congress.

Of the Committee of Five, only Jefferson questioned the Biblical and Blackstone positions on slavery; he speculated that the races may have evolved differently, rather than affirming that all races descend from a common ancestor.

During the same time period that the founding fathers wrote the Declaration of Independence, slavery was denounced as inefficient in economic theory, though entrenched in the southern economy. In *The Wealth of Nations* (1776), Adam Smith demonstrated that slavery was more inefficient than the typical master-servant employment relationships common to the northern parts of America and most of England. The lack of personal incentive and mobility made the slave laborer more unproductive than an at-will employee.

From the employer's standpoint, slave ownership was more expensive. The care of the slaves was part of the employment benefits package. Bad employees could not simply be terminated.

The economic inefficiency of slavery was already evident in the colonies by 1776. The North prospered while the South deteriorated. The notable exception to southern poverty was the Piedmont area of North Carolina. There, German and Scotch-Irish immigrants rejected slavery and worked their own land. By the end of the War for Independence, even the South would have liked to escape slavery.

"ORIGINAL INTENT"

In 1787, the southern delegates at the Constitutional Convention were defending an institution which they did not like, but upon which they were dependent. The northern delegates wanted to abolish slavery altogether, but the southerners could not allow this to happen.

Slavery had developed as both an economic and a cultural issue, drawn along sectional lines. Eventually, the sectional divisions would be constitutionalized in a debate over states' rights.

The "original intent" of the delegates who drafted and ratified the Constitution can be understood so long as it is not oversimplified. The "original intent" was comprised of a number of different opinions which led to a short-term solution. The founding fathers agreed that the slave trade would end in 20 years after the adoption of the Constitution. That would allow current slave owners, including some of the southern delegates to the Constitutional Convention, to make adjustments in how they did business while, at the same time, essentially prohibiting the impairment of current slave contracts. The delegates all planned that slavery would end in a generation.

The debate was heated. Pierce Butler of South Carolina stated the South's position: "The security the southern states want is that their Negroes may not be taken from them, which some gentlemen, within or without doors, have a very good mind to do."

Governour Morris of Pennsylvania, commenting on the passage of the Northwest Ordinance of 1787 that provided that "neither slavery nor involuntary servitude" would be allowed in the new territory between the Ohio River, Mississippi River and the Great Lakes, believed, "it was a mistake to join eight northern republics to five southern oligarchies." Years later, interestingly, a European observer of political institutions and class distinctions, Karl Marx, made the same observation about America's fundamental division while writing in Europe at the time of the Civil War.

George Mason, who owned 5,000 acres in Virginia and 200 slaves, criticized both the North and the South on the slavery issue:

> The present question concerns not the importing States alone, but the whole Union...Slavery discourages arts and manufacturers. The poor despise labor when performed by slaves ...[Slaves] produce a pernicious effect on manners: every master is born a petty tyrant. They bring the judgment of heaven on a country...I lament that some of our Eastern brethren have, from a lust of gain, embarked in this nefarious traffic.

Many northerners eventually agreed that slavery presented a national problem. Senator Daniel Webster acknowledged this in 1820 when he said, "We consider slavery as your calamity not your crime, and we will share with you the burden of putting an end to it."

South Carolina and Georgia refused to enter the Union unless the Constitution recognized the present right to own slaves. By ratification they agreed to abolish the slave trade in 20 years.

Rufus King of Massachusetts and Governour Morris of Pennsylvania bitterly opposed slavery. But because slavery was dying out, and world opinion was moving toward the abolition of slavery, and because the South was so economically depressed compared to the North, they agreed with the majority of delegates that the slavery issue could be avoided until after ratification. One delegate, Elbridge Gerry of Massachusetts, refused to sign the new Constitution. He was partly prophetic when he predicted Civil War which he believed would begin by the time he returned to Massachusetts.

The founding fathers' hopeful predictions that slavery would simply disappear were all made wrong because of a revolution in technology.

In 1793, Eli Whitney invented the cotton gin. A new industry, dependent upon slave labor, was spawned. The South expanded as far west as New Orleans. Alabama and Mississippi entered the Union as slave states. The decision to take New Orleans in 1815 and attack Texas and Florida is traceable to the expansion of the cotton industry.

The tactical decision to postpone the confrontation with the slavery issue because it would die a natural death had proven to be disastrous to the North. The avoidance strategy had failed. An unforeseen technological invention created a new generation of slave owners. The South had passed a point from which it could not retreat.

THE DEBATE POLARIZES

The third phase of slavery in America began in 1820. Daniel Webster, compassionate but uncompromising, defined the issue and the North's hardening position in a speech in Plymouth, Massachusetts commemorating the 200th anniversary of the Pilgrim settlement at Plymouth Rock:

> If there be, within the extent of our knowledge or influence, any participation in The [Slave] Traffic, let us pledge ourselves here, upon the rock of Plymouth, to extirpate and destroy it. It is not fit that the land of the Pilgrims should bear the shame longer. I hear the sound of the hammer, I see the smoke of the furnaces where manacles and fetters are still forged for human limbs. I see

the visages of those who by stealth and at midnight labor in this work of hell, foul and dark, as may become the artificers of such instruments of misery and torture. Let that spot be purified, or let it cease to be New England.

Disunion and civil war was the discussion in Congress in 1820. Henry Clay of Kentucky, the Speaker of the House, maneuvered the Missouri Compromise into law. The specifics of the compromise were that Missouri would be allowed to permit slavery and be admitted as a "slave state" while Maine would be admitted to the Union as a "free state." Furthermore, it stipulated that all Louisiana Purchase states north of Missouri's southern border would be admitted as free states.

Thomas Jefferson prophetically called the Missouri Compromise, "A fire bell in the night, which awakened me and filled me with terror. I considered it at once the [death] knell of the Union...as it is, we have a wolf by the ears, and we can neither hold him, nor safely let him go. Justice is on one scale, and self-preservation on the other."

Jefferson later wrote, "I regret that I am now to die in the belief that the useless sacrifice of themselves by the generation of 1776, to acquire self-government and happiness to their country, is to be thrown away by the unwise and unworthy passions of their sons. My only consolation is that I will not be alive to weep over it." Jefferson died on July 4, 1826, on the 50th anniversary of the signing of the Declaration.

The Missouri Compromise of 1820 was followed by the Tariff of Abominations of 1830. The Tariff of Abominations was, in fact, a number of tariffs passed by Congress which the South Carolina state legislature eventually declared null and void. The South Carolina legislature published the "South Carolina Exposition and Protest," also labeled the "South Carolina Doctrine." It protested the tariff as unconstitutional and advanced the theory of nullification whereby South Carolina asserted it could nullify any act of Congress that it deemed unconstitutional. Their actions were appealed to the United States Supreme Court. Chief Justice John Marshall declared the acts of the South Carolina legislature unconstitutional.

The South attempted to align itself politically with the West. Senator Robert Hayne from South Carolina attacked New England from the floor of the U.S. Senate. Senator Daniel Webster defended New England and articulated the case for an inseparable Union based on the Declaration of Independence. Webster's argument resulted in the defeat of John Calhoun's resolution in the Senate. President Andrew Jackson signed the bill. John Marshall rejected the state of South Carolina's nullification claim.

The North, too weak to defeat the South in war because of the strength of the South's military leaders and the confusion and ambivalence of northerners, had avoided war. And Webster had provided the legal theory that would later be embraced by Abraham Lincoln.

THE THEOLOGICAL ASSERTIONS

The Abolition Movement, led by northern Christian fundamentalists, exposed the disharmony between Christian principle and toleration of slavery. Spiritual revival had sparked the Second Great Awakening in the West during the early 1800s. Revival spread to the North under the leadership and influence of lawyer turned evangelist Charles Finney. The abolitionist movement, led by a Finney protégé, Theodore Dwight Weld, Dean of Oberlin College in Oberlin, Ohio, began to harden the North's antislavery resolve while polarizing the northern moderates—and striking fear in the South.

Slavery was no longer considered an issue separated by church and state. An 1829 "Christian Spectator" article about the separation of church and state and the moral opposition to slavery asked:

> What has religion to do with the state, you ask? In the form of ecclesiastical alliances, nothing. But in its operation as a controlling, purifying power in the consciences of the people, we answer, it has everything to do. It is the last hope of the republics. And let it be remembered, if our ruin shall come, that the questions which agitate, the factions which distract, the convulsions which dissolve, will be the secondary causes. The true evil will lie back of these, in the moral debasement of the people. And no excellence of political institutions, no sagacity of human wisdom, which did not, like that of our Puritan fathers, begin and end with religion, could have averted the calamity.

Boston clergyman Lyman Beecher called for the unification of law and theology in 1831 in his sermon "The Spirit of the Pilgrims:"

> The government of God is the only government which will hold society, against depravity within and temptation without; and this it must do by the force of its own law written upon the heart. This is that unity of the Spirit and that bond of peace which alone can perpetuate national purity and tranquility—that law of universal and impartial love by which alone nations can be kept back from ruin. There is no safety for republics but in self-government, under the influence of a holy heart, swayed by the government of God.

The abolitionists convinced Americans of the heresy of tolerating slavery. At the same time, the United States Supreme Court permanently incorporated slavery into the Constitution in the infamous case of <u>Dred Scott v. Sandford</u> (1857). Based upon the dubious attempt of a freed slave to exercise the rights of a free citizen in the South, the Supreme Court struck down the Missouri Compromise of 1820. It did so by misinterpreting the reason that the drafters of the Constitution had postponed the abolition of slavery. The opinion of the Court misstated Congress' intent to permit slavery for a period of years as an unqualified right to own another person. The Court incorrectly claimed that it created a constitutionally protected right to own a person as property. The Supreme Court's misinterpretation of the drafters' intent is found in the following passage of its opinion:

> The right of property in a slave is distinctly and expressly affirmed in the Constitution. The right to traffic in it, like an ordinary article of merchandise and property, was guaranteed to the citizens of the United States, and every State that might desire it, for twenty years. And the Government, in express terms is pledged to protect it in all future time, if the slave escapes his owner. This is done is plain words—too plain to be misunderstood. And no word can be found in the Constitution which gives Congress a greater power over slave property, or which entitles property of that kind in less protection than property of any other description.

The Supreme Court had, accordingly, extended the property principle beyond the drafters' intent, violated the inherent inalienable right of an entire group of citizens based on race, and constitutionalized the issue such that the ownership of slaves could be extended by Congress and state legislatures but could not be restricted.

The result of <u>Dred Scott</u> was immediate. Slavery could exist anywhere but could not be prevented anywhere, except by the exercise of conscience by white people to not own slaves. Laws were passed in Ohio and Indiana guaranteeing the return of fugitive southern slaves. Maryland and Delaware considered legalizing slavery.

LINCOLN

Lincoln wrote in 1857 that the plight of the Negro had never been worse and was almost hopeless.

> They have him [the Negro] in this prison house; they have

searched his person, and left no prying instrument with him. One after another they have closed the heavy iron doors upon him, and now they have him, as it were, folded in with a lock of a hundred keys, which can never be unlocked without the concurrence of every key; the keys in the hands of a hundred men, and they scattered to a hundred different distant places; and they stand musing as to what invention, in all dominions of mind and matter, can be produced to make a possibility of his escape more complete than it is.

Lincoln called for harmony between law and theology on the issue of slavery and identified the disharmony as the cause of the Civil War. This position can be clearly discovered by reviewing the text of a number of different proclamations and addresses given by Lincoln. The first is from Lincoln's Fast Day and Thanksgiving Day Proclamations.

When our own beloved Country, once by the blessing of God, united, prosperous and happy, is now afflicted with faction and civil war, it is peculiarly fit for us to recognize the hand of God in this terrible visitation, and in sorrowful remembrance of our own faults and crimes as a nation and as individuals, to humble ourselves before Him, and to pray for His mercy—to pray that we may be spared further punishment, though most justly deserved; that our arms may be blessed and made effectual for the re-establishment of law, order and peace, throughout the wide extent of our country; and that the inestimable boon of civil and religious liberty earned, under his guidance and blessing, by the labor and sufferings of our fathers, may be restored in all its original excellence.

Lincoln's Fast Day and Thanksgiving Day Proclamations clearly articulated the theological principle of national sin, followed by repentance, followed by restoration, and then mercy. He asked rhetorically, "May we not justly fear that the awful calamity of civil war, which now desolates the land, may be but a punishment, inflicted upon us, for our presumptuous sins, to the needful end of our national reformation as a whole people?"

In his 1865 Second Inaugural Address given shortly before his assassination, Lincoln quotes Matthew 18:7: "Woe unto the world because of offenses." He said:

The prayer of both could not be answered; that of neither has been answered fully, the Almighty has his own purposes, Woe unto the world because of offenses. For it must needs be that offenses come; but woe to that man by whom the offense cometh!

Lincoln follows by showing that the law had been worked out in our national history:

> If we shall suppose that American Slavery is one of those offenses which, in the providence of God, must needs come, but which, having continued through His appointed time, He now wills to remove and that He gives to both North and South this terrible war as the woe due to those by whom the offense came, shall we discern therein any departure from those divine attributes which the believers in a Living God always ascribe to Him?

Lincoln spoke of national sin as applying to both North and South, as America was one consecrated people, not two halves. His Second Inaugural included a prayer for restoration:

> Fondly do we hope—fervently do we pray—that this mighty scourge of war may speedily pass away.

He referred again to God's will and purpose:

> Yet, if God wills that it continue until all the wealth piled by the bond-man's two hundred and fifty years of unrequited toil shall be sunk, and until every drop of blood drawn with the lash shall be paid by another drawn with the sword, as it was said three thousand years ago, so still it must be said, "the judgments of the Lord, are true and righteous altogether."

Lincoln firmly rooted himself in the Genesis 9:6 concept of expiation. He continued with a plea for reconciliation and forgiveness toward the South:

> With malice toward none; with charity for all; with firmness in the right, as God gives us to see the right, let us strive on to finish the work we are in; to bind up the nation's wounds; to care for him who shall have borne the battle, and for his widow, and his orphan—to do all which may achieve and cherish a just, and a lasting peace, among ourselves, and with all nations.

He calls on a united people "to finish the work we are in." He meant not just the war, but also "the unfinished work" of the first dedication to his proposition, "the great task remaining before us." The Second Inaugural begins the work of carrying out the great purpose of the Gettysburg Address. The work remained unfinished, however, because of John Wilkes Booth's assassination of Lincoln a month and half later.

A COSTLY MISTAKE

The Court had made mistakes in interpreting the law and the Constitution. Others misinterpreted theology and history. And those who were mistaken used the law and raw political power to stifle all opposition, to suppress truth and allow evil to spread. Their actions resulted in a bloody Civil War.

Lincoln's assertion represented two significant principles. First, the slavery heresy was a form of national sin, which, when it had not been corrected, resulted in God's judgment. Second, as argued by Webster, the Declaration of Independence supported the principle of national union, which superseded the then-current states rights arguments advanced by secessionists.

Jefferson foreshadowed the first principle, and his words are inscribed in the rotunda of the Jefferson Memorial:

> Can the liberties of a nation be thought secure, when we have removed their only firm basis, a conviction in the minds of the people that they are a gift of God? Indeed, I tremble for my countrymen, when I reflect that God is just, that His justice cannot sleep forever.

Justice did not sleep forever. The consequences of the slavery heresy, and the injustice it caused, could not be changed by Congress, the Supreme Court, or state legislators. A misguided majority will, as reflected in the legislative support for slavery and hostility to the abolitionists, was not justifiable even though the legislation was democratic. The Supreme Court's pronouncements, even though allegedly based upon fundamental law rooted in the Constitution and the Common Law, were not supreme. America has still not learned these lessons of the Civil War.

The task of maintaining self-government was never believed to be easy or simple. Truth cannot be determined legislatively. Nor can truth be determined by the courts. Truth cannot be determined. Truth must be discovered.

Errors in judgment on issues of law and theology should not be viewed simply or taken for granted. The result of such error can be disastrous beyond the contemplation of those who refuse to see the core of the issue in both theological and legal terms.

CHAPTER 8
The Abortion Heresy

"There also are two gods, exceedingly obscure, Vitumnus and Sentinus—the one of whom imparts life to the foetus, and the other sensation; and, of a truth, they bestow, most ignoble though they be, far more than all those noble and select gods bestow. For, surely, without life and sensation, what is the whole foetus which a woman carries in her womb, but a most vile and worthless thing, no better than slime and dust?"

Augustine, *City of God*

"Those barbarous and savage laws...which conferred honour on thieves, allowed the promiscuous intercourse of the sexes, and other things even fouler and more absurd, I do not think entitled to be considered as laws, since they are not only altogether abhorrent to justice, but to humanity and civilized life."

Jean Calvin

"Marriage is encouraged in China, not by the profitableness of children, but by the liberty of destroying them. In all great towns several are every night exposed in the street, or drowned like puppies in the water. The performance of this horrid office is even said to be the avowed business by which some people earn their subsistence."

Adam Smith, *The Wealth of Nations*

The lesson of the Civil War that Americans learned, and have not forgotten, is that slavery is wrong. People are not chattels. Congress emphasized this when it quickly responded to the end of the Civil War by passing the Civil War amendments.

The Thirteenth Amendment formally abolished slavery. Congress proposed it to the states on January 31, 1865.

The Fourteenth Amendment guaranteed due process and equal protection of the laws to all Americans. Furthermore, it addressed the states rights debate and adopted Webster's and Lincoln's "national rights" theory, proposed to the state legislatures by Congress on June 13, 1866. These Fourteenth Amendment guarantees were superior to the power of the states.

The Fifteenth Amendment guaranteed the right to vote for all adult males regardless of their race. Congress sent it to the states on February 26, 1869.

Congress intended that the Civil War amendments would not only correct the injustice done to slaves, but would also correct errors in constitutional interpretation. States' rights were not superior to natural rights. Inalienable rights were natural rights beyond the states' jurisdiction.

Unfortunately, other Civil War lessons have not survived. Theology that fails to confront serious moral issues results in national sin, and national sin results in predictable negative consequences. Law rooted in expedience and compromise rather than in God's moral law will be resisted by Christian people. The denial of justice will lead to conflict.

Modern Americans deny that ignorance of these principles is a threat to the nation's well-being. We refuse to consider that a departure from the divine attributes of a living God, as Lincoln understood, will lead to any consequences today. In a nation whose very existence was based upon and nurtured on a continuous dependence on divine providence, God is now considered irrelevant. During the somber days at the end of the Civil War, perhaps for the first time, did the American people remember and understand the relationship between the fortunes of a nation and God. That most important lesson of the Civil War has now been dismissed as irrelevant history.

FORGETTING THE FIRST COMMANDMENT

Lincoln spoke eloquently about the continuous merit of acknowledging the divine attributes of the living God, and the necessity for repentance under the divine justice demanded in the context of a great national sin.

Modern Americans need to answer the question, "What happens when the living God is rejected and dismissed as irrelevant history?" Furthermore, "Do the divine attributes of the living God permit injustice to continue merely because the people ignore Him, or disregard the historical record of God's continuous relationship with America's people? Is there any relationship between obedience to the living God and America's national destiny?"

The foolhardy pronouncements by nonbelievers and theologians declaring God's death have been too passively accepted by modern Christians. This is evidenced by their acquiescing to the rebellious demand that God's moral law and truth be dismissed as it applies to the law of the land.

The consequences of denying God have been repeatedly validated over time in civilization after civilization. Abortion, like slavery, has once again presented America with that consequence, and to date, it has been answering the dilemma wrongly, in the same manner as the 1857 Court did in <u>Dred Scott</u>. Why has it happened again?

UNCOMFORTABLE FOG FROM PHONY FOUNDATION

Abortion, as a political issue, makes many Christians uncomfortable. Part of the discomfort is because other issues are more important to some Christians. A constitutional crisis is not as important to many as education or personal healthcare or economic issues.

Abortion is divisive. Abortion, as a political issue, forces each person to also address issues of theology and fundamental law. But, in fact, the theological and legal issues that ultimately must be addressed are not the complex, technical arguments made to support or oppose abortion. The issue is simpler and far larger.

Lincoln's Gettysburg Address and Second Inaugural Address went beyond technical arguments. Slave owners had used Biblical arguments in favor of slavery just as abortion proponents find pastors and theologians to support abortion. As with slavery, abortion advocates use proof-texts of Biblical passages and carefully parsed Supreme Court precedents to obscure the main issue. Recent history confirms that legal arguments originating solely from the Constitution can and are debated with no clear result; and often the wrong analysis becomes law. Theologians and Supreme Court justices are no more infallible than were the Pharisees.

True theology and law are both based on who God is and the predictable effects of God's reality, not just man's partisan prejudiced interpretation of the written text.

Both sides of the abortion debate appear afraid to fully disclose the roots of their stated positions. Their foundationless arguments are rooted in intense emotion, and this reveals a deeper conflict. Many of the assertions and arguments in the political debate fail to address the central issue. The arguments and points made about abortion are often disingenuous, confusing and inconclusive.

Let it be stated plainly: The foundation of the pro-life position is Christian. In contrast, the pro-abortion position is hostile to Christianity, and by extension, to Christian morality. Christians are uncomfortable with the pro-life apologetic because it forces them to unabashedly acknowledge the truth about Christian faith in the face of hostile, Godless skepticism, especially when that means standing firm against friends and relatives.

Understanding the slavery issue required studying the historical beginnings of slavery in Virginia, and then witnessing the sequence of events that ultimately trapped the South in an economic system doomed to failure. Slavery was required to maintain the southern lifestyle. Southerners glossed over their immoral lifestyle and futilely tried to assuage their consciences. Likewise, the abortion issue is also about the lifestyle of our current culture.

OUT OF THE FOG'S MIST

Lifestyle choice sits at the core of the cultural struggle to maintain the system of legalized abortion. This new cultural revolution occurred suddenly. It was not until the 1960s that traditional American culture was rejected and historic American values were attacked. This cultural revolution is at the core of this newest constitutional revolution.

At the core of the American cultural revolution of the 1960s lay the desire of the revolutionaries to substitute a new lifestyle for that which had existed in America for centuries. They celebrated this new lifestyle in their music and art, and claimed the arrival of a new revolution in thought and behavior, free from the moral restraints of the past. This new revolution was promoted and accepted on college campuses and in major sections of America's large cities. The traditionalist establishment was completely unprepared for the revolution.

The only legal obstacle for the revolutionaries was Common Law that had been incorporated into state statutes prohibiting abortion. This obstacle was wiped away in 1973.

On January 22, 1973, a seven vote majority of the United States Supreme Court issued its opinion in <u>Roe v. Wade</u>, over two dissenting opinions. Instantaneously, over 1,000 years of Common Law criminalizing abortion was abandoned. Instantaneously, all state laws criminalizing abortion were declared repealed. A number of rationales were extended to support the unprecedented ruling. None of these rationales have survived the brief test of time. A couple of constitutional theories were presented to support the ruling. Even those constitutional theories had to be amended in later decisions.

Since then, numerous state legislatures have attempted to restrict the practice of abortion. Courts have struck down these attempts. Normal medical procedures have been proposed, such as licensing and informed consent requirements, but medical regulation has been brushed aside as swiftly as Roe brushed aside the Hippocratic Oath.

Because of Roe v. Wade, the obscure, political debate about legal abortion from the late 1950s and 1960s roared front and center into American law, politics and religion. Political party loyalties have been realigned. Churches have split. And American law books have had to be rewritten to explain the new jurisprudence, its philosophy, and the cases that have had to be decided to perpetuate what had been a relatively rare, yet barbaric, and scorned upon medical procedure.

Many abortion opponents consider it to be America's newest and biggest national sin. Yet, all legal and political challenges have been fruitless. The biggest obstacle for abortion opponents has been the lack of knowledge and general apathy of American Christians, exacerbated by fear of confrontation or, a new theology and view that confrontation itself is wrong.

The clear unimpeachable scientific fact that life begins at conception was ignored in Roe and amazingly, has come to be doubted when, prior to Roe, it had been accepted matter-of-factly as scientific truth in school textbooks. To avoid being embroiled in a so-called religious battle, Christians have conceded established scientific fact to allow abortion supporters to debate the undebatable. Most modern Christians would rather avoid any conflict or controversy with abortion supporters than think deeply about the reality of abortion and its larger implications. Modern Christians do not understand that, at the core of the legalization of abortion as a political issue, is a cultural revolution that is not just un-Christian but is anti-Christian.

A RELIGIOUS CONFLICT

The abortion debate, on a broad level, pits religiously-based presumptions favoring the protection of innocent life against modern preferences for the protection of sexual freedom without restriction or consequences. At an even broader level, abortion raises an irreconcilable conflict between fundamentally different philosophical and theological systems, in the nature of what Santayana defined as an "alien fatality." The "alien fatality" results from the fundamental anti-Christian philosophical underpinnings of the abortion culture which cannot coexist with a Christian culture.

Christians have ignored the cultural and philosophical conflict, hoping for compromise. So to not be accused of violating the false "separation of church and state," Christians have instead focused on legal and political issues.

At the practical level of law, the abortion debate centers upon conflicting theories of interpretation of the Constitution. At the political level, the debate turns on who can turn out the most motivated followers.

Common Law and constitutional obstacles to legal abortion had been unquestioned until the 1960s. In 1973, abortion suddenly became a national, constitutional issue. In <u>Roe</u>, the old constitution and Common Law were rejected.

Out of the penumbra discussed in <u>Griswold</u> came a new definition of liberty which provided the framework for <u>Roe</u>. The penumbra gave way to the Fourteenth Amendment in <u>Casey</u>. <u>Casey</u> placed the "rights" to abortion upon a newly defined concept of liberty. The right to liberty, no longer strictly viewed as a natural, inalienable right, now originates from the Court's interpretation of the Fourteenth Amendment, not from the Creator, as stated in the Declaration.

IN THE BEGINNING, THE FOURTEENTH AMENDMENT

The Fourteenth Amendment has had a controversial history. The limits of the scope of the Fourteenth Amendment depend upon whether it is interpreted as a general statement of natural law, enacted in response to the rejected theory of slavery, or as a specific response to slavery as a rejected practice.

Modern proponents of a "living" constitution usually begin with the Fourteenth Amendment. "Right to privacy" cases depend upon interpreting the Fourteenth Amendment as a statement of natural law. But a new libertarian view of nature has been substituted for the old understanding of the law of nature and of nature's God. As a result, the language of the Fourteenth Amendment has been broadly construed in its definitions of "due process" and "equal protection." The courts have liberally forced these new definitions on the states.

Out of context, the Fourteenth Amendment is, in effect, a new constitution.

In context, the Fourteenth Amendment is a logical extension of both the end of slavery and the dispute over the states' alleged right to permit slavery. In context, the Fourteenth Amendment simply guarantees certain minimum rights to all national citizens and prohibits the states from legislating otherwise.

In contrast, the Court in <u>Roe</u> found a right to abortion in the Fourteenth

Amendment. The Fourteenth Amendment, they said in effect, provides a new beginning. They simply passed over the Common Law connection to the Constitution by misconstruing and misstating it. The connection of the Declaration of Independence to the Constitution is also over. The Declaration of Independence is no longer relevant to the Constitution and is often considered in conflict with it. The Fourteenth Amendment was analyzed out of context and established as a new declaration of fundamental law.

THE REAL FOURTEENTH

The Fourteenth Amendment was proposed as a constitutional amendment June 13, 1866 and it became effective July 28, 1868. It was introduced following the passage of the "Black Codes" in numerous state legislatures of the southern states readmitted after the end of the Civil War. The Fourteenth Amendment was also necessary as a response to President Andrew Johnson's veto of the Civil Rights Act of 1866. The "Black Codes" and the Civil Rights Act of 1866 were attempts to circumvent the effect of the Thirteenth Amendment, in effect since December 18, 1865, which abolished slavery.

The Fourteenth Amendment was adopted to clarify the due process debate, the equal protection of the laws debate, and the national rights debate, by settling the issues once and for all. The text of Section One of the Fourteenth Amendment is as follows:

> § 1. All persons born or naturalized in the United States, and subject to the jurisdiction thereof, are citizens of the United States and of the state wherein they reside. No state shall make or enforce any law which shall abridge the privileges or immunities of citizens of the United States; nor shall any State deprive any person of life, liberty, or property, without due process of law; nor deny to any person within its jurisdiction the equal protection of the laws.

To arrive at their tortured decision in <u>Roe v. Wade</u>, the Court had to interpret the Fourteenth Amendment in two contradictory ways. First, they interpreted the Fourteenth Amendment broadly to find a right to abortion under its protection of liberty as a substantive due process protection of an unenumerated fundamental right. Secondly, they saw the inalienable right of an unborn child to its life as not protected under the Fourteenth Amendment, seeing that it refers to "persons born or naturalized." The Court finds no Congressional discussion contemporaneous with the adoption of the Fourteenth Amendment that included references to the rights of unborn children. Their "strict construction" as applied to the rights of unborn children is the opposite of the constitutional noninterpretivism employed to find a vague, undefined right to an abortion. "Life" was narrowly construed for one class—unborn babies—while liberty was broadly construed for another—women carrying unborn babies.

"Strict construction" vs. "judicial activism" has been a polarizing political debate played out in judicial nomination battles since Roe v. Wade. Yet, ironically, two conflicting rules of constitutional construction were used in the same case by the same judges. Roe v. Wade far surpasses Dred Scott for pure judicial dishonesty.

The drafters of the Fourteenth Amendment never debated the rights of unborn children for two reasons. The Fourteenth Amendment was a political response to efforts to nullify the effect of the Thirteenth Amendment that emancipated the slaves—it had nothing to do with the abortion question. The drafters' mental contemplation pertained only to slavery. The law regarding abortion and the rights of the fetus were well-settled and unquestioned. The drafters of the Fourteenth Amendment did not consider the rights of unborn children because the issue never occurred to them.

Until Roe v. Wade, abortion was impermissible from the viewpoint of the medical profession. Abortion, as a medical procedure, was contrary to 2,000 years of medical ethics first established by Hippocrates and part of the Hippocratic Oath.

Roe v. Wade also disregarded legal history. Abortion had been considered criminal from before the time of Bracton. Bracton was the first to attempt to summarize Common Law. The criminalization of abortion had been ingrained in the Common Law for a long time.

At the time of the ratification of the Fourteenth Amendment, every state in the union considered abortion a crime. Connecticut first enacted a sanction against abortion in 1821, but it had been a capital crime under Common Law since at least the Sixth Century, and even earlier. Courts relied on Common Law as the source of criminal law prior to the states' passage of statutory criminal codes during the mid-Nineteenth Century.

For the Court to insinuate in Roe that the drafters intended to omit the well-established rights of unborn children from the application of the Fourteenth Amendment is a gross and impermissible presumption without basis in law or fact. Neither history nor logic supports that presumption.

COMMON LAW DELETED

Contrary to the Court's assertion written in the majority opinion of Roe

v. Wade, that the criminal codes were a reflection of Nineteenth Century "Victorian Morality," and that they were concerned with the safety of the mother because of the medical dangers associated with abortion, the root of the crime of abortion can be traced to the understanding that an unborn child has a right to its life as an inherent, natural right which cannot be interfered with without due process of law. Due process of law in the Eighteenth and Nineteenth Centuries meant that the commission of a crime or civil interference with the right of another had occurred and, accordingly, a deprivation of life, liberty, or property was justified.

Blackstone's *Commentaries*, the legal reference used by lawyers at the time of the ratification of the Fourteenth Amendment, introduced his review of "Absolute Rights" with John Locke's quote that, "Where there is no law, there is no freedom." Blackstone then wrote about "Absolute Rights," beginning with the "Right of Personal Security," set forth below:

Right of Personal Security

Defined. This right consists in a person's legal and uninterrupted enjoyment of his life, his limbs, his body, his health and his reputation.

1. Life. This right is inherent by nature in every individual, and exists even before the child is actually born.

"Rights of Unborn Child. The offense of abortion of a quick child is not murder, but homicide or manslaughter. An infant *in ventre se mere* is supposed in law to be born for many purposes. It is capable of having a legacy made to it. It may have a guardian assigned to it, and may have an estate limited to its use, and to take afterwards by such limitation, as if it were then actually born. The same ruling holds in the civil law.

Blackstone's definition did not depart from the definition and principles of abortion law announced by Bracton, repeated by Sir Edward Coke in his *Institutes of the Laws of England*. Numerous cases involving the rights of an unborn child, outside of the context of the specific issue of abortion, had followed Common Law definitions and principles up to 1973.

Although Roe v. Wade avoided the question of when life begins, it instead adopted a dubious new concept called "potential life." Subsequent cases have upheld Common Law teaching on the rights of a fetus unless the Common Law contradicts Roe v. Wade. If Common Law contradicts Roe v. Wade, the Supreme Court has held that Roe v. Wade supersedes Common Law by implication. To permit abortion, not just the criminal abortion statutes had to be repealed; more than 12 centuries of an accepted body of law had to be set aside.

THE ARBITRARY USE OF RAW POWER

The Supreme Court's failure to exercise its judicial power to protect human life is alarming. The ostensible use of judicial power to attack the democratic process is more than alarming. Until the 1960s, all states had laws criminalizing abortion. The "life of the mother" exception, though rare in practice, had already been either legislatively or judicially recognized. The Jewish and Catholic debate over the translation of Biblical texts had reached a practical compromise that allowed abortion to save the life of the mother. Then dramatically, and unnecessarily, all state legislation as it pertained to almost all abortions was ruled unconstitutional. Since 1973, the Supreme Court has continuously exercised authority to prevent any state from legislating in the abortion arena. There was no urgent reason for the Court to exercise power it should not have used to so dramatically make such sweeping, unnecessary changes. The misuse of its power should have alarmed everyone!

The legal authority relied upon by the Court to strike all state legislation and overturn hundreds of years of Common Law was as tenuous as it was murky. Roe v. Wade was based partly upon policy arguments advocated in studies conducted by the American Medical Association and American Bar Association, and partly upon a purported extension of the constitutionalization of the concept of the "right to privacy" first announced in Griswold v. Connecticut.

The policy arguments relied upon by the Court in Roe v. Wade were first proposed in the 1960s and can be summarized as follows.

> Abortion statutes were based upon a purpose to promote morality but abortion statutes did not, in fact, promote celibacy.
> The permission of abortion would not, at the same time, promote promiscuity.
> The liberalization of abortion laws would promote safety.
> Abortions were not available to the poor.
> Abortion laws were unenforceable because their violation was widespread.

Additional policy arguments included the need for population control, the woman's equal right to not have to unilaterally bear the burden of childbirth, rather than carry a child to term, and the argument by the medical profession that it be allowed to regulate itself.

Historically, policy arguments, by their nature as "policy," suggest legislative solutions. Policy arguments never before suggested a change in fundamental law. By making a policy change and calling it fundamental law, the Court, in essence, took to itself the role as policymaker and decreed that the policymaking body, the legislature, could not overrule it.

WHOSE RELIGION AND WHOSE SCIENCE?

The foundation of the opposition to abortion within the rule of law is Biblical. Human life first exists in the womb. God's relationship to that life contradicts the unscientific assertion that a fetus is not human life.

Science offers proof of the Court's error. The Supreme Court's trimester approach directly conflicts with science. Modern science confirms the early development of all essential organs and features of a living human being within the womb. But the Court refused to address that reality, that a fetus is a living human. To address that issue left the Court bare and without any justification for abortion. So they simply dismissed the question.

The argument that an "unborn" child should be protected by the Fourteenth Amendment was dismissed as theological, beyond the scope of its jurisdiction. But they felt no such restraint when they expanded the scope of the fundamental law and the "right to privacy." With no restraint or parsing of the drafters' words, they dismissed Common Law theory and precedents, and decreed that all state abortion statutes were unconstitutional as part of an evolving moral consensus. Later, in Casey, the Court changed the theoretical basis for a fundamental right to abortion, arguing that it originated in the nature of the right to liberty under the Fourteenth Amendment. Secular philosophy replaced theology as the guideline for constitutional interpretation.

ERRORS COMPOUNDED

The Court's abortion decisions reflect a number of serious errors resulting from the new methods of constitutional interpretation. These errors include:

> The source of fundamental rights is not the Supreme Court, vaguely defined and arbitrarily applied. Rather, rights are inalienable, incapable of being withdrawn or limited, because they are granted by God;
>
> The strict interpretation of the Fourteenth Amendment to deny

the natural right to life of an unborn child, in contrast with the broad interpretation of the same clause to allow abortions, is both disingenuous and hypocritical;

The extension of the prohibition of the government to interfere with the jurisdictional authority of the family in Griswold cannot logically be extended under the same theory to a right to not bear a child as found in Roe v. Wade; and

The new philosophical definition of liberty articulated in later abortion cases, in substitution for the flawed "right to privacy" in Roe, cannot sustain a "rule of law" for general application but must be applied on a case by case basis.

Few serious students of constitutional law support the "right to privacy" theory, though the "right" is still politically popular. The Court originally found the "right to privacy" as "emanating" from a "penumbra" that they asserted surrounded the many Bill of Rights protections for personal liberty.

Griswold struck down a Connecticut statute prohibiting the sale of contraceptives to married couples as infringing on the private right, fundamental to marriage, to determine whether to have a family. No law had ever considered that "begetting" a child was a legitimate function of government. The Ninth Amendment clearly protects the individual from intrusions by the state which are beyond the legitimate exercise of state authority. The problem with the Connecticut statute, for definers of the new cultural morality, was that the statute had nothing to do with the activity of married couples in the bedroom. Rather, the statute merely regulates what married couples could buy at the store. The Griswold opinion ignored fact and analysis, creating a theory that supplied a vague and manipulative precedent for subsequent holdings and rhetoric for political advocacy.

References to "freedom of choice" and "right to privacy" are meaningless buzzwords when used apart from the philosophy that provides context for their definitions. The privacy argument was later used to extend Griswold to unmarried couples, in complete disregard of Griswold's purported attempt to protect marriage.

Contrasting Justice Douglas' arguments that the sanctity of marriage required the privacy protection in Griswold, the Court extended the right to purchase contraceptives to unmarried couples in Eisenstadt v. Baird on dubious equal protection grounds, equating married couples' marital rights with unmarried couples' marital rights. The dicta in Eisenstadt v. Baird gratuitously offered that the "right to bear or beget a child" was within the right of privacy protection. That decision was later cited as precedent in Roe v.

<u>Wade</u>, which matter-of-factly, without discussion, announced that the right to bear a child or not bear a child was equated with the right to beget or not beget a child. By so misconstruing the "right to privacy" concept that had been created to promote the freedom of a married couple as part of the sanctity of family and marriage, the Court used it to permit the termination of human life.

DRED SCOTT PLUS

The strict interpretation of the Fourteenth Amendment to exclude an unborn child from constitutional protection parallels the exclusion of an entire race from constitutional protection in <u>Dred Scott</u>. The only distinction is that <u>Dred Scott</u> was based on a clear misinterpretation of the reason for the 20 year allowance of slavery residing in the 1787 Constitution. This contrasts with the clear noninterpretation of the extant Common Law rights of the unborn child in <u>Roe v. Wade</u> that had existed for a period of 2,000 years. The grave and disastrous political implications of constitutionalizing a misinterpretation or noninterpretation and denying an inalienable right are clear from events subsequent to <u>Dred Scott</u>. With access to all judicial and legislative remedies denied, justice for the child or family members other than the mother is no longer available through any legal process. The only alternative is an inevitable confrontation or a subsequent breakdown of civil society and in slavery's case, Civil War.

Perhaps the most egregious and significant change in legal philosophy in <u>Roe v. Wade</u> is the express transfer of fundamental rights from "inalienable rights" endowed upon humankind by God to "fundamental rights" found by the Court. By definition, a fundamental right must be rooted in a philosophy. Even ignoring, for the moment, the issue of abortion as a fundamental right as a serious conflict with Christian philosophy, what possible important value does abortion symbolize that the will of the majority must yield to it? Although support for abortion is popular with those who oppose population growth and proponents of eugenics, such support is based only on an opinion about what is good for society as a whole, a utilitarian theory, which by definition is antithetical to a fundamental rights theory. The politics of population growth and eugenics is not based on philosophy and it is not widely accepted. One person does not have a fundamental right to deny another person's right to exist merely because of a value judgment and an opinion about the best interests of the majority. A fundamental right to an abortion is as rootless as a slave owner's fundamental right to own another person.

IT'S ABOUT THE CULTURE

The declaration of abortion as a "fundamental" right is related to its importance as a cultural issue. The underlying cultural issue behind all of the legal and political controversy is the drive for sexual liberation of women. This cause is entirely secular. Even honest libertarians place limits on natural law because of the threats of disease, depression and death.

Abortion advocates' initial support for abortion on moral grounds, that abortion laws neither prevent promiscuity nor encourage celibacy, has been discredited by evidence obtained during three decades of experience following <u>Roe v. Wade</u>. Yet, the moral issue relates, in any event, to the scope of the police power and not to the fundamental rights issue.

Exposing the root of this new fundamental right as based on sexual liberation without moral guidelines or restrictions, sets the abortion movement as directly opposed to the law of God. The right to eliminate unwanted offspring, who are considered but a nuisance and an unwanted consequence of sexual freedom, has now been constitutionalized, and doing so blocks the implementation of God's standard of justice. God created governmental institutions to implement justice according to His standard. The Courts have rejected His standard for their own new standard.

What is alarming to legal practitioners is the effect abortion has had on the interpretation of all law. To make room for legalized abortion, well-settled principles of law and set standards of justice had to be removed, ignored or changed, while truth had to be denied and suppressed. In <u>Roe</u>, the Supreme Court said that it need not decide the question of when life begins. Later, in <u>City of Akron v. Akron Center for Reprod. Health</u> (1983), the Court admitted because of scientific advances that the trimester formula in <u>Roe</u> was on a collision course with itself. In <u>Casey</u>, the Court admitted that the <u>Roe</u> analysis was flawed, though its rule would not be overturned lest the Court lose respect.

WORSE THAN SLAVERY

The tolerance for abortion has had a more devastating effect in America than did the tolerance for slavery. The disrespect for life that has resulted from legalized abortion is all pervasive.

The Holocaust in Germany did not occur simply because Hitler was anti-Semitic. The German people did not rise up as a nation against the Nazis, in part, because they were virtually powerless to do so after the courts refused to uphold justice for the Jews. The German courts did not stop the

Nazis from confiscating Jewish property nor did they stop the storm troopers from interfering with Jewish businesses. When the Parliament ceded additional powers to the dictatorship, the German people approved the usurpation of authority over life and death and handed it to one person.

Interestingly, abortion has been determined to be unconstitutional in modern Germany. Citing its history with National Socialism, the German court saw that the respect for life is a prerequisite for justice, and that meant protecting the rights for all individuals, even unborn children.

The right to life did not originate in the German constitution nor does it originate in the Fourteenth Amendment. The right to life certainly does not originate with the decision of the United States Supreme Court. The right to life is antecedent to and superior to any law originating with a human or human institution. The denial of that right to life creates a call for justice.

Injustice caused by mankind creates a need for divine justice. Lincoln saw that principle in Nineteenth Century America. Bonhoeffer saw the same principle in Germany.

Despite the United States Supreme Court's call for finality in <u>Casey</u>, pro-life American Christians cannot stop fighting for the right to life. Opposition to abortion is opposition to tyranny, and is not only integral to the life of the individual Christian but also integral to the continued existence of the nation.

WHY A HERESY?

The term heresy is disturbing because many martyrs were condemned as heretics for attempting to express truth when it conflicted with custom and tradition. The conflict between custom, expressed as the cultural norm, and truth, expressed as principle, continues.

Customs and traditions are useful as constant reminders of ideas and emotions that do not reoccur regularly or spontaneously. To many people, customs and traditions are windows to the past, reminders of truth discovered throughout the centuries. To others, customs and traditions are viewed as "windows to heaven," serving as reminders of matters unseen and discipline to focus upon the divine. The Catholic Church, both eastern and western, has been sustained and stabilized through times of changing ethics and morality because of their customs and traditions. Luther did not reject the customs and traditions of the Roman Catholic Church that did not conflict with doctrine. Customs and traditions that conflicted with doctrine were quickly abandoned or modified. The Catholic Church reformed itself shortly after Luther exposed certain customs and traditions that conflicted with

Scriptural principle.

The written law and the moral basis of a culture are similar to church doctrine and church practice. The customs and traditions set forth in selected case precedents and unrepealed statutes provide evidence of the law.

Common Law has existed and has been maintained for centuries as a guideline for behavior and evidence of "truth." Common Law was built upon reason and Scriptural truth in the light of reason, and not from the dark recesses of judicial chambers, to act as a bulwark, first against barbarism and lawlessness, and then against tyranny. But cultural customs and traditions do not constitute the law. Rather they are evidence of the law. The same is true for written statutes and judicial opinions that conflict with fundamental truth. Erroneous judicial opinions and misguided legislation cannot change immutable truth.

American slavery provided an example of a cultural custom and tradition that violated principle. Neither church doctrine that failed to condemn slavery nor democratically enacted or court adjudicated law promoting slavery provided a firm moral base for a custom that conflicted with principle.

Unlike slavery, abortion proponents had to change custom and tradition to overcome principle. The law had to be changed prior to bringing about changes in the cultural customs and traditions of 1973, because America had historically rejected abortion as an acceptable practice. By 1992, the Supreme Court retrieved the argument that custom and tradition, fully 19 years old by the time of the Casey decision, constituted a law that could not be changed. The same court that changed fundamental law in 1973 to prevent the states from restricting abortion declared in 1992 that it lacked the authority to allow the states to pass legislation that conflicted with the 19-year-old custom and tradition. The Court's strange rediscovery of the importance of "custom and tradition" reflected America's new moral finding that abortion was neither wrong nor socially unacceptable.

Many see the legalization of abortion as the triumph of the 1960s cultural war. Abortion proponents have understood the significance of the symbolism of the abortion issue better than do abortion opponents. They saw that the libertine lifestyle that needs legal abortion is offensive to true Christianity because it is offensive to God.

When Lincoln surmised that God had chosen Lincoln's time to put an end to slavery he still believed in the applicability of the Scripture: "woe to man because of his offenses." The Civil War was a sentence upon this nation imposed for not stopping an institution that had existed in this land since before the arrival of the Puritans. Supporters of slavery could look to Scriptures to see that the practice existed in Biblical times. Yet, Lincoln saw the Civil War as God's punishment of America for tolerating the unjust institution of slavery. In contrast, the institution of abortion is new and unprecedented under Anglo-Saxon law and the Catholic tradition from which Common Law developed.

The conflicts in philosophy, law and theology between the opposing forces that clash in the abortion debate clearly parallel some of the issues that defined the slavery debate. But abortion is worse. Abortion targets the defenseless and demeans the life of every person. At the core of the support for abortion is an opposition to God. *Abortion combines the constitutional philosophy of slavery with the political philosophy of the Holocaust.*

Slavery presented a conflict between principles of the Declaration of Independence against advocates for states' autonomy. Abortion presents a conflict between the principles of the Declaration of Independence against advocates for individual autonomy.

Slavery symbolizes the sin of man against man. Abortion symbolizes the sin of man against God.

When Lincoln warned that the divine attributes of God never changed, his commentary that "woe to that man by whom the offense cometh" reflected an understanding that the judgment of God followed the transgressions of man, even when man was not consciously rebelling against God. The slavery heresy resulted in part from a lack of understanding of the fundamental moral principle that slavery was wrong; in turn, caused in part more from a moral compromise and a lack of diligence in pursuing Scriptural truth.

Abortion, in comparison, represents open rebellion against God and a direct rejection of fundamental principle. To facilitate abortion, America's culture had to be changed, her ethics redefined, and Scripture had to be openly challenged as offensive to the rights of individuals seeking an abortion. Adherence to Scriptural truth is now challenged as bigoted and hate filled.

Abortion rights advocates understand the significance of Biblical truth which they express in an animated and violent intolerance of expressions and application of Christianity. Abortion advocates, to maintain their position, had to use the courts and the law to suppress the opinions of abortion opponents. To win the debate, and they must win, Christians have to go beyond the legal and ethical arguments against abortion and address the more fundamental and significant issue. A loose minority of people, tied together by hostility toward God and a desire for personal autonomy, have changed the law and ethical truth and culture of this country. Because life is a sacred gift from God, the right to life had to be eliminated as an inalienable right, in open rebellion against God. This open rebellion against God has continued to exist because of the passive acquiescence and general apathy of today's Christians.

In slavery, the law protected custom while conflicting with principle. In abortion, the law conflicted with custom and principle, but Christians have refused to resist these changes.

How should we apply the sentiments expressed by Jefferson, Webster and Lincoln against slavery, reflecting upon God's justice, when we try to gain perspective on the greater heresy of abortion? How much worse will it be for this generation, nurtured by the cultural upheaval of the 1960s, that has rejected its Common Law opposition to a practice that had, since ancient times, only been tolerated in barbarian cultures?

CHAPTER 9

EQUALITY

"America, then, exhibits in her social state a most extraordinary phenomenon. Men are there seen on a greater equality in point of fortune and intellect, or, in other words, more equal in their strength, than in any other country of the world, or in any age of which history has preserved their remembrance."

Alexis de Tocqueville, *Democracy in America*

In November 1995, I was invited to speak at a conference at Catholic University in Lublin, Poland. I spoke in the late morning of the second day following a succession of clergyman and politicians. They had talked about trying to understand why the intense, emotional victory of Solidarity in 1989 was losing its influence on politics and culture in Poland. (Two days after the conference ended, Lech Walesa lost his reelection bid.)

The speaker who preceded me was a Scottish Professor from Edinburgh; he was anti-capitalist, anti-American and the author of a new book titled, The New Wealth of Nations, *which he described as the most important book on economics in history.*

When it was my turn to speak, I ignored the professor's anti-Americanism and instead observed, as an American, that I thought it was "odd" that European nations continued to define themselves by their ethnicity. Given that fact, I asserted that the European Union would never succeed. In America, I told them, despite our uniqueness as the most multiracial, multicultural and multiethnic nation in history, we were also the most unified. The reason, I asserted, is that we all agree to be bound by a written set of rules found in the Declaration of Independence and the Constitution.

I talked them through the Declaration, point by point, starting with self-evident truths, and explaining how the American view of equality was different from theirs. I described secular equality as either the French version, symbolized by the guillotine, or the communist version that had more to do with equality of misery than equality of opportunity. I explained that American equality, in contrast, was based on the concept of the brotherhood of man derived from the fact that we all have a common Father. I found that Europeans, stuck in the old world, understood this better than modern Americans.

I added that at its founding, America's New World vision allowed her to rise above European tribalism. What I didn't mention to them was that the founding fathers' lofty idealism had long since been replaced by a new type of tribalism created by the United States Supreme Court, substituting class-based equality in place of the ideal that each individual is equal.

◆ ◆ ◆

The distinctive contribution of American Christianity to political philosophy is the belief in legal equality. The Nazi Holocaust resulted from an exaggeration of a centuries-old European tradition that exalted individuals to dictatorial status while disparaging whole ethnic groups to subhuman status. America's view of legal equality, drawn from a Protestant Christian worldview, rejected both of those traditions in principle.

Adhering to principle has always been difficult. America's critics assert that the principle of equality never really existed, citing the apparent inapplicability of the Declaration of Independence to slaves and women. Their assertion is wrong. The principle is correct. It is the application of the principle that has been flawed.

Non-adherence to the principle of legal equality has caused serious problems. About this, no one can rightfully argue. But, rejecting the uniquely Christian principle of legal equality has caused far more serious consequences for entire nations and peoples, consequences that result in deprivation, oppression and even death.

THE MEANING OF LEGAL EQUALITY

As a practical matter, people understand equality differently.

To some, equality means that everyone must have the same opportunity. They see that inequalities must be manipulated to assure that all persons who attempt to take advantage of opportunities have equality in preparation.

To others, equality means that everyone should have the same outcomes. They believe that society must manipulate the factors that provide some with greater outcomes while others achieve less. Essentially, some people are given benefits to improve their outcomes while others are restricted so as to lower their outcomes.

Neither of these examples adequately defines legal equality.

As used in the Declaration of Independence, equality has a specific meaning. "That all men are created equal," stems from two important Christian theological concepts. All humans are created. Humankind did not evolve into coincidental equal beings. One, all men are equal because God created men equal. Disbelief in the Divine Creation of man is disbelief in human equality, as the founding fathers saw it. Two, the equality of men, as it has been traditionally understood, is based upon the symbolism of brotherhood. The idea of brotherhood implies that we all have a common father. Two people without the same father are not brothers. They may be friends, but they are not brothers.

Equality has a definite theological meaning. Equality, under God, means we all have an equal opportunity for salvation or damnation. God's law judges each person's choice. Equality before God does not mean an equal participation in God's creation, but an equal application of God's justice.

Equality also has a legal definition that is the foundation for man's ministration of justice. The Canon Law term, *jus commune*, embodies the principle of legal equality. It became the foundation of the law in England, known as Common Law.

In America, the colonists attempted to literally follow the equality principle. According to Jesse Root, in his *Report of the Law Cases of the Connecticut Colony*, the American legal system had been purified of the special prerogatives of the English monarchs, the major obstacle to pure equality in England. Americans attempted to eliminate all rules and regulations that granted favorable treatment to a person based on family name, economic status or political affiliation. American law only retained distinctions which were related to a person's ability, ingenuity and willingness to work, provided that such distinctions could not be repugnant to Biblical principles. For example, colonial governments allowed for licensing laws that required training or special skills, but banned licensing laws that required a payment of a fee and could, therefore, favor the rich and powerful.

With the obvious exceptions of slavery, which the founding fathers addressed in the Constitution, and women's equality, which was subject to some peculiar interpretations of Common Law, the early Americans incorporated equality principles into their new American government. As observed by Alexis De Tocqueville in *Democracy in America*, first published in 1831, "Equality is the well-nigh irresistible principle of authority in the modern world."

De Tocqueville, a French aristocrat, had not been impressed by the concept of equality that drove the French Revolution. But in America, equality and democracy worked. True enough, De Tocqueville criticized Americans' lack of tolerance for deviation from an unspoken standard of conformity in habits and ideas. His important point was that equality had survived in the short run because it was a principle rooted in the "goodness" of their character, not in selfishness. He warned that democracy would fail if the motivation for equality changed.

THE SECULARIZATION OF LEGAL EQUALITY

In modern terms, the main proposition of human equality is that all men share a common nature. This is not the same as the Christian theory of brotherhood. The proposition that all men are created equal historically meant that all humans are the same in some things, but not in everything. Lincoln understood that people were not necessarily the same or equal in "color, size, intellect, moral development, or social capacity." That means that individuals could be unequal in many respects, but remain equal with respect to inalienable rights.

Christians also agree that man should not be treated as a god or as an animal. One person cannot treat another as a chattel nor can one person be lord over another unless they are unequal.

Secular equality is different from Biblical equality. The French believed in equality when they executed the nobility and clergy. Karl Marx and Nicolai Lenin collaborated on a theory of equality that advocated elimination of all individual personal and property rights to pursue a collectivist system that was supposed to bring everyone into a state of economic perfection. Only the Biblical model, however, respects the equal rights of each individual.

The concept of "consent of the governed" is the reciprocal of equality. Consent is theoretically necessary because men are theoretically equal. The exercise of authority and submission to authority by equals must be by agreement and consent. Consent to government is a Christian innovation to political philosophy and an addition to the law of nature.

The Massachusetts Constitution of 1780 states, "The body of politics is formed by a voluntary association of individuals; it is a social compact by which the whole people covenants with each citizen and each citizen with the whole people that all shall be governed by certain laws for the common good."

Respect for the rights of others is required before one's own rights can be respected and recognized. Consent is related to equality because individuals who are equal can only consent to a limited government. To grant a special status to a leader or a group without consent violates the equality principle. For leaders to take more power or authority without consent violates the understanding that everyone is equal. Elitism, as a government policy, has been deliberately rejected in America.

The principle of equality is contradicted by "collectivist" theories of government and strict democratic principles. The needs of the group cannot trump individual rights because that makes some people equal and others unequal. A pure democracy, without a reservation of individual rights, can also make some people not equal. Communism inherently violates the equality principle. Democracy can, in practice, violate the same principle.

The founding fathers were more concerned with the special status granted to some that are based upon inherent privileges resulting from either birth or appointment. Principles of equality stand in opposition to the concentration of power and wealth. The opposition to the concentration of political power is the theme of Madison's commentaries on factions in the Federalist Papers. The opposition to the centralization and concentration of wealth is evident in the writings of George Mason and Jefferson. They argued in favor of including provisions outlawing public and private monopolies in the original Constitution. Political and economic freedom both flow from the decentralization of political and economic power. The founding fathers argued for preserving the rights of citizens to participate politically and economically while being protected from the inequalities suffered at the hands of the nobles and monarchs in Europe.

RACIAL EQUALITY

In 1776, the common enemy of all of the colonies was England. The colonists were united against the monarchy. The colonists were also in agreement about the unfairness that they had no ability to participate in the political process. Because England was the object of their immediate concern, the political debate focused on the inequality of wealth and power resulting from status and privilege.

The colonists postponed the debate about slavery so as not to detract from the main issue at hand—the imminent war with England. The debate about slavery was among themselves. The debate would last until the outbreak of the Civil War.

A fundamental, theoretical conflict arose between North and South in

Congress relating to the concepts of consent of the governed and equality. The disagreement over these fundamental core principles of the Declaration arose because of the debate about continued legalization of slavery. The South emphasized the concept of consent of the governed. Southerners argued that the North's attempt to restrict and ultimately abolish slavery was being done over the opposition of the interests of the South. In essence, they argued that the abolition of slavery would be accomplished without their consent.

The North, on the other hand, emphasized the principle of equality. Obviously, the existence of slavery was a blatant example of inequality. Equality applied equally to the slaves and the slave owners. For northerners, consent of the governed must exist in harmony with equality. Otherwise, American equality was no better than the equality of the French Revolution.

The North had always adhered to the equality principle. The 1779 Vermont Constitution explicitly prohibited slavery. In 1780, the Massachusetts Constitution unabashedly declared that, "all men are born free and equal, and have certain natural, essential, and inalienable rights which are the right of enjoying and defending their lives and liberties, that of acquiring, possessing and protecting property." Their action abolished slavery in Massachusetts.

The North's concession to slavery, by omission in the Declaration, and partial commission in the Constitution, was for political expediency. For the sake of independence in the first instance, and the Union in the second, the North reluctantly agreed with the South. The original Constitution bears witness that acceding to this agreement was temporary. To maintain their economic status quo, the South refused to compromise.

During that time, many Americans were becoming less certain about the creation/equality theory. Jefferson typified a southern view that, though it was not sinister in appearance, was devastating in principle. Publicly critical of slavery, Jefferson stated his intention to free his slaves in his will, but at his death, his executors sold his slaves to pay his debts.

Clergymen who based their opposition to slavery on the Biblical principle that all races had descended from Adam and Eve, opposed Jefferson's 1800 presidential candidacy. This, because Jefferson had speculated that the races may have evolved differently. One clergyman wrote:

> [Jefferson] does not adopt, as an article of his philosophy,
> the descent of the blacks as well as the whites from...[Adam and
> Eve] which came immediately from the hands of God. He is not

> sure...Now, how will all this accord with revealed truth? God,
> says the Apostle Paul, 'hath made of ONE BLOOD ALL
> NATIONS of men, for to dwell on ALL the face of the earth.'

The theory of racial evolution conflicts with the principle of Biblical equality and the story of creation. Serious pastors had to reject it, and reject those who advocated it as truth, like Jefferson.

Once the principled position of racial equality had won the day through a bloody Civil War, the debate did not simply dissipate. Racism replaced slavery.

Though Congress and the states quickly passed the Thirteenth Amendment in 1865, many southern states enacted "Black Codes" to nullify its effect. In response, Congress enacted the "Civil Rights Act of 1866," that declared that the newly freed man was a citizen and, as such, was entitled to the "same right...to make and enforce contracts, to sue, be parties, and give evidence, to inherit, purchase, lease, sell, hold, and convey real and personal property, and to full and equal benefit of all laws, proceedings for the security of person and property, as is enjoyed by white citizens."

President Andrew Johnson vetoed the 1866 Civil Rights Act, saying it went beyond Congress' authority. Congress overrode the veto. Then Congress began the process of enacting the Fourteenth Amendment to prevent states from denying the equal protection of the laws to the freed slaves. Thus, they thought, a legal mandate would resolve racial issues. They were wrong.

THE FOURTEENTH AMENDMENT SOLUTION

The improvement of race relations in America since the Civil War has been slow; the United States Supreme Court has actually blunted this improvement by its Fourteenth Amendment decisions.

The lessons of the Civil War should have been clear. The Constitution did not allow states to infringe upon the fundamental rights of its citizens, no matter their color. The fundamental rights of all Americans were superior to the police power of individual states to limit them. The Declaration of Independence had made that clear. Any lingering doubt about the conflict between an individual's natural rights and the power of tyranny should have been settled by the mandates of the Fourteenth Amendment which states:

> § 1. All persons born or naturalized in the United States,
> and subject to the jurisdiction thereof, are citizens of the United
> States and of the state wherein they reside. No state shall make

> or enforce any law which shall abridge the privileges or immu-
> nities of citizens of the United States; nor shall any State deprive
> any person of life, liberty, or property, without due process of
> law; nor deny to any person within its jurisdiction the equal pro-
> tection of the laws.

"Persons" means humans. "All" means all. The amendment left no room for a different legal standing based on a person's skin color.

Congress meant to disallow states their ability to base nullification claims on a desire to impose tyranny on any of their citizens. The original Constitution had mandated that all states adopt a republican form of govern-ment. The amended Constitution added the requirement of states to recog-nize fundamental rights. It further defined those rights by forcing states to adhere to the principles of due process, equal protection and the recognition of the privileges and immunities attached to the status of being a United States citizen. The Constitution required that any rebel state, as a condition of its re-admittance to the union, and any territory that desired to become a state had to acknowledge these same legal principles. The Fourteenth Amendment nationalized fundamental rights.

So it seemed that the issue of legal equality had been settled, until the Court began to meddle. Their retreat from the broad and hopeful sweep of the Fourteenth Amendment, as with the Declaration of Independence, was swift and decisive.

The United States Supreme Court restricted the scope and impact of the Fourteenth Amendment in two major rulings known as The Slaughter-House Cases (1873) and the Civil Rights Cases (1883). The Slaughter-House Cases ruling, resulting from a challenge to state-granted monopolies in the New Orleans packing plant industry, created an arbitrary distinction between the privileges and immunities of national citizenship and the privileges and immunities of state citizenship. As a result of that decision, the constitution-al distinction between state and national citizenship is still left uncertain. Slaughter-House also limited challenges to class-based discrimination, rather than individually suffered equal protection discrimination. *The Court had thereby granted fundamental rights to individuals only as members of a class.*

The Court further agitated against individual rights and for class-based rights in Yick Wo v. Hopkins (1886). It became the cornerstone of modern equal protection jurisprudence and the central reason for our modern class-conscious culture.

JUSTICE DELAYED: THE CIVIL RIGHTS CASES

In the Civil Rights Cases, the Supreme Court consolidated the prosecutions of five different citizens in cases pertaining to the denial of access to inns, public conveniences and amusement parks on the basis of race. In its Civil Rights Cases ruling, the Court overturned the prosecutions on the basis that no state action had been involved. Although the Thirteenth Amendment required the elimination of slavery and "all badges and incidents of slavery," the Court did not consider the denial of access to public accommodations as a "badge of slavery" until Jones v. Alfred H. Mayer Co. (1968). Thus, the Court left grey an area that otherwise seemed black and white.

At the time of the ratification of the Thirteenth and Fourteenth Amendments, discrimination against former slaves was aimed at the particular race that had been subject to slavery laws, i.e. Negroes. The Thirteenth Amendment prescribed a uniquely different civil rights issue than issues faced by non-Negro citizens. If the Court had enforced the law that subjected private action to the provisions of the Civil Rights Act, which actions were made unconstitutional by the ratification of the Thirteenth Amendment, the unique discrimination faced by former slaves and their descendants could have been seriously improved in the 1860s. The Civil Rights Cases prevented that solution by seriously retreating from the original intent of the Civil Rights Act by limiting liability for violators of the Act and making it harder for victims to sue. The expansive civil rights rulings in the 1960s should not have been necessary.

The Supreme Court later held that states could not be sued directly under the Civil Rights Act for violations of individual civil rights, because of the Eleventh Amendment. The dual holdings that directed states to take action, but made it impossible to sue states that refused, negated the impact of the Fourteenth Amendment and the Civil Rights Act until modern times. Prior to the Civil War, states enforced laws restricting individual rights based on race. After the Civil War, race discrimination was not so much a matter of direct government action, but a matter of private conduct that became commonplace when the government refused to enforce the laws that could have restrained unlawful private discriminatory conduct. Racial discrimination was carried forward not just by direct individual action, but also by actions directed at businesses or individuals that had no interest in discriminating against black people. Discrimination laws were replaced by discriminatory enforcement of the laws. The states denied justice indirectly rather than directly.

JUSTICE FURTHER DELAYED: "SEPARATE BUT EQUAL"

The Court's "separate but equal" doctrine further inhibited progress toward racial equality by allowing the state and local governments to continue to regulate individuals based on their race. In Plessy v. Ferguson (1896), the Supreme Court stated that:

> Laws permitting, and even requiring, their separation in places where they are liable to be brought into contact do not necessarily imply the inferiority of either race to the other, and have been generally, if not universally, recognized as within the competency of the state legislatures in the exercise of their police power.

The first Justice John Harlan's dissent in Plessy rejected the hypocrisy of the separate but equal theory. Harlan's dissent encompassed a Nineteenth Century version of natural law when he argued that the Constitution must regard "man as man," and be "color-blind."

Acts 17:26 addresses this separate but equal doctrine rendering it without theoretical substance. "God hath made of one blood all nature of men for to dwell on all the face of the earth."

Furthermore, Blackstone never recognized racial classifications under Common Law. The northern delegations to the Continental Congress and the Constitutional Convention had condemned the slave trade. The abolitionists had rightly condemned slavery as unbiblical. But the Court still persisted in permitting racial classifications, making them a basis for discrimination claims. This defied law, logic and legacy.

THE FOURTEENTH AMENDMENT
REPAIRED, BUT NOT RESTORED

In 1954, in Brown v. Board of Education, the Court overturned Plessy, rejecting the "separate but equal theory." Although Brown has been considered a landmark decision and the most important modern case applicable to racial equality, Brown still did not adopt Harlan's Plessy dissent, nor was it based on the views of Blackstone or the founding fathers. Brown simply declared that statistical evidence did not support the separate but equal premise that different facilities for different races could be made equal. Brown rejected the Plessy hypocrisy, but did not modify the states' police power to enact laws and regulations based on race classifications.

The Court refused to adopt Harlan's advocacy for a "color-blind" Constitution until 1995. In <u>Adarand Constructors, Inc. v. Pena</u> (1995), the Court disallowed the use of federal government financial incentives paid to general contractors that favored minority-owned businesses based solely on race. In fact, the Court disallowed all government attempts to regulate based on race: "To pursue the concept of racial entitlement even for the most admirable and benign of purposes—is to reinforce and preserve for future mischief the way of thinking that produced race slavery, race privilege and race hatred."

Concurring, Justice Clarence Thomas attempted to square the principle of equality with the Constitution:

> Government cannot make us equal, it can only recognize, respect, and protect us as equal before the law...that these programs may have been motivated, in part, by good intentions cannot provide refuge from the principle that under our Constitution, the government may not make distinctions on the basis of race. As far as the Constitution is concerned, it is irrelevant whether a government's racial classifications are drawn by those who wish to oppress a race or by those who have a sincere desire to help those thought to be disadvantaged. There can be no doubt that the paternalism that appears to lie at the heart of these programs is at war with the principle of inherent equality that underlies and infuses our Constitution.

<u>Adarand</u> did not rule out the possibility that the government may still undertake the promotion of diversity, perceived as a legitimate objective in <u>Regents of Univ. of Cal. v. Bakke</u> (1978). The Court, in fact, did elevate diversity to a constitutional right in the recent case of <u>Grutter v. Bollinger</u> (2003). This single issue perpetuates the problem of the Court's refusal to resolve the issue on proper grounds. It does not have to be this way.

Historically, many justified slavery on the basis that the races might have evolved differently, contrary to the assertion of the Declaration of Independence; as a self-evident truth, "all men are created equal." <u>Brown</u> struck down the separate but equal doctrine because it did not work, not because the state should be prohibited from making race a legislative consideration. But it failed to address the equally dubious purpose of promoting diversity, which in practice, still obstructs promoting the purist form of individual equality. The equality of the Declaration sees no racial distinctions at all, because all individuals are equal before God.

GENDER EQUALITY

CHRISTIANITY AND PATERNALISM

Christianity has been inaccurately portrayed as paternalistic and anti-female. This is because detractors see no distinctions between men and women, basing their philosophy on a misunderstanding of the meaning of legal equality.

Historically, gender inequality has been correctly linked to paternalistic political theory. As well, it is easy to observe that legal inequality based on gender is a regular practice in most non-Christian cultures. But paternalism was first identified as a political theory under the absolutist theory of government advocated by the Stuart kings of England. The Stuart kings and their supporters advanced a political theory that attempted to justify the dynasties that controlled Seventeenth Century Europe, some of which continued until the Twentieth Century. The absolutist supporters, which included such notable scholars as Hobbes and Bacon, linked the leadership role of the male in the family to political leadership. They based their theory of government on the argument that the appointment of Adam as the head of the family in Genesis also entitled Adam to have dominion over the entire human family. The subjects of the absolute monarchs were forced to view them as divinely appointed sovereigns who traced their position and authority to Adam.

In contrast, the political theory foundational to the Declaration of Independence rejected the paternalistic Adamic model. In his *Two Treatises of Government*, Locke rejected paternalism, which he saw as contrary to Reformation thought. Locke's theory directly refuted Hobbes' and Robert Filmer's argument that attempted to justify paternalism as a political theory. Locke acknowledged the obvious differences between male and female, and saw that both offered essential functions in support of the family structure. Locke agreed that a distinction existed between Adam and Eve within the family structure—a structure that places the male as head of the household and is central to Jewish thought. He saw that such a distinction was vitally necessary for the maintenance of a civil and ordered society. But the role of Adam as the political leader and first monarch was rejected. Locke separated the structure of civil government from the structure of a family.

America rejected paternalism as a political theory but accepted the English Common Law as legal theory. The early American lawyers and judges ignored the references in Blackstone's *Commentaries on the Laws of Eng-*

land describing the English monarchy and political system, but they adopted Blackstone's Common Law principles that were related to private conduct.

Common Law placed both political and economic restrictions on women. Early American law placed those restrictions on women for the express purpose of preserving and protecting the family. As a result, the Constitution forbade women from voting or holding office until the Nineteenth Amendment had been ratified in 1920.

Although the stories of Adam and the patriarchs of Genesis were used to justify the "divine rights of kings" political theory, the rest of the Old Testament offered little support for Common Law restrictions on women. Women's suffrage and Common Law could both be argued to be in conflict with Scripture. Old Testament models were not dispositive. Miriam held the office of prophet. Deborah held the offices of prophet and judge, although she was not required to lead an army into war. Athalia, however, was deposed as her status as queen was contrary to law. Shortcuts in establishing a simple principle were not possible. There did not appear to be any legal restrictions on women from the time of the patriarchs until the time of the kings under the laws of Old Testament Israel.

What application of constitutional law could be found in the conflicts in the law of Israel? English Common Law considered the husband and wife as one person. Therefore, a married woman could not own property or enter into contracts. Common Law drew this distinction not between men and women generally, but was aimed at married women in particular. The purpose of Common Law was sometimes to protect women and sometimes to protect the family; women were, as a consequence, prevented from participating in the economic life of the community. Common Law restricted the inalienable rights to total liberty and the pursuit of happiness to males, seeing them as necessary to the attainment of male virtue.

GENDER EQUALITY UNDER THE NEW FOURTEENTH AMENDMENT

Laws restricting females, passed to protect women and the family structure, were not challenged until after the passage of the Fourteenth Amendment. The first challenges against gender inequality were based on both the Fourteenth Amendment due process and equal protection clauses. The body of judge-made law that followed these challenges is both confusing and contradictory, interweaving principles of due process and equality while attempting to focus upon sex discrimination issues, while at the same time trying to continue to balance its traditional concern with the protection of the family. The Court has attempted to balance protected rights with the expansion of the government's police power, all the time shifting its focus between clauses of the Constitution and who the court is attempting to protect. No clear consensus emerges of a unified theory resolving the goals of these conflicts. As a result, an irreconcilable conflict emerged as the Court reasoned between gender equality cases and the protection of family cases. The conflict deepened as the Court formally abandoned tradition and changed its view of the traditional family. The modern unification of disparate theories advocating female equality, sexual freedom and a new overarching philosophical principle of individual autonomy collided with each other, and, moreover, became irreconcilable with Biblical mandates.

The Supreme Court's Nineteenth Century philosophical conservatism obscured all distinctions between political and economic equality, and the protection of the family unit and the rights of women. This is observed in its first consideration of these issues in a constitutional case. The Court rejected the first legal attempt to use the new Fourteenth Amendment to secure equality for women in <u>Bradwell v. Illinois</u> (1873). <u>Bradwell</u> addressed the attempt of a married woman to obtain a license to practice law in the state of Illinois. The argument of her counsel was simple: the declarations of the Fourteenth Amendment applied to all persons, including women. The Court ignored that argument. Instead, the Court reaffirmed Common Law stating, that "a woman had no legal existence separate from her husband, who was regarded as her head and representative in the social state; and, notwithstanding some recent modifications of this civil status, many of the special rules of law flowing from and dependent upon this cardinal principle still exist in full force in most states."

During the same session, the Court had rejected the concept that fundamental rights were a privilege and immunity under the Fourteenth Amendment in <u>The Slaughter-House Cases</u> (1873). The Court had misinterpreted the argument in <u>Bradwell</u> as an argument in favor of women's suffrage and continued to reject the literal meaning of the Fourteenth Amendment in order to restrict its application. The Court reasoned that because the right to vote was not universal—males under 21 could also not vote—therefore, women's suffrage could not, therefore, be a right. The Court shelved the Fourteenth Amendment argument.

The Court's political conservatism was also philosophical, as is apparent in Justice Bradley's concurring opinion. There he explained the dilemma faced by attempting to balance the fundamental rights of the female with the maintenance of the family:

It certainly cannot be affirmed, as a historical fact, that this has ever been established as one of the fundamental privileges and immunities of the sex. On the contrary, the civil law, as well as nature herself, has always recognized a wide difference in the respective spheres and destinies of man and woman. Man is, or should be, woman's protector and defender. The natural and proper timidity and delicacy which belongs to the female sex evidently unfits it for many of the occupations of civil life. The constitution of the family organization, which is founded in the divine ordinance, as well as in the nature of things, indicates the domestic sphere as that which properly belongs to the domain and functions of womankind. The harmony, not to say identity, of interests and views which belong or should belong to the family institution, is repugnant to the idea of a woman adopting a distinct and independent career from that of her husband. So firmly fixed was this sentiment in the founders of the Common Law that it became a maxim of that system of jurisprudence that a woman had no legal existence separate from her husband, who was regarded as her head and representative in the social state; and, notwithstanding some recent modifications of this civil status, many of the special rules of law flowing from and dependent upon this cardinal principle still exist in full force in most states. One of these is, that a married woman is incapable, without her husband's consent, of making contracts which shall be binding on her or him. This very incapacity was one circumstance which the Supreme Court of Illinois deemed important in rendering a married woman incompetent fully to perform the duties and trusts that belong to the office of an attorney and counselor.

It is true that many women are unmarried and not affected by any of the duties, complications, and incapacities arising out of the married state, but these are exceptions to the general rule. The paramount destiny and mission of woman are to fulfill the noble and benign offices of wife and mother. This is the law of the Creator. And the rules of civil society must be adapted to the general constitution of things, and cannot be based upon exceptional cases.

The humane movements of modern society, which have for their object the multiplication of avenues for woman's advancement, and of occupations adapted to her condition and sex, have my heartiest concurrence. But I am not prepared to say that it is one of her fundamental rights and privileges to be admitted into every office and position, including those which require highly special qualifications and demanding special responsibilities. In the nature of things it is not every citizen of every age, sex and condition that is qualified for every calling and position. It is the prerogative of the legislator to prescribe regulations founded on

nature, reason, and experience for the due admission of qualified
persons to professions and callings demanding special skill and
confidence. This fairly belongs to the police power of the state;
and, in my opinion, in view of the peculiar characteristics, destiny and mission of woman.

In this decision, the Supreme Court confused personhood with citizenship and police power with the law of the Creator. Citizenship grew out of
Locke's concept of a political community. Citizenship includes voting
rights and the ability to participate in the political community. Personhood
includes the right to own property, enter into contracts and to pursue the
common callings. These rights, defined by Jefferson as the pursuit of happiness, are inalienable and encompass the ability to participate within the
economic community.

Although the distinction between personhood and citizenship has never
been defined clearly, the Court completely blurred all distinctions in Bradwell. Similarly, the Court completely blurred all distinctions between the
police power and the law of the Creator.

The law of the Creator needs to be studied and understood. Justice
Bradley simply assumed that the government's exercise of police power was
related to the preservation of the family. An analysis of the government's
limited role in regulating professions requiring special skills is not necessarily related to the preservation of the family. Whatever connection between
job skills and the preservation of the family that may exist were not established nor considered in Bradwell. Justice Bradley's philosophy favoring
the family over individual rights of women was not pertinent to the issue in
the case. The Court's inflexibility eventually caused a backlash.

GENDER EQUALITY AND THE LAISSEZ FAIRE COURT

Following Bradwell, the Court's conservatives shifted their focus from
politics to economics. Women's suffrage was a constitutional issue for Congress. In the late Nineteenth Century, the Court redefined its role, viewing
itself as a bulwark protecting economic freedom against the expanding regulatory framework of the state's police power. As a result, economic conservatives were among the first to disregard laws that sought to uphold the
traditional protection of females when laws requiring different work standards for women restricted employers.

The Court eventually struck economic restrictions that attempted to
maintain gender distinctions as unequal and unconstitutional. In Muller v.

Oregon (1908), the Court had upheld wage and hours laws restricting women on the basis that they were, "properly placed in a class by herself, and legislation designed for her protection may be sustained, even when like legislation is not necessary for men, and could not be sustained," and, "the reason runs deeper, and rests in the inherent difference between the two sexes, and in the different functions in life which they perform."

Newer members of the Court ignored Muller, refusing to sustain similar legislation in Adkins v. Children's Hospital (1923). Adkins is usually remembered by constitutional lawyers as an example of extreme economic conservatism because the Court refused to allow police power to regulate private contracts. But the political philosophy of the Court had actually become quite modern:

> But the ancient inequality of the sexes, otherwise than physical, as suggested in the Muller Case has continued 'with diminishing intensity.' In view of the great—not to say revolutionary —changes which have taken place since that utterance, in the contractual, political, and civil status of women, culminating in the Nineteenth Amendment, it is not unreasonable to say that these differences have now come almost, if not quite, to the vanishing point. In this aspect of the matter, while the physical differences must be recognized in appropriate cases, and legislation fixing hours or conditions of work may properly take them into account, we cannot accept the doctrine that women of mature age, *sui juris* require or may be subjected to restrictions upon their liberty of contract which could not lawfully be imposed in the case of men under similar circumstances. To do so would be to ignore all the implications to be drawn from the present day trend of legislation, as well as that of common thought and usage, by which woman is accorded emancipation from the old doctrine that she must be given special protection or be subjected to special restraint in her contractual and civil relationships.

Oliver Wendell Holmes, in his dissent, showed less modernity in his political philosophy, declaring, "It will need more than the Nineteenth Amendment to convince me that there are no differences between men and women, or that legislation cannot take those differences into account."

The Court reversed Adkins in West Coast Hotel Co. v. Parish (1937), turning onto the present bumpy road which the Court has since followed down two separate paths. Following one path, the Court began interpreting the equal protection clause in conjunction with the right to privacy principles found in the due process clause. On the other path, the Court attempted to protect the family under the due process clause. Ultimately, the two theories conflict with themselves and with historical Christianity.

Scripture assigns different roles to men and women within the family structure. Could the court reconcile external political and economic equality for women while respecting internal family differences? The answer could possibly be "Yes," but only if Biblical principles of equality and Biblical principles of family are considered and reconciled in each case. Guided only by secular considerations, the answer has evolved to a clear and unequivocal "No!" The secular mandates of equal protection and right of privacy instead came to mean that to be equal, childbearing responsibility must also be equal for men and women. Roe became the logical extension of a secular equal protection and right to privacy analysis. Abortion became Rousseau's method to obtain equality when confronted with the gender equality question.

THE STRUGGLE FOR COMMON SENSE

In West Coast Hotel Co., the Court upheld minimum wage legislation for women and treated sex classifications with the same minimal scrutiny applied to other economic legislation that it announced during the same term in United States v. Darby (1937). Years later, in United States v. Dege (1960), the Court would find that a husband and wife were capable of a criminal conspiracy, rejecting the presumption that a wife acted under the coercive influence of her husband and could not be a willing participant, signaling a change in Common Law theory. But a year later, in Hoyt v. Florida (1961), the Court upheld a legislative classification that treated men and women differently for jury duty; it allowed a woman to determine "her own special responsibilities" in deference to traditional family roles. The Court reasoned, "despite the enlightened emancipation of women from the restrictions and protections of bygone years, and their entry into many parts of community life formerly considered to be reserved to men, woman is still regarded as the center of the home and family life." As recently as 1961, the Court was still attempting to protect the family, by protecting the woman's role as center of the home and family, but also allowing women to fully participate in the life of the economic community.

Both the rules and the process began to change during the 1960s. Congressional passage of Title VII of the Civil Rights Act of 1964 coincided with a judicial activism that pushed the Supreme Court beyond the democratic process. In Reed v. Reed (1971), the Court struck down, on equal protection grounds, an Oregon probate statute that preferred males to females in the selection of executors. The argument in favor of the statute was simply administrative convenience for the courts. The Court ruled that the legisla-tion was not rationally related to the purposes of the statute and was discrim-inatory. The theory was, in fact, the same as in West Coast Hotel Co. But the language in Reed v. Reed would lead the Court beyond economics, as it was cited as the basis for striking federal military regulations in Frontiero v. Richardson (1973). Citing to both Reed v. Reed and Title VII, Justice Bren-nan announced that the Court would equate sex discrimination with race dis-crimination and review legislation aimed at the newest "suspect classifica-tion" with "strict scrutiny." Justice Brennan referred to the views of Jeffer-son and de Tocqueville, and Justice Bradley's opinion in Bradwell, as "paternalistic" and "archaic." Justice Brennan, by reference, incorporated the unratified Equal Rights Amendment into constitutional equal protection jurisprudence.

Justice Brennan's view was not adopted by a majority of the Supreme Court until United States v. Virginia (1996). Prophetically, three concurring justices in Frontiero, had specifically cautioned against judicial pre-emption of the democratic process: "[a] major political decision which is currently in process of resolution does not reflect appropriate respect for duly pre-scribed legislative processes." Perhaps the failure to ratify the Equal Rights Amendment caused the Court to uphold, temporarily, differences in analysis of sex discrimination cases from race discrimination cases. The Court had shown some deference to Congress' constitutional authority over national defense by permitting Congress to exempt women from draft registration in Rostker v. Goldberg (1981), though they restricted congressional authority to issues of actual combat and not administration, but even that view is now doubtful because of the recent case of United States v. Virginia.

The Court has not yet eliminated all gender distinctions. Though grudg-ingly granted over three dissenting opinions, state statutes relating to rape were recently upheld because of the differences between men and women in Michael M. v. Superior Court of Sonoma County (1981). In that decision, the majority analyzed Reed v. Reed and the decisions subsequent to Reed and concluded that:

> Underlying these decisions is the principle that a legislature may not make overbroad generalizations based on sex which are entirely unrelated to any differences between men and women or which demean the ability or social status of the affected class. But because the Equal Protection Clause does not 'demand that a statute necessarily apply equally to all persons' or require 'things which are different in fact...to be treated in law as though they were the same' this Court has consistently upheld statutes

where the gender classification is not invidious, but rather realistically reflects the fact that the sexes are not similarly situated in certain circumstances. As the Court has stated, a legislature may provide for the special problems of women.

In his concurring opinion, Justice Stewart stated what had once been obvious, that:

> . . . detrimental racial classifications by government always violate the Constitution, for the simple reason that, so far as the Constitution is concerned, people of different races are always similarly situated. By contrast, while detrimental gender classifications by government often violate the Constitution, they do not always do so, for the reason that there are differences between males and females that the Constitution necessarily recognizes.

The Court cannot resolve its struggles to obscure the legitimacy of scientific gender distinctions. By refusing to acknowledge scientific distinctions, such as the self-evident truth that women can become pregnant while men cannot, then the Court need not factor into their equal protection theory that legal distinctions can be made. Legal distinctions can be justified if scientific distinctions exist. Therefore, the Court must adopt Rousseau's concept of equality; the distinctions must be suppressed.

SOCIOLOGY VS. THEOLOGY AND THE NEW PRIVACY JURISPRUDENCE

The changes in the rules and processes resulting from the Court's change in worldview are more clearly evident in the right to privacy cases than in the sex discrimination cases. Under modern jurisprudence, secular theory precludes consideration of the theological underpinnings of the role of the family as an institution. The exclusion of theological consideration has paved the way for the inclusion of modern evolving sociological concepts. The assault on the institution of the family results from linking gender equality to sociology. The substitution of sociology for theology can be traced through the Supreme Court's due process cases.

Gender discrimination, as an equal protection issue, became a due process issue in Roe v. Wade. The Supreme Court based the legitimacy of its decision in Roe v. Wade on Griswold v. Connecticut.

In Griswold v. Connecticut, the Court first announced its theories regarding the right to privacy, freedom of choice and constitutional penumbras. But Griswold was not about gender discrimination and equal protection; it concerned due process and the protection of the family. In Bradwell, the Supreme Court ignored the issue of discrimination against women in order to protect the family unit. In Roe, the Supreme Court, having dismissed Bradwell as archaic, ignored the philosophical principle and purpose that it previously announced in Griswold that it intended only to protect the family. In a philosophical about face, the Court in Roe used the principle of privacy to establish a new philosophy based on personal autonomy.

Originally, the Constitution and legal system excluded marriage and family from government intervention, seeing them as a liberty right. The source of the liberty right remained undefined until 1923. Following Blackstone's outline, the jurisdiction of the family was never in conflict with the jurisdiction of the government. The government could not interfere with the jurisdiction of the family unless the family unit had been abandoned. The family unit could be abandoned in fact or inferred by acts of abuse or neglect by parents.

The consideration of the issue of parental rights came before the Court in two 1920s cases. In Meyer v. Nebraska (1923), the Court invalidated a Nebraska statute prohibiting the teaching of normal subjects in non-English languages. In Meyer, Nebraska had convicted a private Lutheran school teacher of a misdemeanor for teaching reading to a ten-year-old child in German. The Court's reference to the parents' right to educate their child without interference was not attributed to any specific constitutional provision but to a general right to liberty extant in many areas of life:

> While this court has not attempted to define with exactness the liberty thus guaranteed, the term has received much consideration and some of the included things have been definitely stated. Without doubt, it denotes not merely freedom from bodily restraint but also the right of the individual to contract, to engage in any of the common occupations of life, to acquire useful knowledge, to marry, establish a home, and bring up children, to worship God according to the dictates of his own conscience, and generally to enjoy those privileges long recognized at Common Law as essential to the orderly pursuit of happiness by free men.

The Court reiterated this position two years later in Pierce v. Society of Sisters (1925). It struck down an Oregon statute that had mandated that all children attend public schools. The claim to the right to raise one's own children was clear:

> The fundamental theory of liberty upon which all govern-
> ments of this Union repose excludes any general power of the
> state to standardize its children by forcing them to accept
> instruction from public teachers only. The child is not the mere
> creature of the state; those who nurture and direct his destiny
> have the right, coupled with the high duty, to recognize and pre-
> pare him for additional obligations.

The Court protected Blackstone's intention that the education, safety and welfare of children were both the responsibility of parents and constitutionally protected.

The protection of the family issue evolved from education to procreation and the new privacy jurisprudence evolved with it. The Court struck down mandatory sterilization laws in Skinner v. Oklahoma (1942). The Court had upheld mandatory sterilization for imbeciles in Justice Holmes' opinion in Buck v. Bell (1927), but it could not tolerate the same as a penalty for economic crimes in Skinner. Justice Douglas' majority opinion in Skinner saw the Oklahoma law as a violation of "one of the basic civil rights of man...Marriage and procreation (were) fundamental to the very existence and survival of the race" and a new "fundamental rights" theory was announced. Justice Douglas relied upon an equal protection theory based on arbitrary classifications of different crimes. In a concurring opinion, Justice Stone relied on a due process theory, reasoning that the legislative fascination with eugenics may have been based on bad science. Justice Jackson also concurred, agreeing with both in result, but based his theory on the limitations of police power:

> There are limits to the extent to which a legislatively repre-
> sented majority may conduct biological experiments at the
> expense of the dignity and personality and natural powers of a
> minority——even those who have been guilty of what the majori-
> ty define as crimes.

The justices, to their credit, were refusing to acquiesce in a result and endorse a theory that had been authorized by the Nazi German courts. The Court reasoned that the consideration of genetics does not raise a due process issue. If the penalty was inappropriate to the crime, natural inalienable rights should be secure and police power should be blocked.

Marriage and procreation became an expressed constitutional right when Justice Harlan's dissent in Poe v. Ullman (1961) became the majority view in Griswold v. Connecticut (1965). In Griswold, the Court struck down Connecticut's contraceptive statute on the basis that it was a denial of married persons' "right to privacy" and "freedom to choose" in matters of marriage and procreation. What had been previously self-evident as Biblically based rights outside the purview of government, the Court upheld by mixing pantheistic philosophy with Christian tradition. Justice Douglas' majority opinion found the right to privacy in a "penumbra" of related provisions throughout the first eight amendments. Justice Harlan, as he did in <u>Poe</u>, found the right to privacy in the Fourteenth Amendment. In a separate concurring opinion, Justice Goldberg argued that the Court should not strain to find the right to privacy in other amendments but believed that more properly, the Court should acknowledge the existence and importance of the Ninth Amendment, which reserved all rights not expressly granted to the states or federal government as resident with the people. Ninth Amendment rights, he argued, could be found by looking to the "tradition and [collective] conscience of our people." He reasoned that:

> The entire fabric of the Constitution and the purposes that clearly underlie its specific guarantees demonstrate that the rights to marital privacy and to marry and raise a family are of similar order and magnitude as the fundamental rights specifically protected. Although the Constitution does not speak in so many words of the right of privacy in marriage, I cannot believe that it offers these fundamental rights no protection. The fact that no particular provision of the Constitution explicitly forbids the State from disrupting the traditional relation of the family— a relation as old and as fundamental as our entire civilization— surely does not show that the Government was meant to have the power to do so. Rather, as the Ninth Amendment clearly recognizes, there are fundamental personal rights such as this one, which are protected from abridgment by the Government though not specifically mentioned in the Constitution.

The Court did not base its holding on the Ninth Amendment. Recognizing the inherent rights of individuals as antecedent to the Constitution left too much outside of the Constitution. Basing its decision on the "penumbra" left the power to grant rights to the only people who could interpret the "penumbra:" the justices themselves. The Court's new pantheistic due process philosophy was quickly combined with its new secular equal protection theory. In <u>Griswold</u>, protection of the family came to mean that the married couple's right of procreation also meant the right to contraception.

The Court quickly extended the right to contraception to unmarried couples in <u>Eisenstadt v. Baird</u> (1967), decided on equal protection grounds. Any questions about whether Biblical tradition had been abandoned for secular philosophy were answered when unmarried couples, as a class, had the same constitutional right to contraception as married couples. In four years, <u>Griswold's</u> pro-family pretense had given way to the cultural revolution of the 1960s. The pantheistic penumbra in <u>Griswold</u> remained while the pretext of upholding Christian tradition was discarded. In addition, <u>Eisenstadt v. Baird</u> signaled another extension by offhandedly, in dicta, stating that the right to "beget" and "bear" children was protected by the new right to privacy. <u>Roe</u> followed quickly.

By these decisions, the Court guaranteed this new secular theory of the equality of women, but discarded its previous guarantee of protecting the institution of the family. By its new edicts, the Court decided that the right to life of unborn children, like the clerics and aristocracy in Rousseau's Paris and the Jews in Nazi Germany, cannot coexist when their presence defies the prevailing secular worldview.

THEORIES IN CONFLICT

The conflict between competing theories of equal protection and due process became absurd theater in <u>Bray v. Alexandria Women's Health Clinic</u> (1993), which involved the prosecution of protesters at an abortion clinic. The protesters were advocating for the due process rights of the unborn children. The clinic's representatives charged that the protesters were guilty of animus and discrimination towards women. The Court rejected the clinic's characterization, but did not resolve the theoretical conflict. The Court simply ruled that opposition to abortion could be based on a philosophical view that was not necessarily grounded in hostility towards women. Even though only women were targets of the protest, the Court distinguished between discriminatory intent and discriminatory effect.

<u>Bray</u> illustrates the tortured contentions that result from the wanderings of the Court as it tries to interpret the Equal Protection Clause and the Due Process Clause under secular theories outside of their original context. From the beginning of its Equal Protection Clause interpretations, the Court has required class-based animus rather than focus on the denial of the substantive due process rights of individuals. To limit litigation, the Court, starting with <u>The Slaughter-House Cases</u> and <u>Yick Wo v. Hopkins</u>, and ultimately on to <u>Bray</u>, slowly substituted Karl Marx for the founding fathers which has now been ingrained into our modern political and legal systems.

The Court's requirement for and fixation with class discrimination has led it to the logically disconnected conclusion that abortion protests may be directed against women, rather than support for unborn children. As the

Court pointed out, only women become pregnant; therein lies the irreconcilable conflict between gender equality and the right to privacy in marital and family matters.

The Court dramatically changed the pretext that due process protected marriage and the family in the decisions of Eisenstadt v. Baird (1967) and Roe v. Wade (1973) and in Planned Parenthood of Central Mo. v. Danforth (1976), where it ruled that the consent of the husband to his wife's abortion could not be required. These decisions are based on the old decisions of Skinner, Griswold and Justice Harlan's dissent in Poe, but the fundamental philosophy is entirely different. The Biblically-based tradition underlying the early cases, that traced its roots in American history and was grounded in the protection of the family, was simply replaced by the new sociological revolution of the 1960s and 1970s. America's cultural revolution was rooted in the liberation and autonomy of women, both morally and politically.

To many of the new revolutionaries, male and female cannot be equal so long as women bear the burden of childbirth. Therefore, any opposition to abortion is seen as hostility toward women as a class. Equality no longer defines every individual's standing; liberty no longer defines every individual's right. Rather, equality is liberty under the modern view and any violation of equality in fact is considered to be an infringement of due process according to the modern gender equality view.

◆　◆　◆

Justice Brennan was probably correct, commenting in Frontiero, attributing America's history of sex discrimination as a rationalization of an attitude of "romantic paternalism" which, in practical effect put women, "not on a pedestal, but in a cage." But Brennan's observation was no more than an acknowledgment of Blackstone's observation about the limits of positive law to promote righteousness. Blackstone similarly regretted that Common Law, in protecting parental rights and the family, did not also require parents to fulfill the parental obligations that corresponded with their individual liberty to raise and educate their own children. But Blackstone understood that the role of Common Law was to protect rights; not promote virtue.

Locke discredited paternalism as a political theory long ago. Political and economic restrictions that apply only to women, that put women "in a cage," violate due process as well as the equal protection of the laws for individual women. Proof of class-based animus should not be necessary.

The error in Bradwell, compounding the error in The Slaughter-House

149

<u>Cases</u>, created additional problems. By failing to recognize the Fourteenth Amendment as a reassertion of the fundamental principles of the Declaration of Independence, equal protection became a concept in search of a new philosophy. In the last years of the Nineteenth Century, the Court made economic freedom the first principle and the rights of employers would be valued more than the protection of the family. In the latter years of the Twentieth Century, the Court adopted the new philosophy that personal autonomy for women required equality in fact. But this new modern philosophy adopted by the Court is not only in conflict with science, but is in conflict with Biblical truth.

The concept of due process of law originated in English Common Law and is Biblically based. The concept of equal protection originated with the Declaration of Independence and is also Biblically based. By cutting the concepts of due process of law and equal protection loose from their Scriptural moorings, these constitutional concepts are inevitably applied to the current philosophy of the day. The changing philosophy, used as a means to reinterpret the Constitution, was admitted by the Court in <u>Casey</u>. Unfortunately, these wandering constitutional principles that must be adapted to changing philosophies are often in conflict. The law is no longer a guidepost to be followed but merely a political tool to be manipulated.

The concepts of gender equality and the fundamental law of protection of the family were principles that were not in conflict when the Scriptures were used as the point of reference. Under the new definition of liberty as expressed in <u>Roe</u> and <u>Casey</u>, equal protection and due process cannot be reconciled. One side must lose.

Unless Biblical equality that acknowledges gender distinctions, with both genders subordinate to God rather than one to the other, is restored, some members of society inevitably get left out. The demand for secular equality/liberty exceeds the Biblical standard of equality. For some, the liberty right to be equal in some respects not originally guaranteed as fundamental rights, such as economic equality or equality in child-bearing, means some others are less equal—or have no rights at all. When that happens, slavery is justified, or the Holocaust or Reign of Terror can occur with legal sanction. Without a change in perspective that reinvigorates equal protection and due process with Biblical principles, the Court can no longer prevent that from happening and may, in fact, be the cause.

PUBLIC MONOPOLY

In modern times, equality as a concept applies to the restrictions and denials of inalienable rights by governments, institutions and private persons because of race, national origin or gender. At the time of the Declaration of Independence, the founding fathers viewed equality differently. They referred to equality almost entirely in the sense of denying government the right to grant special privileges to certain individuals, and these were most often economic principles. For instance, they abolished economic privilege based on titles of nobility or special inheritance laws. But the founding fathers' most difficult task was eradicating the privilege inherent in monopoly.

Monopolies, as a grant from the government, violate the basic premise of equality. Privileges are extended to one individual or legal entity to the exclusion of all others. By the time of the Declaration of Independence, monopolies were rejected in principle and characterized in theory as repugnant to a people created free and equal. Except in the examples of patents, copyrights and trademarks, which were protected as products of individual invention and could be protected for a limited time, the special prerogatives that were issued by the English kings were excluded from the enumerated powers of the new American government. Political patronage and special interests, in theory, could not exist.

Monopolies were always present in England. The abuse of granting special prerogatives to friends of the monarch increased under the reign of Elizabeth I and accelerated with the ascension of King James I in 1601. The attacks on the king's privilege were as vigorous as was the resistance to his interference with the religious freedom of the Presbyterians and the Puritans. Parliament passed anti-monopoly statutes, beginning with the Statute of Monopolies in 1603, and restricted monopolies for new manufacturers to 14 years. The Kings Bench, under the leadership of Sir Edward Coke, argued that monopolies violated the spirit, if not the letter, of Magna Charta.

American authority followed the lead of the English anti-monopolists. In the first era of legislation by the American colonies, monopolies were prohibited. In the *Coppie of the Liberties of the Massachusetts Collonie in New England* (1641), at section 9, it was written, "[N]o monopolies shall be granted or allowed amongst us, but of such new Inventions that are profitable to the Countrie, and that for a short term." In one of the earliest reported American cases on the subject of monopolies, monopolies were found to violate Common Law. In <u>Norwich Gaslight Co. v. Norwich City Gas Co.</u>, (1836), an exclusive grant for the right to lay pipes in city streets was declared to constitute a monopoly. The court declared that it was of no consequence that Connecticut had "no direct constitutional provision against monopoly" as the "whole theory of free government is opposed to such grants." The court believed it sufficient that the English Statute of Monopolies, "which declares such monopolies to be contrary to law and void...has always been considered as merely declaratory of the Common Law."

THE EARLY AMERICAN VIEW

At the Constitutional Convention of 1787, George Mason, who later refused to sign the Constitution, unsuccessfully moved for a prohibition of monopolies, objecting that:

> Under their own construction of the general clause at the end of the enumerated powers, the Congress may grant monopolies in trade and commerce, constitute new crimes, inflict unusual and severe punishment and extend their power as far as they shall think proper . . .

A pamphleteer responded by interpreting the Privileges and Immunities Clause in a way that would later be rejected by the Supreme Court in The Slaughter-House Cases, and defended the absence of an express monopoly prohibition in the Constitution:

> I find it expressly provided, 'that no preference shall be given to the ports of one State over the ports of another,' and that 'citizens of each State shall be entitled to all privileges and immunities of citizens in the several states.' These provisions appear to me to be calculated for the very purpose Mr. Mason wishes to secure. Can they be consistent with any monopoly in trade or commerce.

Anti-federalist opposition to the Constitution included prophetic concerns over government monopolies and an expansive interpretation of the Commerce Clause, expressed in the Letter of Agrippa, published in 1788:

> By sect. 8 of article I, Congress are to have the unlimited right to regulate commerce, external and internal, and they may therefore create monopolies which have been universally injurious to all the subjects of the countries that have adopted them, excepting the monopolants themselves.

Thomas Jefferson was a consistent opponent of monopolies. In letters dated February 1, 1788 and February 12, 1788, Jefferson argued that a declaration of rights should include a guarantee of "freedom of commerce against monopolies." After the first set of amendments, which would form the Bill of Rights, were proposed, Jefferson wrote from his post in France to Madison, "I like it as far as it goes; but I should have been for going further. For instance the following alterations and additions would have pleased me..." Among these, "[M]onopolies may be allowed to persons for their own productions in literature and their own inventions in the arts for a term not exceeding __ years but for no longer term and no other purpose."

THE BEGINNINGS OF POPULISM

Opposition to monopolies continued in the first half of the Nineteenth Century. The limitations of the first bank of the United States were the result of intense opposition to the monopolization of banking. President Andrew Jackson opposed the second bank for the same reason. Jackson, and the other opponents of the second bank, argued that it was not only a legal monopoly, as its charter guaranteed that the federal government would not create any other banks, but that it was also a monopoly in the broader political sense since it was too big and too rich. Thomas Hart Benton of Missouri, the bank's chief opponent in the Senate, argued that it was objectionable not only "on account of the exclusive privileges, and anti-republican monopoly, which it gives to the stockholders," but also "because it tends to aggravate the inequality of fortunes" and was "an institution too great and powerful to be tolerated in a Government of free and equal laws." Jackson, when he vetoed the bill renewing the bank's charter, emphasized the "great evils to our country and institutions [that] might flow from such a concentration of power in the hands of a few men irresponsible to the people." The political maneuver of repeatedly condemning the bank as a "monster monopoly," and a "moneyed power" that would establish an oligarchy and eventually a monarchy, defeated the bank's supporters and led to its destruction.

Until the Civil War, public opposition to monopoly was regularly expressed, including opposition to the existence of corporations as separate legal entities. Chief Justice Marshall used the commerce power, under Article 1 Sect. 8, to break a state-licensed monopoly in Gibbons v. Ogden (1824). But Marshall upheld the validity of the corporation, and protected the corporation from regulation by the state in Dartmouth College v. Woodward (1819), under the guarantee that the state had no power to impair the obligation of contracts. These cases are not in conflict, and Marshall had no case before him to reconcile the relationship of the commerce clause to the contracts clause or monopoly power with corporate structures. Gibbons was based on legal equality while Dartmouth College was based on the inalienability of property rights. Subsequent Supreme Court cases confused the principles rather than reconcile them, and the conflict between equality and due process still exists in cases involving corporations as well as in gender discrimination cases.

The problem has not been resolved and the conflict between antitrust law and the scope of permissible corporate conduct is unreconciled. Although the status of personhood was denied on the basis of race and gender, and is still not available to unborn children, personhood has been granted to corporations with few restrictions or questions. Hayek perceptively noted the unresolved conflict in the following section in his *Road to Serfdom*:

> The functioning of competition not only requires adequate organization of certain institutions like money, markets, and channels of information—some of which can never be adequately provided by private enterprise—but it depends, above all, on the existence of an appropriate legal system, a legal system designed both to preserve competition and to make it operate as beneficially as possible. It is by no means sufficient that the law should recognize the principle of private property and freedom of contract; much depends on the precise definition of the right of property as applied to different things. The systematic study of the forms of legal institutions which will make the competitive system work efficiently has been sadly neglected; and strong arguments can be advanced that serious shortcomings have, particularly with regard to the law of corporations and of patents, not only have made competition work much less effectively than it might have done, but have even led to the destruction of competition in many spheres.

In a corporation, a group of individuals can combine together as a single person but they cannot legally conspire. The rights of individuals inure to a potentially large group of individuals. Individual patronage becomes group patronage and an elite class is created. The grant of exclusive privileges to private corporations, and the subsequent refusal by the courts to prevent anticompetitive conduct, has contributed to the growth of monopolistic and oligopolistic industries in America.

POPULISM LOST

It is commonly considered that following the Civil War, the Supreme Court began a new process of constitutional interpretation to facilitate the industrialization of America. If that consideration by the Supreme Court is true, in fact, the facilitation of industrialization by relaxing impediments to expanded government power and the concentration of wealth was not achieved by the consent of the people, as evidenced by the rise of populism in the West. Nor was it accomplished with any clear guidelines of constitutional interpretation. At the same time as the Supreme Court expanded the Commerce Clause power and police power to regulate, exclusive franchises and political patronage increased.

The broad expansion of the commerce clause would not occur until the Twentieth Century. But the expansion of police power in Stone v. Mississippi (1880) (implied power to amend state contracts) and The Slaughter-House Cases (inalienability of police power) would mark the beginning of the decline of substantive due process as a legal basis to defend against government regulation and against government favoritism. Equality, as a concept to protect individuals from government prerogative, would disappear as a factor in opposition to monopoly after The Slaughter-House Cases, but would exist only to strike legislation or regulations that discriminated on the basis of classifications set forth in the Fourteenth Amendment after Yick Wo v. Hopkins [licensing statute not in violation of substantive due process as regulation beyond scope of police power but was found to be unconstitutional under the equal protection clause as the regulations intended to discriminate on the basis of race]. Because individuals could not complain about inequality, individuals could not object to the newfound government prerogative exercised to grant exclusive licenses and franchises and political jobs for supporters.

Today, monopolies are sanctioned, encouraged and promoted by public authorities. The existence of nations that operate as monolithic corporate enterprises, such as those that existed in the former Communist countries and in some current African nations, distract us from the realization and understanding that a large part of the work of our own government, from the local to the federal level, consists of the granting of special privileges and the regulation of many industries to exclude competition, which is the core definition of a monopolistic enterprise. In New State Ice Co. v. Liebmann (1932), the court struck down an Oklahoma law that required a license for entry into a business of manufacturing, selling and distributing artificial ice. The statute was based on public utility criteria, which allowed a license to be denied if existing facilities were sufficient to meet the public needs. Justice Brandeis dissented, turning classical economics on its head, reasoning and postulating that an economy of scarcity had been supplanted by one of over-abundance and that unregulated entry into certain occupations could bring "destructive competition" warranting state intrusion to stabilize the market.

❖   ❖   ❖

Justice Brandeis' constitutional noninterpretation in economic matters corresponded to the rise in popularity of theories proposed by British economist John Maynard Keynes. Keynes' theory justified short-run manipulation of the economy by the government in the implementation of taxing and spending policies to affect prices and wages. Keynes' theory was not concerned with, nor intended to apply to, long-run effects of short-term policy. As economic and political theory, many of Keynes' core theories relating to the anticipated benefit of government intervention have been questioned and largely discredited by the work of Milton Friedman and Fredrick Hayek. Hayek, writing in 1944, compared the rise of government involvement in the management of British and American economies with national socialism in Germany and the state-run economy in fascist Italy.

The "destructive competition" theory first announced by Justice Brandeis would define the problem, and "managed competition" would be the solution. Two years after New State Ice, the Supreme Court reversed direction in Nebbia v. New York (1934), and abandoned all interest in the topic of publicly granted monopolies, stating that "[W]here the policy of the State disclosed that a monopoly should be granted, statutes having that effect have been held inoffensive to the constitutional guarantees." Government officeholders and bureaucrats had retrieved the prerogative lost by King James I, and the era in America of government regulating the economy as a positivist, corporate enterprise had begun.

Just as the Court replaced the Biblically based "all men are created equal" with secular definitions in matters of racial and gender equality, secular considerations now dominate the discussion in economic issues. Only economic theory, not inalienable rights, is factored into modern theories of monopoly, and the principle of equality counts for little. In contrast to the reinvention of theories delved into by the Court when addressing issues of racial and gender equality, the Courts have little interest and have taken a minor role when addressing economic issues. There appears to be no memory that economic rights have any connection with the Declaration of Independence and that the fundamental principles of equality and inalienable rights could have any relationship to the field of economics. Resulting from the abandonment of a judicial role, economic equality is now a matter entirely left to the legislative branch and democratic rule.

CHAPTER 10
THE LIMITATION
OF GOVERNMENT

"To compel a man to furnish contributions of money for the propagation of opinions which he disbelieves is sinful and tyrannical."

Thomas Jefferson

"The abuse of the power to tax is tyranny. No tax can be levied without the consent and authority of the people."
James Madison, *Memorial and Remonstrance*
Against Religious Assessments

"The Constitution was, from its very origin, contemplated to be the frame of a national government, of special and enumerated powers, and not of general and unlimited powers."

Justice Joseph Story

All Americans understand the battle cry, "No taxation without representation." It was a primary dispute that led to the American Revolution. It also was a primary cause of the English Civil War of the 17th Century. In these instances, taxpayers' anger resulted in revolution. Apparently, American judges have not studied history; increasingly, courts have ordered taxes to be levied, bypassing legislatures and Congress. Recent Courts have been consistent in this one thing; bypassing legislators and writing their own laws.

The United States Supreme Court created the constitutional right to an abortion in 1973. Congress, however, had made sure since 1978, that no federal taxes are used to pay for abortions. In 1980, a divided U.S. Supreme Court held that the right to an abortion did not include a right to public funding.

In Minnesota, the legislature made sure that no tax dollars were used to pay for abortions, but the Minnesota Supreme Court, in *Doe v. Gomez*, struck down that law. The Minnesota Court ordered the government to pay for abortion.

I brought suit on behalf of James Tarsney, President of Lawyers for Life and 46 other plaintiffs; we challenged the Minnesota Supreme Court order and asked the federal court to issue an injunction and reinstate the Minnesota statute that prohibited state-funded abortions. What I argued in *Tarsney v. O'Keefe* was not just that religious beliefs were offended by taxpayer-funded abortions. I objected to the authority of the court to impose on Minnesotans an obligation to pay taxes. By ruling against us, the Minnesota courts not only struck down the legislature's will, but it ignored Congress and the United States Supreme Court's rulings. The Minnesota Supreme Court, instead, expressly opined that it liked the dissenting opinion in the 1980 U.S. case better; it interpreted the Minnesota constitution to adopt the dissenting view.

In oral argument before the 8th Circuit Court of Appeals, one of the judges in *Tarsney* asked me why I thought opposing taxpayer-funded abortion was any different from opposing capital punishment. I said that legislatures chose to make capital punishment legal, and the decision to apply it in any case is up to the judge and the jury, as the constitution and statute specified. The court, on the other hand, had simply decreed that Minnesota will fund abortion, contrary to the specific will of the legislature and the political process in general.

Another judge asked why state courts couldn't make their own decisions and interpret their own constitutions. I argued that state courts can't simply make up their own laws. Neither can they take the losing side of a United States Supreme Court case and call it state law, at least without attempting to base the distinction between a state and federal law in the states' own history or tradition. In my petition for certiorari to the United States Supreme Court, I pointed out that 19 states had done what the Minnesota court had done, but none with such blatant disregard for the existing law and principles of due process as in Minnesota.

We lost the argument. *Tarsney's* outcome proves that Americans now have taxation without representation. The people never granted the courts any authority to tax or spend; these are legislative duties. Until the legislatures find the courage to confront the courts and take back their sole power to tax, courts will continue to abuse taxpayers, and leave us no legal remedies for relief.

◆ ◆ ◆

The final phrase in America's great paragraph of political philosophy attempts, in the most ambitious and aggressive covenant with organized government ever made, to limit the extent and sovereignty of the government.

> We hold these truths to be self evident, that all men are created equal, and are endowed by their Creator with certain inalienable rights. That to secure these rights, governments are instituted among men, deriving their just powers from the consent of the governed.

In England, as a direct result of Parliament's long civil war with the Stuart kings, culminating in the Glorious Revolution of 1688, Parliament became the political sovereign. The transfer of political sovereignty from the monarchy to a legislative assembly was a dramatic change from the medieval status quo.

In America, for the first time, according to the Declaration of Independence, the people were identified as the sovereign. The placement of political sovereignty with the people was radical and unprecedented in history.

Equally unprecedented, from the standpoint of political history, was the establishment of the institutions of government by written agreement. In England, constitutional government evolved and, to this day, contains as its constitution both written documents and oral tradition. England's constitution is a product of a thousand years compilation of charters, petitions and precedents that slowly recognized the natural rights of individuals and limitations on the power of political institutions. Other nations evolved from tribal relationships and the seizure of power by individuals and groups who simply claimed sovereignty by force. In America, the people claimed sovereignty. The governing principles were established deliberately. And the rules were all put in writing.

The first great practical task, after peace with England was established in 1783, was to organize the new institutions of government. The states had adopted new constitutions because their governing documents, based on colonial status, were no longer in effect. In addition, the theories of law and politics that had invigorated the Continental Congress involved major changes from English constitutional law. State governments were reorganized. The Articles of Confederation, which had temporarily united the colonies during the war with England, was incapable of governing a nation.

A Constitutional Convention was convened in Philadelphia in 1787 for the purpose of organizing the new nation and to establish a new government based on the unique American principles that had been used to justify independence from England in the first place. The result was a Constitution that laid out a republican form of government, federal in its organization. The republican principle was based upon representation, pursuant to the equality mandate in the Declaration of Independence.

The federal format was based upon a fear of centralized government which appeared, from the observation of the European experience, to be antithetical to the theory of government by consent. The Bill of Rights, incorporated into the Constitution as part of the ratification process, secured the inalienable rights of individuals. The establishment of a federal, republican government, limited in its power by the Bill of Rights, was entirely consistent with the nation's charter, the Declaration of Independence.

There were no clear legal precedents at the time of the adoption of the Constitution and the Bill of Rights to guide the courts and legislatures in the interpretation of the original principles that were the foundation of the Declaration of Independence and the Constitution. Today, the courts and legislatures voluntarily bind themselves to legal precedents, vague in their origin, and unclear in their general application. They often ignore the original principles and political theory that laid the foundation for the institutions of government and the federal Constitution. The "rule of law" evolved by severing legal precedents from original principles.

The modern expansion of government occurred suddenly during the 1930s through a series of Supreme Court decisions. These new precedents, that now serve as the foundation for a "new" constitution, were ostensibly based upon prior precedents. These new precedents, unfortunately, were supported by selective reference to historical precedents and to original reinterpretations of the founding fathers' debates.

The Court, in these new cases, reinterpreted the "general welfare" clause to equate the federal police power with that of the states, eliminated the application of the Tenth Amendment, and ignored the principle of consent when applied to issues of taxation. It expanded the commerce clause to guarantee that all federal economic legislation would be sustained. To support this radical law change, the Court resurrected old debates and decided them the other way, then pronounced the debate over.

FEDERALISM

Perhaps de Tocqueville's most noteworthy political observation concerned the decentralization of power in American government. The decentralization of power and authority was intentional. The federalist theory of government and the deliberate structure of the institutions of American government mandated decentralization. Centralized authority leads to corruption and elitism. This is why the powers of the United States government are specifically listed in the Constitution. Those powers not listed are not presumed to remain as federal power, but, rather, are limited by the general reservation of powers to the states in the Tenth Amendment. All government power, federal and state, is further limited by the general reservation of rights, too numerous to list, which remain with the individuals because of the general reservation of rights in the Ninth Amendment.

THE HISTORICAL DEBATE

Neither Hamilton nor Madison argued against the need for a national government. In "The Federalist Papers", both wrote in favor of ratification of the new Constitution. Both wrote of the need for a national body to deal with some important issues that could not be addressed by the loose affiliation of states that had come together under the Articles of Confederation. Madison participated in the drafting of the Constitution and debated its provisions in Congress.

The first Congress did not answer all of the early constitutional questions. Inevitable questions and conflicts that arose between adverse parties had to be settled in court. They knew, and history has more than adequately shown, that debates about constitutional issues are unending and always being litigated. An impartial judiciary is a necessary component of constitutional government. The debate about the extent of the Court's role in interpreting the Constitution continued for the first 150 years after its enactment.

The earliest significant cases attempted to answer questions about the extent of federal power. Chief Justice John Marshall provided precedent-setting analysis and applications. In the Marbury decision, Marshall questioned the constitutionality of an act of Congress as a necessary part of the court's duty to adjudicate conflicts. Then, he addressed the nature and scope of the express constitutional powers of Congress in Gibbons v. Ogden. McCulloch v. Maryland addressed the nature and scope of Congress' incidental constitutional powers. In McCulloch, Marshall held that once Congress had the power to regulate, it also had the power to tax and spend to implement its express enactments. In Gibbons, Marshall denied the attempt of the state of New York to regulate navigation on the Hudson River contrary to the power of Congress to regulate interstate commerce under the Commerce Clause of Article I, Section 8.

The Gibbons, McCulloch and Marbury opinions began by citing the explicit constitutional authority for the legislative enactment, and Marshall based his rulings on the logical relationship of the legislation to the written Constitution. The limitations of federal power on what and how Congress could legislate remained clear and respected, for the most part, for 150 years, until the Court reinterpreted the Constitution and reanalyzed the principles of federalism as part of the ratification of the New Deal.

THE OLD DEBATE REDECIDED: FEDERALISM REDEFINED

Congress strove to end the Great Depression during the 1930s. The Court faced multiple challenges to Congress' efforts to expand the power of a centralized federal government as the answer to the nation's financial dilemma. As a result of both Congressional and executive pressure, the Court abandoned the prior theory of federalism.

In the early days of the republic, widespread opposition to a national government had required ratification of the Ninth and Tenth Amendments. These two amendments were unambiguous. In essence, they were the assurances of Madison in the first Congress, publicly recorded in "The Federalist Papers," that the federal government's power was limited to national concerns, such as war and interstate and foreign commerce.

Marshall had taken great care to apply the written text of the Constitution to the cases that came before the Court when he was shaping principles of federalism as Chief Justice. The early debates about federal power were not limited to whether the Court had the power to interpret the Constitution or whether that power belonged to the legislature. Proponents of legislative power, such as Jefferson and Madison, never conceded that the Court could declare a legislative act unconstitutional or make pronouncements of what the Constitution means any more than a congressman or president could. Marshall, in the tradition of Coke before him, cautiously and conservatively used judicial power to apply the law to the facts of a case, even if that meant analyzing the meaning of a constitutional provision for the first time.

Federalism was a new theory in the early days of the republic. Even though the loose affiliation of states under the Articles of Confederation worked poorly, opposition to a stronger, central government was widely held. Assurances by Madison that the national government had limited power, and by Hamilton, who favored a stronger, central government, were necessary for ratification of the Constitution. The Ninth and Tenth Amendments were required as written confirmation of these principles.

THE BUTLER CASE
THE RESURRECTION AND REDEFINITION

Notwithstanding the lengthy history of the debate and its extensive documentation, showing how it was cautiously settled by the application of those principles in <u>Gibbons</u> and <u>McCulloch</u>, the Court continued its redefining process. The Court, in 1936, undertook its redefinition process and the debate was resurrected in <u>U.S. v. Butler</u>. Foreshadowing a technique used a decade later to redefine the First Amendment in <u>McCollum</u> and <u>Everson</u> in 1947 and 1948, the Supreme Court gave the initial political victory to the conservatives, but set the stage for major changes by how the principles were analyzed and the decision made.

In <u>Butler</u>, the Court declared as unconstitutional a federal act regulating agriculture. Until that time, the regulation of agriculture was a matter for the states under the Tenth Amendment. But <u>Butler</u>, while reaffirming that agriculture was a matter for the states, decided to review and reinterpret the General Welfare Clause. Madison had argued that the power to tax for the "general welfare" was limited to the express powers of Congress detailed in Article 1, Section 8 of the Constitution. Hamilton had argued that the General Welfare Clause contained a power to tax, separate from the grant of Congressional power. Hamilton carefully qualified that the purpose of the tax was to be general, not local. The 1937 Court criticized Madison's approach, stating "in [t]his view the phrase is mere tautology, for taxation and appropriation are or may be necessary incidents of the exercise of any of the enumerated legislative powers," without explaining why Marshall found it necessary to carefully explain the relationship of the taxing power, under his "necessary and appropriate" analysis, in <u>McCulloch v. Maryland</u>.

Justice Joseph Story was a contemporary of John Marshall on the Supreme Court and author of the treatise, *Commentaries on the Constitution*, that was as influential as Blackstone. Without further explanation or reference to Story's cautious analysis, the 1926 Court declared that Justice Story supported Hamilton's position; Madison and Marshall were respectable but incorrect. The General Welfare Clause would, henceforth, be interpreted broadly. The Court then decided that the legislation before the Court was unconstitutional as it concerned matters too local for Congressional discussion.

By separating the taxing power from the enumerated powers, the taxing power had been released from it moorings. The Court had created a new test. No longer would the Court ask whether the tax was necessary and proper to effectuate Congressional power, but rather, whether the legislation was national or local in character. The new limitation was weak and temporary.

The first time the Court considered and upheld Hamilton's and Story's position, in <u>Butler</u>, it declared the tax to be unconstitutional because it was too local in character and beyond Congressional power. The second time it considered the issue, in <u>Helvering v. Davis</u> (1937), the Court upheld a national unemployment tax, endorsing the idea that unemployment had become a national problem. The Court gave Congress the power to define "national," thereby giving Congress complete control over the limits of its own power. "When money is spent to promote the general welfare, the concept of welfare or the opposite is shaped by Congress, not the states."

Hamilton and Story, like Madison, believed that federal power should be limited. The Supreme Court in the 1930s did not agree with any of them. Disregarding Marshall's cautious conservatism as well as his insistence on exercising judicial power only when appropriate, the 1937 Court pulled out of the federalism debate altogether, stating, "[o]ur concern here as often is with power, not with wisdom." Hamilton's and Story's generality and locality distinction was obliterated by the new maxim: "so the concept be not arbitrary, the locality must yield."

WICKARD V. FILBURN AND ABSOLUTE FEDERAL POWER

By 1941, the new federal power became absolute in fact. In <u>Gibbons v. Ogden</u>, Marshall had invoked the Commerce Clause to show the legitimate right of the federal government to regulate navigable waters flowing between two states. In 1941, in the case of <u>Wickard v. Filburn</u>, the Supreme Court used the same Commerce Clause to regulate a local farmer's produce grown for his own consumption. Marshall had reserved to the federal court the power to adjudicate conflicts between states and to determine whether the issue presented a federal question. In 1941, federalism meant that Congress could define federal power and the court would not intervene. Every question had the potential to become a federal question. Because Congress was given absolute authority to define its own federal power, Congress no longer debated the question of federal power. Because the Court gave Congress absolute authority to define its own federal power, the Court also quit debating the issue and, instead, assumed Congress had whatever power it determined appropriate.

The focus on rights rather than wisdom had been changed to a focus on power rather than wisdom. Madison's limitation on federal power relied on the specific enumeration of Congress' powers in Article I, Section 8. In <u>But-</u>

ler, the Court arbitrarily rejected Madison, declaring that Hamilton and Story had the better argument. But Hamilton's and Story's limitation on federal power, repeatedly referred to by Story in his 1833 *Commentaries on the Constitution*, provided an obvious distinction between local and general concerns. The Court wiped clean those distinctions in <u>Helvering v. Davis</u>. As the dissenters in <u>Helvering v. Davis</u> concisely pointed out, the majority holding had nullified the Tenth Amendment. All that remained of state power was any power delegated to them by the federal government. Even the states, however, had not legislated as broadly as the new, reinvented federal government.

THE POLICE POWER

The power of the states to legislate is derived from their inherent power to protect their citizens, and is called the police power. The police power of the state governments was never unlimited. The original states obtained their limited powers from their colonial charters. After the formation of the United States, the individual states wrote their own constitutions, as did states admitted to the Union in later years. Each new constitution had to conform to the national standard expressed in the U.S. Constitution that guaranteed individual rights and freedom, and a republican form of government. Western expansion in America was preceded by legal documents, such as the Northwest Ordinance of 1787, that guaranteed that no state could violate America's unique standards of natural and fundamental rights. The ratification of the Fourteenth Amendment reconfirmed these principles of national standards of liberty, due process and equality. Individual rights were not created by the Fourteenth Amendment but existed prior to the grant of statehood. In the tradition of the Declaration of Independence, which was enacted because Parliament had violated the God-given inalienable rights of the colonists, the Fourteenth Amendment was enacted because the states had violated the God-given inalienable rights of slaves. The modern Court's insistence that it look for and find the source of fundamental rights from the Fourteenth Amendment is misplaced.

Expansion of state power occurred rapidly in the Nineteenth Century. Even Jefferson had allowed for government power to allow taxation for the "necessities" of the people. The ambiguity inherent in the word "necessary" lent support for two new conflicting political theories.

"Necessary" is a word of considerable flexibility. "Necessary" can mean "indispensable," or "necessary" can mean "convenient." "Necessary" relates to the word "need." People may perceive a need for safety, public morality or welfare. If political power is measured by what is "necessary" or by the "needs" of the people, the nature of political power changes in accordance with the changing perceptions of needs.

By the end of the Nineteenth Century, the Judeo-Christian worldview that had predominated throughout the country's founding had changed. The New England Puritans and southern aristocrats could agree on government by consent, limited to protect public morality and individual rights. But western expansion and new waves of immigrants brought new political philosophies. Western settlers worried more about personal safety than maintenance of the established public order.

Immigrants in the mid-Nineteenth Century were more familiar with Europe's socialist political philosophy than with John Locke and Thomas Jefferson. Public welfare became increasingly more important to them while public morality became less important. Europe's traditional form of private Christianity took hold in Twentieth Century America until morality became irrelevant in its secularized courts and legislatures.

A MEANINGLESS LIMITATION

The Court has pretended to create exceptions to unlimited power. In balancing individual rights with government power, the Court conducts an academic exercise to pretend to balance the needs of the individual with the needs of the government. In some cases, the Court will apply a "rational basis" test, which is essentially no balancing at all. If the legislation is somehow connected to a public purpose, which it broadly defines, it is sustained and the individual loses.

Under its strict scrutiny test, the Court examines the conflict more closely and rules on a case by case basis. Inevitably, strict scrutiny decisions are completely arbitrary and predicated entirely on the judge's own political principles.

By balancing, the Court has permitted legislatures and executives almost unlimited power, limited only by the withholding of consent to the use of that power—by the Court itself.

HOBBES OVER LOCKE

The modern view of police power results from a dramatic shift away from Locke's philosophy of government back to the political philosophy of Hobbes.

Locke advocated limited government. The term "police power" limits the functions of government. The limited purpose of government is to restrain the lawless, punish lawbreakers and to intervene in emergencies. Jefferson's use of the term "necessities" inadvertently expanded Locke's limitation. That undefined expansion has gradually evolved into the antithesis of Locke's original premise.

Hobbes saw government's role as to maintain order and enforce the unlimited will of the sovereign. The Supreme Court decided the debate between Hamilton and Madison by ruling and announcing that Hamilton was the victor. The Court, without announcement, and perhaps unknowingly, rejected Locke in favor of Hobbes. If Hamilton preferred Hobbes to Locke, that opinion was never made known. Instead, the modern Court misinterpreted Hamilton to allow Hobbes' absolutist philosophy to be substituted for Locke's theory of limited government.

Rather than placing absolute sovereignty in the hands of a monarch as in the Seventeenth Century, the modern Supreme Court quietly and quickly placed absolute sovereignty into its own hands. The Court had assumed the role of Hobbes' Leviathan. Justice Marshall's assertion of the Court's right to interpret the Constitution, in its capacity as adjudicator of legal cases, had evolved into an oligarchy that determined all law. The process of lawmaking had become assumed to be under the Court's supervision. Because all concerns had become national, police power was also nationalized. Although the states retain an abundance of broad power to legislate anything that the Court deems "rational," the state's police power is now as mandated by Congress itself. The centralization of American government is now complete, exercising police power without limitation.

CONSENT OF THE GOVERNED

An express declaration of power, by necessity, also defines enforcement powers and the taxing authority to finance it all. The United States Constitution meant to define the extent of federal government power. McCulloch v. Maryland and Helvering v. Davis discuss whether the constitutional power should be narrowly or broadly interpreted. In McCulloch, Marshall viewed the taxing power narrowly cautioning that "the power to tax is the power to destroy." Marshall allowed that the government had the implicit power to tax, but only to effectuate the grant of authority as expressed in the Constitution's clearly defined enumerated powers. If the power was validly granted, then the taxing power was implied.

The discussion of federal constitutional power must relate back to the individual's inalienable right to be free of taxation without consent. When

Marshall implied that the taxing power was necessary, but limited to implementing the express provisions of Congress' enumerated powers unquestionably granted by the people to Congress, no one disputed the reasonableness of his logic. However, when Congress assumes the authority to define its own power, the consent to its absolute authority to tax cannot be assumed, because it is not beyond debate, and arguments that no one consented to be taxed this broadly are well-founded.

LEGAL CONSENT

The modern Supreme Court has corrupted the term "consent of the governed" to mean, "consent to govern." The term "consent of the governed" appears in the Declaration of Independence and is based upon the legal term "consent," a term in common usage in contract law. The term "consent," as used in contract law, formed part of the foundation of Common Law.

In American constitutional law, government power cannot exist independent of the people's "consent." It is the people who granted the government its power.

In contract law, consent is not vague and ambiguous. Consent has a specific meaning. Consent refers to an identifiable state of mind necessary to bind a person to a contract. "Consent" requires the use of reason in which a person has deliberated and weighed the benefits and liabilities of each side of an issue before entering into an agreement. "Consent" is more than passive acquiescence to a contract, but rather, specific authorization of an act. Legal consent implies more than a mere formal agreement of the mind or a signature on a contract. It is an act made freely, unhampered by fraud, duress, or sometimes, even mistakes. Under contract law, contracts cannot be imposed upon unwilling parties. The freedom to enter into or reject an agreement can only be relinquished by consent.

POLITICAL CONSENT

America is distinguished from other nations by its reliance on "consent" at the core of its political theory. Many nations have constitutions. Only America's Constitution is defined by the Declaration of Independence. A recent European observation of America's success highlights this fact of history:

> There is an important lesson also to be learned from the
> United States; the only country in which the attempt has ever

been made to convert a multi-ethnic, multi-lingual, multi-cultural and multi-national society into a single nation by consent. Once you lose the homogeneity, the common understandings which stem from a shared history, a shared language and a shared culture, you have no alternative but to write down a detailed set of rules by which your relationships are governed.

That observation reflects the unique difference between American government and traditional European political communities. Neither Congress nor the Supreme Court has the authority to define government power. Government power had already been defined as limited in the Declaration of Independence.

RUTHERFORD

The language of the Declaration of Independence is a pure application of John Locke's theory and language. Locke had expanded upon the Biblical theory of Rutherford in *Lex Rex*. Rutherford had based constitutional government on the model of Israel's constitutional monarchy established during the time of Samuel.

In I Samuel 8:3, the elders asked for "a king to judge us like all the nations." Instead, God instructed Samuel to install a covenant king as foretold and described in Deuteronomy 17:14-20. After Israel made Saul its king, Samuel "told the people the manner of the kingdom, and wrote it in a book." I Samuel 10:24. God had defined the form of civil government and wrote it in a book to guide and bind both the civil ruler and the governed. The governed were required to obey the civil ruler so long as the ruler acted in accordance with the delegated authority obtained through consent. They could refuse to obey if the ruler acted outside of the legitimate authority granted under the written guidelines. Rutherford's theological basis for "consent" and civil disobedience later formed the foundation for Locke's political theory.

LOCKE

Locke's theory began with options differing from Rutherford's Biblically-based model. Locke rejected the limited alternatives about which Hobbes wrote in *The Leviathan* and Robert Filmer's paternalistic "divine right of kings" theory. Locke simply stated that legitimate government must be derived from: (1) paternal rights, (2) consent of the people or (3) the unusual case of the appointment by God Himself. The origin of the theory of con-

171

sent arose from the elevation of mankind from a disorganized natural society to a political society formed for the specific purpose of mutual protection. Locke's basic statement resonates in the Declaration of Independence:

> Men being, as has been said, by Nature, all free, equal and independent, no one can be put out of this Estate, and subjected to the Political Power of another, without his own consent. The only way whereby any one devests himself of his Natural Liberty, and puts on the bond of Civil Society is by agreeing with other Men to joyn and unite into a Community, for their comfortable, safe, and peaceable living one amongst another, in a secure Enjoyment of their Properties and a greater Security against any that are not of it. This any number of Men may do, because it injures not the Freedom of the rest; they are left as they were in the Liberty of the State of Nature. When any number of Men have so consented to make one Community or Government, they are thereby presently incorporated, and made one Body Politick wherein the majority have a right to act and conclude the rest.

Locke's theory of the beginning of political society was the ownership and possession of real property. The necessity of securing those rights to property against those continuing to live in a state of nature was the primary reason for forming a government.

JEFFERSON AND MADISON

Locke's property rights theory, as a basis for the requirement of consent to be governed, was expanded to "ideas" by Jefferson and Madison. In their opposition to taxation for religious purposes, Jefferson and Madison openly argued that the liberty attached to property ownership, which could not be taken without consent, should also include the liberties of thought and religious belief. Jefferson argued that the attempt to regulate religious belief was tyranny of the mind. Madison, too, equated "ideas" and conscience as a property of one's mind and that liberty should attach to "ideas" as well as property. Under either argument, they established the principle that a person could not be taxed for the support of ideas repugnant to the taxpayer.

THE EVOLUTION OF CONSENT

Madison's emphasis on "ideas" as a right of liberty formed the basis for Twentieth Century cases about freedom of conscience. But Madison's philosophical underpinnings of that belief, as well as Locke's analysis of property ownership in the state of nature and the necessity of consent, are no longer relevant. The Court no longer sustains objections to payment of taxes for offensive ideas. Reminiscent of one of the majority opinions in The Ship Money Case, the necessity to fund the government is seen as more important than the political theory of consent.

Two recent cases reconstruct the concept of "consent" within new philosophies. The first case, Gillette v. U.S., considered the right to resist the draft during the Vietnam War. The second case, Casey v. Planned Parenthood, concerned the "right" to abortion. In both cases, the Court premised the decision on a theory of consent of the governed, but neither even remotely relate to the theories of Rutherford, Locke or Jefferson.

As in Griswold, Justice William O. Douglas advanced his legal theory in Gillette to support the right of an individual to resist a law enacted legislatively and democratically. The right to resist, incidentally, does not apply to religious beliefs. In Employment Division, Dept. of Human Res. v. Smith, the Supreme Court specifically disallowed a free exercise objection to a lawfully enacted statute that reflected the democratically established majority will. Since the fundamental right permitting resistance to a lawfully enacted statute cannot come from Biblical beliefs, this superior, fundamental "right" must come from somewhere else. To have a "right" to resist a technically correct legislative enactment, the "right" must be superior to any "right" of the majority to bind an individual to the majority's will. To override the general will, the individual's right must be so "fundamental" as to be supreme and beyond the scope of political power. The "right" must have a philosophical origin and must be identifiable. Otherwise, the "right" will simply be the result of the will of the judge.

Douglas presented his argument in Gillette in a dissenting opinion in a case in which the Court majority upheld the constitutionality of the Selective Service Act. In supporting resistance to the draft, Douglas constructed a jurisdictional defense to government intrusion based on a right of conscience derived from a liberal expansion of the First Amendment. Douglas stated:

> Free expression and the right of personal conscientious belief are closely intertwined. At the core of the first amendment's protection of individual expression, is the recognition that such expression represents the oral or written manifestations of conscience. The performance of certain acts, under certain circumstances, involves such a crisis of conscience as to invoke the protection which the first amendment provides for similar manifestations of conscience when expressed in verbal or writ-

ten expressions of thought. The most awesome act which any
society can demand of a citizen's conscience is the taking of a
human life.

Government, Douglas asserted, has complete power that can be
opposed only by the assertion of an individual's right of conscience. Neither Douglas nor the majority discuss the "just war" doctrine. Just as Douglas leapt from a statutory challenge to restrictions on the sale of contraceptives in stores to a "right of privacy" to activities in a married couple's bedroom in <u>Griswold</u>, he leapt from a statutory challenge to draft registration to
a generalized objection to killing. What happened in either case factually or
legally is no longer important. *The change in legal philosophy, however, is
dramatic.* The objection to the draft was not based upon personal Christian
beliefs nor traditional Christian opposition to unjust wars, because the draft
objector was not a Christian. Rather, the objection was vague and pantheistic.

Justice Douglas refuses to appeal to Judeo-Christian theology for support of his assertion. Such an appeal would have legally placed anti-Vietnam
draft resistance in harmony with the Declaration of Independence and Christian theology. Medieval theories regarding just wars and due process could
have supported resistance to the draft for purposes of fighting in the Vietnam
War. The Vietnam War was opposed by many on constitutional grounds and
by others for traditional philosophical reasons. Douglas, however, rejected
traditional legal philosophy and relied on a higher law of nature, comprised
of all religions. Quoting Tolstoy, he wrote:

> Tolstoy wrote of a common man, one Van der Veer, 'who,
> as he himself says, is not a Christian, and who refuses military
> service, not from religious motives, but from motives of the sim-
> plest kind, motives intelligible and common to all men, of what-
> ever religion or nation, whether Catholic, Mohammedan, Bud-
> dhist, Confucian, whether Spaniards or Japanese.'

Douglas continued: "Van der Veer refuses military service, not because
he follows the commandment, 'Thou shalt do no murder,' not because he is
a Christian, but because he holds murder to be opposed to human nature."
Again quoting Tolstoy, Douglas went on to say:

> Van der Veer says he is not a Christian. But the motives of
> his refusal and action are Christian. He refuses because he does
> not wish to kill a brother man; he does not obey, because the
> commands of his conscience are more binding upon him than the

commands of men...Thereby he shows that Christianity is not a
sect or creed which some may profess and others reject; but that
it is naught else that a life's following of that light of reason
which illuminates all men. 'Those men who now behave rightly and reasonable do so, not because they follow prescriptions of
Christ, but because that line of action which was pointed out
eighteen hundred years ago has now become identified with
human conscience.'

Douglas' references to Tolstoy and the characterization of Van der Veer
as a non-Christian are unnecessary and confusing. Tolstoy's experience as
a Russian Christian, disillusioned with the tsarist Nineteenth Century Russian establishment, is interesting but inapposite to America's own history.

Douglas' new theory ultimately needed to be grounded in Christianity
and its moral teachings. Instead, he relied on a new pantheistic philosophy.
But the origin of the "right" remained Christian. For Douglas, "consent"
was not based on Christian teaching but on an undefined "freedom of conscience." Like the "right to privacy" created in Griswold, the "freedom of
conscience" theory had no precedent or apparent limitations.

Twenty years later, in Casey, the Supreme Court shifted back to the
covenant theory of government in America, but attempted to bind persons
who were neither party to the original contract nor in agreement with its
principles.

> Our Constitution is a covenant running from the first gener-
> ation of Americans to us and then to future generations. It is a
> coherent succession. Each generation must learn anew that the
> Constitution's written terms embody ideas and aspirations that
> must survive more ages than one. We accept our responsibility
> not to retreat from interpreting the full meaning of the covenant
> in light of our precedents. We invoke it once again to define the
> freedom guaranteed by the Constitution's own promise, the
> promise of liberty.

The Court, therefore, permits abortion because the women who seek
abortions have not consented to government interference into matters centered upon their own personal belief. The origin of the right to an abortion,
according to the Court in Casey, was found in the liberty of conscience. But
to protect the liberty of conscience, the Court departed from more than a
thousand years of Common Law theory and proclaimed, without precedent,
that actions resulting from that belief must also be protected. The new theory is pantheistic. The government's obligations under this covenant evolve

in accordance with the Court's opinion of a nation's evolving worldview. The theory is also entirely libertarian. According to <u>Casey</u>, each and every individual should be able to resist the authority of government each time they refuse to consent to the legitimacy of the exercise of any government authority. A necessary and inevitable result of that theory is chaos and disorder, leading to tyranny by government. Hobbes' Leviathan was the necessary solution to a disorderly, lawless world.

By failing to ground their theory of fundamental law in a plausible philosophical theory, the right identified in <u>Casey</u> is both arbitrarily identified and incapable of integration into a systematic legal theory. If autonomy is an individual decision, individuals can give their consent randomly and arbitrarily as well. Whether a choice to consent is good or evil is irrelevant, because the choice, which is the result of the liberty of conscience, is protected. If the choice cannot be judged wrong, then the consequences of that choice, manifested in actions, must also be protected. If each individual choice becomes the law of the land, then all other law becomes irrelevant. All personal "rights" are fundamental and supreme over any legislative act, unless the individual voluntarily and expressly consents to the legislation. Under such absurd rules, all laws can be challenged by someone. Obviously, the Court did not intend <u>Casey</u> to be that far reaching. It is probably safe to assume that the radical precedent was intended to only apply to abortion. But the precedent is there. Following <u>Casey</u>'s precedent, only the reluctance of the Supreme Court to strike all statutes can preserve legislation. The Court has taken unto itself absolute power. But is has no theory to direct that power.

CONSTITUTIONALLY IMPLIED CONSENT

A proper Biblically based understanding of "consent of the governed" is not so difficult, vague and fluid as recent Supreme Court decisions make it appear. The *Two Treatises of Government* and the Declaration of Independence clearly require an agreement or contract between people and their government based on the contractual principle of consent. One party to the agreement, the institutions of government established by the United States Constitution, has not changed. Institutions are perpetual in character and cannot unilaterally, by actions or re-interpretation, change the terms and obligations of the agreement to which they are already bound, except by amendment.

As for the people, Locke's own theory indicates that the consent must be obtained for the individual and not for the people as a collective. The people operate collectively through legislatures, but consent comes from the individual and it should be intelligently granted. Locke wrote, "...that every Man, that hath any possession, or enjoyment, of any part of the Dominion of any Government, doth hereby give his *tacit Consent* and is as far forth obliged to Obedience to the Laws of that Government, during such Enjoyment, as anyone under it." [Emphasis added] The modern day shift from voluntary and intelligent consent to submission results partly from citizens' lack of knowledge of the contents of the social contract.

Individuals do not re-interpret the terms of the Declaration of Independence and Constitution from generation to generation any more than they each physically sign a new document. Our form of government does not require newborn babies to sign their palm prints to the Constitution, nor does it require their parents' signatures. By virtue of their birth as American citizens, they have signed the Constitution. Like the government, each signer is obligated to abide by the terms of the Constitution, as originally understood.

Each individual consents to the old documents or knowingly at some point in life refuses to consent to be governed. The government offers to the citizen the right to live in peace secure from infringements on life, liberty or property by lawless people. The lawless are free to live within the community upon the same terms as a foreigner; life, liberty and property will be maintained and secured for that individual by the same laws that protect the citizen, but they are not citizens.

CONSENT TO TAXATION

The irony of recent court decisions which mandate the payment of taxpayer money for abortions and an entitlement to public benefits for illegal aliens is that the requirement of "consent" has been ignored, and entitlement to protection by the political community has been applied to the wrong person. Taxpayer-funded abortions are offensive to the religious beliefs and conscience of most Christians and constitute an expropriation of property; it is repugnant to Common Law.

Under Jefferson's and Madison's theory, mandatory tax payments violate the idea of consent. Yet individuals today who live in a state of nature or reside as illegal aliens, contrary to Biblical principles, Common Law and the Declaration of Independence, win an entitlement from the political community courtesy of the courts. In both examples, the benefits and protections of the political community have been extended to those who refuse to consent, but have been withdrawn from those abiding by the social contract.

At the same time that the Court eliminated the distinction between national and local issues, it eliminated the right of the individual to object to taxation on the basis of lack of consent to the tax. England had emphatically established that principle by the Long Parliament's reaction to The Ship Money Case. The American colonists ratified that principle by their response, at the Boston Tea Party, when Parliament had imposed taxes without their consent after it had repealed the Townshend Acts in 1773. The colonists did not just object to taxation without representation in Parliament. "Taxation without representation" was about sovereignty and the right to resist taxation imposed without consent. A tax imposed by a political body without authority was illegitimate and could not be obeyed—or paid.

The Long Parliament and the Boston Tea Party are two of the most famous events in America's political history. Both events stood on the same principle; no person can be forced to divest his property, or have his property expropriated without the consent of the individual. The 1936 Court missed the precedents established by the Long Parliament and the Declaration of Resolves of the First Continental Congress in Steward Machine Co. v. Davis, decided the same day as Helvering v. Davis.

PROXY TO CONGRESS

In Steward Machine Co., the Court upheld the unemployment compensation tax and payment provisions of the Social Security Act. In Helvering v. Davis, the Court upheld the old age benefit provision of the Social Security Act. In Steward Machine Co., the Court upheld congressional power based upon any matter that was of national concern and, by its holding, indicated that almost all matters involving economic regulation were now of national concern. In Helvering, the Court essentially rejected the Tenth Amendment as a limitation upon federal power.

In Steward Machine Co., the Court admitted that its holding conflicted with previous decisions from Massachusetts, but attempted to distinguish the precedents from the jurisdiction that provided national authority, the Suffolk Resolves, for inclusion of the natural rights theory for the Declaration of Independence, as limited only to Massachusetts. Ironically, in one day, the United States Supreme Court elevated to national concern an individual's employment status but localized an individual's claim to inalienable rights. Essentially, the Court declared that each individual had given a proxy to Congress to levy any tax Congress, in its discretion, wanted.

Justice Cardozo rejected the appellant's appeal to history and constructed his own. Citing the Revenue Act of 1777, passed by Parliament, not the

Continental Congress, and by colonial legislatures in Virginia (1786), North Carolina (1784) and Georgia (1778), America's historical objection to taxation based on natural rights was dismissed.

In one day, in the <u>Steward Machine Co.</u> and <u>Helvering</u> decisions, the Supreme Court ignored the most important cases and events in American constitutional history and focused on the obscure. Consent to taxation became subordinate to government's police power. Federal police power, with the broadest possible interpretation of the General Welfare Clause and the Commerce Clause, became virtually unlimited, trumping state and local laws. The Court, in this broad stoke, swept away America's long history of limited and decentralized government, referencing instead the authority to tax wielded by King George III in 1777. The Court's 1937 reinterpretation of the Constitution's General Welfare Clause had left the Declaration of Independence reference to "consent of the governed" without meaning.

Generally, courts attempt to interpret contracts to give effect to all of the contractual provisions. The assumption of courts is that parties to contracts and legislatures who enact laws intend to provide meaning to all of the provisions in their contracts and statutes; otherwise, they would not bother to incorporate them into the document. Once the Court ignored the "consent of the governed" language, it could no longer, nor has it attempted to, reconcile Locke's and Madison's vision of "consent of the governed" with modern government's demand for more power and centralized administration.

A Theological Concept
Stripped of Theological Content

The requirement of "consent to be governed" began as a theological statement about sovereignty. Rutherford's and the Long Parliament's response to <u>The Ship Money Case</u> were based on a Biblical model. The fact is that Christians cannot be forced to submit to unlawful exercises of authority. Christians may choose to so submit by "consent," but they cannot be forced.

Locke expanded Rutherford's premise by extending the act of consent to taxation to property in general. The political community existed as an association of property owners who paid taxes for institutions to protect their property. They empowered institutions of justice and defense as a necessary and mutually beneficial result of consensual delegation of and submission to a neutral authority.

America's First Amendment is a necessary result of Jefferson's definition of "religion," enacted in Virginia, that combined Locke's property theory with Locke's religious liberty theory. It extended consent to ideas as well as to property. Madison saw ideas as an individual's property, and consent could not be forced to support ideas repugnant to an individual's personal conscience.

Today, consent no longer has a theological context. In <u>Gillette</u>, the current vision of consent has no relationship to Rutherford's Old Testament analysis. Today's identification of consent is an undefined, vague pantheistic feeling of objection to something that the judge dislikes in harmony with the litigant. In <u>Casey</u>, that objection based on consent was specifically identified as an objection to laws restricting abortion, an objection shared by the Court. Consent had changed from a theological concept, established as a foundational principle applicable to all people, to a personal opinion shared by a lucky litigant who agreed with the personal political opinions of the judges.

Opposition to taxation survives as a constitutional right but this principle has also changed from a religious idea to an express, secular theory. <u>McCollum</u> and <u>Everson</u> were both taxpayer lawsuits, brought by taxpayers objecting to taxes for religious purposes. In <u>Flast v. Cohen</u> (1968), the taxpayers' objection to taxation for religious purposes was declared a constitutional right. Although the Court would claim, in <u>Valley Forge Christian College v. Americans United for Separation of Church and State, Inc.</u> (1982), that there was no hierarchy of constitutional values, in the recent 8th Circuit Court case of <u>Tarsney v. O'Keefe</u>, a hierarchy of constitutional values was established granting taxpayer standing to atheists only. In 1952, in <u>Zorach v. Clausen</u>, Justice Hugo Black stated that the law would not allow Christians to be favored over atheists. By 2001, atheists were favored over Christians.

In <u>Tarsney</u>, a challenge by 47 taxpayers to a State Supreme Court imposed tax funding abortions in Minnesota, the Court expressly declared that only objections based on the Establishment Clause would be heard. The practical result is that atheists are protected and Christians are not. Atheists' objections based on their being offended by religion continue to be heard. In contrast, Christians' objections to the expenditures offensive to their religion would not even be considered by the Court. The Biblical model has been juxtaposed and the proxy to Congress to spend for whatever it wants can continue despite being offensive to Christians. The Court has declared Jefferson to be an antiquity.

RESTORED CONSENT

If America is to remain a land of liberty, it must recognize certain truths. A limitation upon the power to tax is critical to limiting the exercise of government power. Ultimately, political power is defined by the people. Just as the founders never considered that Congress and the Court had the authority to define "truth," neither Congress nor the Court has the authority to define "consent." "Truth" can be objectively known and commonly understood, but "truth" cannot be implemented by decree. Similarly, "consent" that is first implied and then decreed, conflicts with the First Amendment.

Jefferson's admonition against taxation that conflicts with opinion was based on theology and political philosophy. This reference to "sin," as well as to tyranny, squares his viewpoint about freedom of religion with Samuel Adams' viewpoint about consent. Justice Douglas and Tolstoy could have (and should have) rested their objections to killing upon Christianity. And Douglas could have rested a Christian's objection to killing on the First Amendment. Christians who object to tax-payer funded abortions can cite to Jefferson and Samuel Adams. The Court's analysis of "consent" in Casey cannot.

The Court will never retreat from nor sort out the constitutional mess it has created unless "We the People" reclaim our sovereignty. The Court's decisions have served to transfer sovereignty from the people to state governments. State sovereignty, because of the supremacy clause, is subject to federal power. The Court has never stated, in so many words, that individual religious convictions are subordinate to the taxing authority of the states or federal government, but in effect, religious convictions have become private and secondary to government needs.

The Court has disregarded the opinions of Locke and Madison, traceable to Rutherford. To return to Rutherford's principles and The Ship Money Case precedent in modern America requires a new reinterpretation and limitation of Court precedents. The Court must begin to render decisions based on sound philosophy with their roots in historical Christianity, to restore the Declaration of Independence and Constitution to their original purpose of limiting government to the powers granted by the "consent of the governed." To leave this undone, to support the status quo, is to render the future of American progeny to government by the powerful; America, then, will have gone full circle back to George III.

CHAPTER 11
THE ROBIN HOOD HERESY

" 'Where there is no property there is no justice,' is a proposition as certain as any demonstration in Euclid."

John Locke

"Government is instituted to protect property of every sort; as well as that which lies in the various rights of individuals, as that which the term particularly expresses. This being the end of government, that alone is a just government which impartially secures to every man, whatever is his own."

President James Madison

"A state of equality as to property is impossible to be maintained, for it is against the laws of our nature...Civil government is not entitled, in ordinary cases, and as a general rule, to require the use of property in the hands of the owners, by sumptuary laws, or any other visionary schemes of frugality and equality."

James Kent

I have been deeply involved in the title insurance industry. I represent clients who examine title to real estate, and I insure real estate transactions. As well, I clean up titles so property can be transferred and people can obtain mortgages. I have handled dozens of cases involving the resolution of conflicting interest of property owners to particular parcels of real estate.

Real estate law has been developing for centuries. Judges and lawyers usually do a very good job of sorting things out and reaching a just result. Disputes with the government, however, are a very different story. Title insurance companies won't insure against any governmental action, and for a good reason. The practical reality is that the government can do with your property whatever it wants to do.

I have found that it is possible to fight city hall and win, but litigants had better be prepared to fight long and hard. Otherwise, they are wasting their time and money. The rules are slanted in favor of the government and courts have given it a lot of discretion. Successful private litigants know the rules better than the government and also know how to use the rules against it.

It is difficult to make the argument that private property rights are Biblically based, but Aquinas and Locke did so, and our Puritan founders incorporated those principles into American law. I wrote in "Economic Freedom and the Reign and Rule of Law" that private property rights are the basis of the American Dream because they form the foundation for the independence of the family.

In discussing with policy makers from formerly Communist countries the problems faced in transitioning from communism to capitalism, I always encourage them to pay as much attention to establishing a good system of private real estate ownership as they did to establishing capital markets. It isn't capitalism that built America; rather, individuals that pursued the American Dream of property ownership built this country. It is this inherent belief in private property ownership that continues to drive our pursuit of the American dream; it keeps fueling America's national prosperity, making her the envy of the world.

◆ ◆ ◆

T he founding fathers saw the right to own and use property as an inalienable right. The Leviathan state attacks and in many ways, destroys this right. While property rights still exist, the right is qualified, highly regulated and always subject to alienation for a higher government purpose. And governments tax property when it is used, sold, and purchased. Even if it sits idle, the owner still gets an annual tax bill. Compare Locke's assertion that government exists to protect property with Leviathan's actions that deem property as something to be exploited to provide for those who do not own property.

The right to own and possess property is an element of the Declaration's assertion of the inalienability of the right to pursue happiness. For a time, property rights were protected as a substantive due process right under the Fourteenth Amendment. But the "blessings of liberty" have been separated from liberty itself and redefined as a requirement imposed on some individuals to provide and transfer the blessings to others. The result has been the creation of a dependent class, the recipient of the transferred "blessing of liberty," and the loss of liberty for the providers.

As a matter of law, property rights were established by Chapter 39 of Magna Charta: "No freeman shall be arrested, or detained in prison, or deprived of his freehold, or in any way molested, and we will not set forth against him, nor send against him, unless by the lawful judgment of his peers and by the law of the land."

The rights to own and use property, free from expropriation and divestiture, were first set forth in the Coronation Charter of Henry I, also known as the Charter of Liberties (1100). The Charter included provisions for unjustly acquired property, stating it must be returned to its legitimate owner.

Further developments in property law date to the reign of Edward III (1352). Using Magna Charta as authority, private individuals could not oust another person "on petition or suggestion to the king or his counsel by powerful individuals," ending a common practice from that time.

Colonial America rejected feudalism, the European system of property ownership. Feudalism, as a real property system, is analogous to franchising as a marketing distribution system. The state owned the patent to land. Territories were granted to noblemen in exchange for loyalty in time of war, and royalties to maintain the central government. The nobility, in turn, would grant sub-territories to another class that worked the land, in exchange for loyalty to the noblemen.

The feudal system met much opposition. The rise of mercantilism and tradesmen was antithetical to feudalism. The Puritan middle class that settled New England was fiercely democratic and anti-feudalistic. The Puritans who stayed in England had reduced the importance of the royalty and nobility by the mid-1600s.

The Bill of Rights of 1689 provided expressly for the protection of life, liberty and property. It was drafted with the assistance of John Locke, as counsel to William and Mary, at the same time as he published his *Two Treatises of Government*. Locke's writings were cited extensively in America. But property rights were already expressly protected in the First Virginia Charter of 1606, the Charter of New England of 1620, the Charter of Massachusetts Bay of 1629, the Charter of Maryland of 1632, the Charter of Maine of 1639, the Charter of Connecticut of 1662, the Charter of Rhode Island of 1663, and the Charter of Carolina of 1663.

The Declaration of Independence, the Constitution and the Bill of Rights reaffirmed the right to own and use property. Blackstone wrote that inherent rights include the right to personal security, personal liberty, and the ownership and use of private property.

Blackstone defined property as that which "consists in the free use, enjoyment, and disposal of all [personal] acquisitions" and he spoke of the "sacred and inviolable rights of private property." The Constitution of Pennsylvania of August 10, 1776, the Delaware Declaration of Rights of September 11, 1776, and the Constitution of Vermont of July 8, 1777 specifically repeated the Blackstone three-part definition of property. The Declaration and Resolves of the First Continental Congress (1774) included "the inhabitants of the English colonies in North America, by the immutable laws of nature, the principles of the English Constitution, and the several charters or compacts" were "entitled to life, liberty and property."

Property rights, as a matter of law relied on the Bill of Rights of 1689 and Magna Charta as legal precedent, but also the immutable laws of nature, Blackstone's definition and Locke's arguments, to establish property rights as an inalienable right.

AMERICA'S INNOVATION IN PROPERTY LAW

The "pursuit of happiness" in the Declaration of Independence meant that every individual was created with the inherent right to live in accordance with the laws of eternal justice. This concept of eternal justice differs significantly from modern concepts of social justice. Also differing significantly is our understanding of the term "happiness."

"Happiness" in Eighteenth Century England did not mean the same thing as it does today. "Happy," in England, was derived from the Latin "*beatis*," as is the term "beatitudes." The pursuit of happiness can be best explained as the right to pursue virtue in accordance with the Sermon on the Mount; this contrasts with our contemporary understanding of the pursuit of happiness which modernists take to mean the pursuit of pleasure, with all individuals defining pleasure in their own way. The pursuit of happiness was included in the Declaration of Independence to guarantee the entire range of economic rights, including property rights, the right to contract, and the freedom to use one's labor as one chooses—that is, income is also our property.

As a practical matter, the theoretical source of property rights had to be determined to implement the nation's settlement after independence was obtained. Most of the new land sat unsettled. The right to possess land in America was to be based on ownership, not just on possession. Evidence of ownership of land was to be based on documented records; these records were to be maintained in each municipal subdivision. Access to the records would always be open to public inspection and notice to the world of each individual's ownership rights. Laws relating to title to property are still based on record evidence found and maintained at the local courthouse.

Documentary title evidencing ownership of land begins with a grant from the state. Vesting title in the state was a legal fiction developed to permit the state to facilitate a process transferring private property rights to individuals. Until the patent was issued to an individual, the legal title remained in the United States or the individual state as trustee only. The equitable title was considered to be in the eventual holder of the certificate of entry. The certificate was issued by the registrar of the land office and that entitled the claimant to the patent. The patent holder became the original owner of the property and was entitled to buy, sell or encumber the property at his choice.

At the time of Blackstone, the field of study now known as property law was undeveloped. To lawyers in the Eighteenth Century, property law was limited to conveyancing. The function of the law was to facilitate the transfer of real property in accordance with principles laid down when feudalism still prevailed, although feudalism had disappeared in Eighteenth Century Western Europe and never was practiced in the New World. The rules were archaic but practical. In facilitating the transfer of individual parcels of real estate, conveyancing was a necessary and useful part of Eighteenth Century legal practice.

Pragmatism and conveyancing had to give way to legal philosophy and modern property law when the new American nation prepared for settlement and expansion. The expansion into the Northwest Territory following the French and Indian War, and into the Great Plains following the Louisiana Purchase, presented opportunities for new settlements and practical problems of transferring ownership to the new settlers. The question of who was entitled to possession and ownership of the new territories needed to be addressed philosophically.

A cornerstone of modern property law is the United States Supreme Court decision, <u>Fletcher v. Peck</u> (1810), written by Chief Justice John Marshall. In <u>Fletcher</u>, the developing principles of contract law and property law were merged. The result was a holding that established constitutional principles securing the rights of property owners and the establishment of property ownership as a fundamental right under the new federal constitution that could not be jeopardized by state legislation.

The holding in <u>Fletcher</u> was simple. The Court denied the state's attempt to rescind a previously issued patent to land. The grantee to land had an indefeasible interest in real estate. The patent was a contractual obligation. The government could not breach its contractual obligation once the patent was issued. Combining principles of contract law with developing principles of real property law that prohibited restraints on alienation, the patent transferred all of the government's interest in the property to the owner that could not be qualified, conditioned, or rescinded.

An explanation for the unsurprising but revolutionary holding in <u>Fletcher</u> can be seen in the writings of early Nineteenth Century legal philosopher Jeremy Bentham. Bentham had redefined "property" to a legally protected "expectation" which could be realized "only from law." Legal philosophy and practical lawyering were united. The practical necessity for a fixed rule of law, as the only means of securing property rights, took on constitutional significance. The direct mandate of government, as set forth in the Declaration of Independence, that governments are instituted to secure rights, became a fixture of private property law.

THE SOURCE OF PROPERTY RIGHTS

Though the <u>Fletcher v. Peck</u> decision presented an issue of legal philosophy as it pertained to private property, the legal philosophers were in disagreement as to the source of individual property rights. At least five separate theories were prevalent in the early Nineteenth Century.

The debate over property rights by early English and American legal scholars raised many points which never reached an ultimate conclusion. Henry St. George Tucker, noted legal scholar and editor of an edition of Blackstone's *Commentaries* in the early Nineteenth Century, wrote, "[I]f the laws of the land were suspended, we should be under the same moral and natural obligations to refrain from invading each other's property, as from attacking and assaulting each other's person."

Justice James Wilson wrote, "the general property of man and animals, in the soil, and in the productions of the soil, is the immediate gift of the bountiful Creator of all." Wilson saw the economic decline and failures in the Virginia and New Plymouth colonies in the 1600s as the result of communal theory. He made the practical observation that Virginia and Plymouth were revived by the establishment of private property rights. He argued, "Exclusive property prevents disorder, and promotes peace."

James Kent, another early authority on real property law, believed that Genesis supported the theory that the Bible was the source of private property rights, and that the right of property included, and was confirmed by the Biblical right of inheritance.

John Locke, in Chapter 5 of Book Two of the *Two Treatises of Government*, believed in "private Dominion, exclusive of the rest of Mankind." He asserted that God gave the earth to mankind in common, but that the property right derived from the liberty right to the fruit of one's labor. Property rights are not found in a divine chain of title, but as part of the expansive rights derived from the individual's right to liberty.

Blackstone was unclear as to whether property rights were based on the law of nature or social compact, but that "necessity begat property."

Justice Joseph Story stated that in nature, all things were held in common. A theory of possession and use could only justify a temporary claim. Story further maintained that the social contract theory was unsupported theory. "The truth, however, seems to be, that, in a state of nature, each man actually appropriates to himself whatever he desires, and can get, and then holds it by the title of the strongest, and no other person respects his title any longer than it can be so maintained." Story adds, the "first rudiments of exclusive property began in the fact of actual possession and power."

Modern legal scholars and jurists are reluctant to attribute property rights to Biblical principles. Modern defenders of property rights, as a defense to government encroachments through either the exercise of expanding police power or socialist philosophy, argue only that economic efficiency mandates a system of private property ownership. The collapse of international communism lent credence to the practical conclusions of modern economic efficiency advocates, but the philosophical questions remain unaddressed.

THE THEOLOGICAL FOUNDATION
FOR AMERICAN PROPERTY LAW

A review of the records of the debates over the ratification of the United States Constitution and the passage of the Bill of Rights clearly indicates that the political leaders of the time were subordinating their personal economic interest to larger philosophical considerations. Studies show that Scripture was the primary reference of the debaters. America resulted from a political reformation more than it could be characterized as a political revolution. By the late Eighteenth Century and early Nineteenth Century, American lawyers and political leaders relied not on new precedents and principles but on a clearer understanding of old ideas.

The American understanding of property law was not new, but almost entirely based upon John Locke's *Two Treatises of Government* and the medieval Catholic Church position on property law. John Locke and Thomas Aquinas both based property theory on the Old Testament.

The practical debate over property law theory continues in the Catholic Church, but the official position was settled long ago. The early Catholic Church believed that the concept of "inalienable" rights appeared too Greek

189

and pantheistic. More specifically, the Dominicans and Franciscans dis-agreed whether property ownership was a gift from God or a result of man's fall into sin.

The Dominicans, following Thomas Aquinas, advocated that property was part of the law of nature and had nothing to do with man's innocence or sinfulness. Pope John XXII's issuance of the *Quia Vir Reprobus* in 1329 set-tled the Catholic debate in favor of the Domincans.

The Calvinists later adopted the Dominican view; they considered prop-erty ownership as a divine blessing for which individuals had obligations as stewards to care and nurture their property, free of government or the inter-ference of other individuals. The Dominican position became part of Eng-lish Common Law.

The early legal philosophers debated whether property devolved from God to the individual or to the community. There is no clear answer to that question. In Israel of the Old Testament, the land was partitioned and con-veyed to the separate families, identified as the 12 tribes of Israel. The Bib-lical model had set the pattern for Christian, medieval Europe. But the medieval institution of feudalism was paternalistic. The initial partition in Israel, as in Europe, was followed by a paternalistic institution and central-ized administration.

Locke rejected paternalism and pioneered the inalienable rights theory. The concept of the inalienable right to property was the result of a philo-sophical and theological concept Locke developed, based upon Catholic property rights theory and Reformation equality principles.

The secular debate had to, as a practical matter, also decide the issue whether to grant land to individuals or the community. The secular theorist had no philosophical answer. The grant of individual rights to land was based upon privilege or power. Individual equality was not possible. On the other hand, community ownership of all land has been proven to result in either totalitarianism or communism.

Locke centered the right of property ownership on the individual fami-ly as the clearest parallel to Old Testament economics. Property rights, which Locke saw as including the right to the proceeds gained from one's own labor, were easily combined with a theory of individual inalienable rights. There is no inherent initial conflict between the rights of the man as head of the individual family and the rights of an individual. Both stand opposed to a collectivist theory and a statist theory. Collectivism, as it relat-ed to property ownership, was in conflict with the Old Testament. Locke also discredited the idea of statism, based on the paternalistic concept that all humanity since Adam—including entire nations—derived from the growth of individual tribes.

America had begun, and then grew as a gathering place for all nationalities that agreed to adhere to common principles found in the Declaration of Independence, Constitution and Bill of Rights, and Common Law. It could not, by observable evidence, have evolved to nation status from tribal status as had occurred in Europe. As well, the collectivist theory conflicted with Puritan theology and with early constitutional precedents. All of the early American and English legal philosophers were right: American property law theory is more American than Scriptural, but it has a Scriptural foundation.

EXPROPRIATION AND DIVESTITURE

American real estate law is still more practical than philosophical. Real estate law continues to be a combination of possession and record title.

Because of <u>Fletcher v. Peck</u> (1810), title examiners trace the source of title to the original grant from the government. Title examination does not include guarantees and assurances that title and ownership will be secure from divestiture or expropriation by the government. By whatever source early Americans justified private property ownership, initial ownership rights were complete and indefeasible. Successive owners were granted the same complete rights as the original owner.

Property lawyers understand that the terms "inalienable" and "indefeasible" mean that property cannot be taken away. Rules were established under Common Law and English statutory law requiring that estates in land be inalienable and indefeasible. Restraints against alienation are still disfavored under the law as between competing private interests. In early America, the same rules were applied to the government. That principle was constitutionalized into rules against expropriation and divestiture which were rigorously enforced.

Under American law, expropriation is "taking property from A and giving it to B." Divestiture is "taking property from A and giving it to the benefit of the public at large." Expropriation is unconstitutional and has been since the early days of the republic, as seen in the case of <u>Calder v. Bull</u> (1798). In a later Justice Story opinion, the Supreme Court invalidated a Virginia statute that attempted to defeat the title of the Episcopalian Church to property in the case of <u>Terret v. Taylor</u> (1814). <u>Terret</u> was based on the contract clause of the Constitution but the principle was anti-expropriation.

Divestiture of property was also strictly prohibited. In <u>Fletcher</u>, the state could not rescind a transfer of property subsequent to a federal land grant. In <u>Dartmouth College v. Woodward</u> (1819), a corporate charter did not include a right of the state to regulate the corporation. In <u>Dred Scott v. Sandford</u> (1857), Section 8 of the Missouri Compromise was struck down as an unconstitutional divestiture of property.

The shaky philosophical foundation of American property law became apparent after the Civil War. Popular criticism of <u>Dred Scott</u> discredited property principles in general as well as the proper conclusion that a person is not property.

Marx and Engels and other utopian philosophers popularized the opposition to property rights intellectually. At the same time, utilitarians and economic interests expanded the government's role in using and manipulating public property for economic growth. In addition, religious groups sought the assistance of the state's police power to eradicate alcohol abuse. The principles of <u>Fletcher</u> and <u>Dartmouth College</u> were impediments to be either distinguished from new principles or ignored entirely.

The two fundamental constitutional principles of property law that have been ignored are the principles of expropriation and divestiture. Expropriation refers to simple transfer of property of one person to another by force. The principle of divestiture refers to the loss of use of property by one person because of a larger purpose belonging to the public at large. Expropriation was necessary to facilitate economic expansion. The principle of divestiture was used first to regulate, then abused to justify the redistribution of wealth.

The steady expansion of the state's police power used to tax and regulate property eroded the principle that expropriation and divestiture are unconstitutional. All branches of government eventually came to ignore the bulwark that had stood against the power to tax and regulate. Principles developed by the Puritans and held firm by the founding fathers, those of the "inalienable right to property" and the principle that no taxation or delegation of authority was allowed without the consent of the people, have now been ignored—even discarded. Pre-Civil War property theories and principles are hardly even considered worthy of discussion as legal arguments before modern judges and are rarely taught in law schools. *The result has been that the government now exercises almost unlimited authority over property and can levy any tax for any purpose without restraint by the courts.*

UTILITARIAN PHILOSOPHY REPLACES THE INALIENABLE RIGHTS THEORY

The decline in individual rights and the expansion of government power did not develop until after the Civil War. Legal theory changed because of the decline in a firm belief in the law of nature and of nature's God, and the rise in popularity of the theory of utilitarianism, as presented by the British legal scholar Jeremy Bentham and philosopher John Stuart Mill. The Supreme Court began compromising earlier courts' holdings by failing to adhere to the written constitutional text and not grounding its newer decisions in the legal philosophy of Jefferson, Webster and Lincoln. Rather, the Court began issuing a series of conflicting and confusing opinions and precedents not grounded in text or theory. No clear sense can be made from these cases. Without "inalienable rights" and "consent of the governed" as a reference to what the law should have been, compared to the way it was actually decided, cases can be discussed and analyzed, but not reconciled.

In colonial times and in the early days of the republic, government could not force its way onto private property except by the power of eminent domain. Public use of private property could be required, but compensation after the fact was also always required. Public purpose was synonymous with eminent domain. Property appropriated or destroyed in a time of war was justified on principles similar to the tort defense of necessity. The comparison with "necessity" disappeared in the late 1800s.

After the Civil War, the public purpose doctrine was expanded to include the regulation of public utilities. Public utilities were public companies permitted to exercise monopoly power for the benefit of the citizenry. The standards were continually relaxed until, under today's holdings, any business or development that creates at least one job will be upheld as a public, rather than a private purpose, which essentially redefines expropriation out of existence. When benefits for one individual, or corporation, are considered to benefit all, the old distinctions disappear.

Most citizens benefit from the products generated by these utilities. These monopolies could not, it was argued, be created without the assistance of government. Public lands were conveyed to the monopolists. When necessary, the power of condemnation was exercised to force the conveyance of private land. The government intervention in this manner, which would not have been permitted in the early 1800s, was justified in the name of industrialization rather than necessity in the traditional sense. Necessity became grounded in economic theory rather than the effect of public necessity that affected private property rights.

The expansion of the "public purpose" definition essentially created a public enterprise theory. Any government activity that is expected to provide a benefit to anyone can be justified as a public purpose. This has allowed government agencies not only to expropriate real property, but tax dollars which it then appropriates to private businesses in the hope that someday those businesses might produce jobs. The government calls this "economic development."

At the time of Fletcher v. Peck, the possession of property by the government was custodial until ownership could be claimed by private individuals. The Court has since reversed the idea of custody and ownership of property. Private individuals now possess property as custodians unless and until the government claims ownership for some public purpose or public enterprise. Nowadays, the government authority to zone essentially eliminates most uses of property of which the zoning authority disapproves. Zoning restrictions can eliminate discretion in the size and color of structures as well as the types of uses permitted on the property. Police power cannot only regulate what can be done on private property in the future, but can change existing uses such that a change in plans by the government for use of property can eliminate any use of the property by the property owner. Individuals can buy property but may not be able to use it. Balancing is now always in favor of the government.

The expropriation and divestiture of private property in furtherance of government enterprise was only the first step toward the ultimate purpose of redistributing wealth. First, the right to own property was made subject to the power of the government to convert private property to a general public use. Next, private use of property became subordinate to the government power to regulate. The source of government power to regulate property was linked to the government's inherent police power to secure safety, health and morals, which now included economic development.

GOVERNMENT REGULATION
REPLACES COMMON LAW PROHIBITIONS

As with freedom of speech and religion, property rights and contract rights are expressed in America's founding documents in absolute terms. As the Court distanced itself from the legal philosophy of Jefferson, Madison and Marshall, the ability to distinguish and adjudicate between the property and contract rights of individuals versus government interest, expressed in the police power, became more difficult.

In Fletcher v. Peck and Dartmouth College v. Woodward, Marshall carefully made clear that government grants in the nature of land grants and corporate charters were absolute. The prohibition of impairment of contracts could not be violated by the government. In Stone v. Mississippi (1880), the Court had to retreat from Marshall's absolute terms when the question of the

interest of the public and the government were in conflict with a lottery contract granted by the legislature in its administrative capacity. In <u>Stone</u>, the
Court was careful to distinguish between traditional property rights and
dubious contractual obligations created by the legislature. What remained
after <u>Stone</u>, however, was the principle that government police powers were
inalienable. But police power and individual rights and contract rights cannot both be inalienable. Balancing of interests had begun.

After the Civil War, the focus on the problems in the South was replaced
with discussions about how to most directly approach the more pleasant
problem of effectively facilitating the settlement of the West. The government immersed itself in the process of western settlement by issuing exclusive franchises to build railroads, establish industries and, at the same time,
issue small individual land grants to induce settlers to move. The unintend-
ed consequences caused by government sponsored monopolies seemed hypocritical. It was difficult to take seriously the argument that contract rights
and property rights were fundamental and superior to government power to
regulate when those rights were only recently benevolently granted by the
government. Any reference to the pursuit of happiness as a principle of
adjudication seemed hypocritical. The Court's function moved from adjudicator to policy maker. Similarly, to balance the competing interests of the
monopolists and the public, the legislatures had to regulate the businesses it
had helped to develop, moving from lawmaker to manager. The focus of the
courts shifted from the rights of the parties to the reasonableness of the regulations.

In the case of real property, the shift in the emphasis from individual
property rights to reasonableness of regulation can be seen in the evolution
of the law of eminent domain to the current emphasis on the law of zoning.

Under Common Law, government power to take away or interfere with
the use of property was limited to the principle of eminent domain. While
the encroachment against private property under eminent domain laws can
be traced from an expansion of Common Law tort doctrine of necessity,
much of modern zoning and building regulations can be traced to the Common Law tort definition of nuisance. But the beginning of the expansion of
the regulation authority under the police power was not based upon necessity or nuisance, but can be traced to a purported concern for safety.

The resulting proliferation of regulatory laws can be directly traced to
the failure of the courts to administer justice in two ways. The Court gradually reversed the balancing of private and public interest to favor the government, rather than individuals, by rejecting the principle that property
ownership was inalienable. Instead, government power became inalienable.

The principle of "inalienability" of <u>Dartmouth College</u> was reversed by <u>Stone</u>. Only one side to the balance could have a right or a power that was inalienable. John Marshall had vested that inalienable right with the individual. That inalienable right was converted to an inalienable power that was given to government in the last half of the Nineteenth Century.

Second, the courts refused to judge the merits of bad science. The law of evidence is supposed to be based upon the evaluation of good versus bad science. By adopting the "rational basis test," the court abandoned any evaluation of the merits of the legislatures' hypotheses. In contracts involving private litigants, the court always assumes the responsibility to seek the truth, as best as it can, to administer justice to the furthest extent possible. Cases between litigants involve the same theories and same scientific issues as cases involving suits against the government. But judicial deference to legislative discretion has led to the withholding of justice.

Government power is not absolute. The burden is on the government to show if necessity or nuisance is absolutely evident in a case. One party to the case cannot have absolute discretion to define the facts to a case and to have more power or rights than the other. In the area of regulation of property, the balance was supposed to favor the individual. On the contrary, the balance, and the rules, have been now given to the other party—government—and the court, unlike Marshall in <u>Marbury</u>, refuses to perform its constitutional duty to apply the correct principles of law to each case.

THE REDISTRIBUTION OF WEALTH

The unchallenged power to regulate eventually led to the use of the coercive power of government to transfer property for the purpose of redistributing wealth. Legislation upheld in the name of public safety had eroded property rights sufficiently to allow the legislature to enact legislation in the name of public charity. The Court did not permit this redistribution of wealth in the name of charity until 1937. Ironically, legislation enacted to support public morality, the basis for the <u>Mugler</u> decision, was dealt a crushing blow by the passage of the Twenty-first Amendment in 1933 which repealed Prohibition. Legislation for charitable purposes had been proposed but rejected prior to 1937. In 1937, the Supreme Court reversed its prior holdings and permitted federal public assistance in the name of general welfare. Laws supporting public assistance arose at the same time as laws against the sale and distribution of alcohol were repealed.

The decision to stop regulating morality and to install a system of public welfare is doubly symbolic to Christians. Traditional Common Law principles that applied to morality could only be based upon an acknowledgment and adherence to Divine law. Following the repeal of Prohibition, adherents of a form of moral license began claiming that legislating morality does not work. Madison's challenge to see whether a nation could govern itself according to the Ten Commandments had been answered— "No!"

At the same time, charity, an outgrowth of cultural Christianity that had existed in America since its founding, was transferred from private to public hands, even though private charities had not been proven to be ineffective. But the Great Depression's hardships were used to justify that change. Until 1937, the federal government had no power to compel taxation for charity. It is likely that an exercise of state power for the same purpose would have also been unconstitutional until that time.

Madison and Marshall were not the only authorities abandoned in 1937. The dissenters, in <u>Steward Machine</u>, simply recited an oft-quoted veto message of Franklin Pierce, issued in 1853, which warned of the dangers of abandoning principle for emotion in the name of charity:

> [It is] my deliberate conviction that a strict adherence to the terms and purposes of the federal compact offers the best, if not the only, security for the preservation of our blessed inheritance of representative liberty.

He further declared that it was the duty of the president to uphold the rule of law over tyranny of men.

> The question presented, therefore, clearly is upon the constitutionality and propriety of the Federal Government assuming to enter into a novel and vast field of legislation, namely, that of providing for the care and support of all those among the people of the United States who by any form of calamity become fit objects of public philanthropy.
>
> I readily and, I trust, feelingly acknowledge the duty incumbent on us all as men and citizens, and as among the highest and holiest of our duties, to provide for those who, in the mysterious order of Providence, are subject to want and to disease of body or mind; but I cannot find any authority in the Constitution for making the Federal Government the great almoner of public charity throughout the United States. To do so would, in my judgment, be contrary to the letter and spirit of the Constitution and subversive of the whole theory upon which the Union of these States is founded.

Pierce also declared that the Constitution was superior to rhetoric regarding the General Welfare Clause.

> I shall not discuss at length the question of power some-
> times claimed for the General Government under the clause of
> the eighth section of the Constitution, which gives Congress the
> power 'to lay and collect taxes, duties, imposts, and excises, to
> pay debts and provide for the common defense and general wel-
> fare of the United States,' because if it has not already been set-
> tled upon sound reason and authority it never will be. I take the
> received and just construction of that article, as if written to lay
> and collect taxes, duties, imposts, and excises in order to pay the
> debts and in order to provide for the common defense and gen-
> eral welfare. It is not a substantive general power to provide for
> the welfare of the United States, but is a limitation on the grant
> of power to raise money by taxes, duties, and imposts. If it were
> otherwise, all the rest of the Constitution, consisting of carefully
> enumerated and cautiously guarded grants of specific powers,
> would have been useless, if not delusive . . .

President Pierce's principles, which had been deemed the best explanation of the issue for years, were only a eulogy, in the form of the dissenting
opinion in <u>Steward Machine Company v. Davis</u> (1937). The majority opinion, written by Justice Cardozo, simply invoked emergency powers to combat unemployment in the Great Depression and would not consider the historical theory and precedent in opposition to the grant of federal power. As
an emergency measure, rather than attempt to limit congressional power by
reference to principles of necessity, the Court found an unlimited grant of
authority in the term "general welfare" in the Preamble to the United States
Constitution.

The General Welfare Clause, as it is called, is now commonly invoked
to support any and all welfare programs. The legal error in claiming authority from the General Welfare Clause in the Preamble to the Constitution,
which did not grant any specific powers to the federal government and no
corresponding power can be found in enumerated powers in the body of the
Constitution, created an unlimited authority to create a welfare state. The
new police power to tax and regulate had been "discovered" in the Preamble; a discovery that had been rejected for years. The reinterpretation was
openly announced, in the name of necessity, because the Supreme Court
declared it so and would not listen to any contrary arguments. The principle
of necessity, which had been limited to the use of buildings and vessels in
the time of war, and required reimbursement from the government in the
name of eminent domain, had been transformed to support the confiscation

of property for the purpose of the redistribution of wealth.

PRIVATE OR PUBLIC CHARITY?

The arguments in favor and in opposition to public welfare cannot be simply stated. Franklin Pierce's sober analysis based on principle now appears cold hearted to Americans. Though individualistic and self-reliant, America's kindheartedness cries out for an interventionist solution. The image of Robin Hood appeals to enough voters unfamiliar with Franklin Pierce, much less his position of private property, to politicize wealth redistribution. With no judicial recourse to protect property rights from coercion, Robin Hood's thievery has been legalized. It makes no difference whether wealth was obtained legally or illegally—individuals have always had the right to sue to get back property taken illegally. The image of the wealthy as villainous, merely because of their wealth, and the political leaders as Robin Hood has led to the triumph of perception over principle. Private property ownership is no longer an inalienable right, but a result of democratic judgment.

The inalienable right to property, included in the right to pursue happiness, is not so much a theological principle as an English and American legal principle with roots in the Protestant Reformation. The vigorous support for property rights argued by Locke and practiced by Anglicans and Puritans alike was not supported by either the Catholic immigrants of the Nineteenth and Twentieth Century or the new secular theories of the Twentieth Century.

At the core of the idea of the inalienable right to property are two principles fully accepted in earlier America. One, individual wealth was a "blessing" of liberty resulting from each individual's own personal relationship with God. Property and wealth were not obtained through the benevolence of the church or the state but because of God's benevolence. For the state or any person to interfere with an individual's relationship with God was deemed inappropriate.

Two, charity is the result of acts of love. Love cannot be coerced. An individual does not demonstrate love or fulfill any duty to God by paying taxes. The fruits of individual love and charity are evidenced by private giving rather than submission to coercive taxation. The modern mindset that compassion can be demonstrated by taking property from one individual and giving to another has no theological significance for either Robin Hood or his victim.

In a Christian nation, private charity is both necessary and evident. Private charity still exists in spite of misguided government policies. The government cannot overcome the flawed premise of the modern welfare state. Poverty is not only an economic problem. The Bible identifies poverty as a spiritual problem. The elimination or reduction of poverty requires a spiritual solution that must accompany economic aid. Economic aid alone will not rehabilitate an individual nor will it even meet the individual's economic needs. America's experience with the welfare state proves that the transfer of resources for the maintenance of a standard of living, rather than to provide for an emergency situation, cannot succeed. The transformation of individuals, rather than mere sustenance, is necessary to cure poverty.

The Robin Hood philosophy satisfies no one. The transferee's needs remain unmet. Robin Hood gets nothing. And the victim, the property owner, decides to forgo God's blessings because it is too dangerous.

In America, as in most of Europe, the debate between the Dominicans and Franciscans had been decided in favor of the Dominicans. The Dominicans' private property view, treated as an inalienable right to own property under English and American law, was then rejected by an unholy alliance between modern liberal theologians and secular collectivists.

The image of Robin Hood, so appealing to modern Americans, is incomplete without a broader view of the primitive and corrupt economic and sociological culture from which the image is derived. Private property ownership is not only the foundation for economic success, but it is also the foundation for liberty and freedom. That view, held as fundamental by America's founders, has been rejected because it is irreconcilable with the modern Robin Hood heresy blessed by the Supreme Court in the 1930s and protected and cultivated by political leaders from both major political parties ever since.

CHAPTER 12

THE ROBBER BARON HERESY - I
THE RISE AND FALL OF FREEDOM OF CONTRACT

"Also riches joined with liberality is Power, because it procureth friends and servants; without liberality not so, because in this case they defend not but expose man to envy as prey."

Thomas Hobbes, *Leviathan*

"There might be times of such great public calamities and distress, and of such extreme scarcity of specie, as should render it the duty of government, for the preservation of even the most valuable part of its citizens, in some measure to interfere in their favor,...to render regulations of this kind necessary...to prevent the wealthy creditor and the monied man from totally destroying the poor though ever industrious debtor."

Luther Martin

"Probably nothing has done so much harm to the liberal cause as the wooden insistence of some liberals on certain rules of thumb, above all the principle of laissez faire."

F. A. Hayek, *Road to Serfdom*

◆ ◆ ◆

The image of Robin Hood in America could not have been resurrected had it not been for the dominant portrayal in American culture for more than 50 years of the Robber Barons. The Robber Barons arrived on the American scene after the Civil War. Just as the blame for the revival of Robin Hood can be placed on the Supreme Court of the 1930s, the blame for the existence of the Robber Barons can be placed on the Supreme Court of the Nineteenth Century.

Changes in Supreme Court precedents usually result from a change in basic principles that can be traced to the abandoning of existing fundamental theories of law and government in favor of a new theory. At the time of America's founding, the underlying theory was Christian, rooted in Catholic teachings on natural law with Reformation principles of individual liberty and equality. Individual enterprise had replaced the aristocratic elitism of the Old World. The gifts of life, liberty and property, which included the ability of each individual to reap the benefits of one's labor and to make contracts, were held sacred.

In the Twentieth Century, modern theories of socialism and collectivism combined with Keynesian economic principles, which require significant government intervention in the regulation of the economy, doomed private property rights in favor of the transcendent needs of the welfare state.

In the Nineteenth Century, the dominant philosophical influence had been utilitarianism, which was later influenced by the scientific philosophy of Darwin. Darwinism soon infiltrated the fields of philosophy, economics, law and government. The conflict between utilitarianism and Darwinism, and the demise of Christian principles, can be found in the manner in which courts have treated the law of contracts.

The fundamental courses of legal instruction in English and American jurisprudence have not changed since medieval lawyers and judges began recording the decisions that resulted from the litigation of disputes between private individuals. American law schools still teach, as their foundational courses of legal instruction, the law of property, contracts and torts. The law of property centers upon the rights of possession and ownership of real and personal property. The law of contracts and the law of torts are similar to each other. The law of contracts governs the conduct and relationship of individuals who enter into agreements consensually. The law of torts focuses upon the conduct and relationship of individuals who interact with each other without consent. An assault and a trespass are both invasions of the rights of an individual by another without the consent of the victim. A breach of contract is a violation of a consensual relationship. Law books still maintain decisions rendered in the Middle Ages adjudicating conflicts arising from these fundamental principles.

All American students, without reference to the law, have been taught as history, lessons learned from the actions of the Nineteenth Century by the

Robber Barons. They are taught that the Robber Barons were restrained and broken by the politics of the Twentieth Century, culminating in the New Deal. They are taught that the unrestrained freedom and liberty to contract results in the inevitable exercise of abusive authority by private enterprise; and that government must intervene to protect the people from "Robber Barons." That lesson is incorrect.

Part of the blame for the demise of the Robber Barons is their own misapplication of Common Law understanding of contracts. In the Nineteenth Century, the courts and the parties to lawsuits forgot the understanding of contract law that led to the intervention of government in contracts, as adjudicators, in the first place. The Courts also forgot the theory of contracts that the early judges relied upon to decide cases—principles based on consent, not liberty. As a result, today, individuals have only a license to contract rather than a liberty to contract. Contractual licenses are issued legislatively under the supervision of the courts.

The Principles of Contracts

To interpret the relationships of consensual undertakings, which is what contracts are, the parties to contracts had to also consent to submit disputes to adjudication. Because of administrative problems of modern court systems, parties to contracts often consent to non-judicial adjudication by arbitrators and mediators. Today's practice resembles the various informal courts common to the Medieval period—courts of the monarchs, manorial estates and churches.

Early judges established rules of interpretation that guided their understanding of not only appropriate remedies, but also whether an agreement was entitled to legal protection. The first recognized form of legal action was a suit based on covenant. A lawsuit brought because of a breach of covenant was used to enforce contracts made under seal. Once a written promise was sealed and delivered, the action of covenant was available to enforce it. It made no difference whether the person who was sued had bargained for or received anything for his promise, or whether the person suing had relied on the promise or had in any way changed his position in reliance on it.

Two functions were performed by the legal formality of the seal. The first was an evidentiary function. A covenant would include trustworthy evidence of the existence and terms of the contract. Secondly, a seal introduced a cautionary, solemn aspect to contracting. A contracts professor explained that a person entering into a covenant would have "the circumspective frame of mind appropriate in one pledging his future."

Early courts also extended their jurisdiction to hear cases based on non-payment of debts. No seal was required to enforce promises to pay a definite sum of money. A "debt" included a promise for money that had been loaned, a promise to pay for goods delivered, or payment for work that had already been done. Courts interpreting the transaction concluded that when an exchange had already been completed by one side, the promisor, or debtor, had something that belonged to the promisee, or creditor. The creditor was permitted to seek the assistance of the court to enforce the transaction.

Later, courts began to recognize a form of contract based on implied obligations and duties arising from typical commercial relationships. This third form of legal case, under contract law, was called "assumpsit." In an action on assumpsit, the promisor sought damages for physical injury to a person or property based on a consensual undertaking. An example of an act for assumpsit might be a ferryman who undertook to carry a person's horse across a river. If the ferryman overloaded the boat and the horse drowned, he would be liable to the owner for the value of the horse. If a carpenter agreed to build a house, he would be liable to the owner if the house was built unskillfully, regardless of whether any specifications or warranties were included in a written contract. If a nonconsensual invasion of person or property was suffered, Common Law recognized a legal action under tort law, and was known as trespass. An assumpsit contained elements of contract law and tort law.

The underlying theme of assumpsit decisions was misfeasance. A promisor, having undertaken to do something, must not do it in a manner inconsistent with the undertaking to the detriment of the promisee. While early decisions did not impose liability for nonfeasance, where the promisor did nothing, by the latter half of the Fifteenth Century the courts made the extension to nonfeasance if the promisee incurred a detriment in reliance on the promise; for example, the owner sold his old house while the carpenter built a new house. By the end of the Sixteenth Century, courts made a second extension, holding that a party who had given a promise in exchange for a promise had incurred a detriment by having his freedom of action limited, as he was bound by his own promise.

THE SCRIPTURAL CONNECTION TO CONTRACT LAW

The contractual forms developed by Common Law judges were infused with a contractual theory consistent with Scripture. Common Law judges relied on the Biblical concept of the vow. Hugo Grotius, the Seventeenth Century Dutch legal philosopher, wrote:

> On this subject we are supplied with noble arguments from the divine oracles which inform us that God, himself, who can be limited by no established rule of law, would act contrary to his own nature if he did not perform his promises. From whence it follows, that the obligation to perform promises, spring from the nature of the unchangeable justice, which is an attribute of God, and common to all who bear his image in the use of reason...It is a most sacred command of nature and guides the whole order of human life, that every man fulfill his contracts.

Emerich de Vattel, the Eighteenth Century Swiss legal philosopher, introduced the connection of the theological basis of contract law, to the language and theory later used by Blackstone and the Declaration of Independence:

> It is shown by the law of nature, that he who has made a promise to anyone, has conferred on him a true right to require the thing promised...there would be no more security, no longer any commerce between mankind, did they not believe themselves obliged to preserve their faith and to keep their word.

That the "natural law" of sanctity of promise was rooted in the belief that "failure to perform a promise made by a free act of the will was an offense against the Deity" is still cited in contract law treatises.

Biblical references to the concept of vow supported the legal philosophers and the decisions of Common Law judges.

> "When thou shalt vow unto the Lord thy God, thou shalt not slack to pay it: For the Lord thy God will surely require it of thee; and it would be sin in thee." Deuteronomy 23:21.
>
> "You should be careful to perform what goes out from your lips, just as you have voluntarily vowed to the Lord your God, what have you promised." Deuteronomy 23:23.
>
> "Better it is that thou should not vow, than that thou should vow and not pay." Ecclesiastes 5:5.

Common Law judges knew the Bible and were guided by its principles. Contract Law was developed during that time period when Scripture provided the foundation for legal judgments. Our common understanding of core contract principles has changed, though basic contract law has not been significantly changed.

THE CONNECTION OF LIBERTY TO CONTRACT LAW

Only Chief Justice John Marshall upheld the link between the law of contracts under Common Law and the Constitution. The Constitution was to be a contract restraining government interference with individual liberty, binding the government to its contract with individual citizens under Common Law principles of contract law. The interpretation of a contract, with the government as a party bound to it, provided the basis for the decision in Fletcher v. Peck. John Marshall's understanding of contract law was that the liberty of contract must be in harmony with the sanctity of the obligation created by the liberty. Marshall's view of contract law formed the basis for his interpretation of constitutional law. The "nonsanctified contract," or a contract which has as its end a purpose contrary to the purposes of God or in violation of the life, liberty or pursuit of happiness of others, was repugnant to Common Law and unenforceable. The liberty of contract was not without limits. This limitation on the unrestrained freedom to contract was ignored, despite Marshall's vigorous dissent, in Ogden v. Saunders (1827).

Rules governing contracts to prevent the enforcement of certain types of contracts were created first by Common Law judges, and later by legislatures. Rules that were designed to protect individuals from unfairness were based both on the status of the contracting party, and on the wrongful behavior of one or both parties. Contracts based on status included contracts with infants, the insane and intoxicated persons. These contracts were void under Common Law and are still void under modern statutes. Contracts with women, which were void under Common Law, are now enforceable. Similarly, attempts to enforce contracts against a nonconsenting spouse are unenforceable by application of the same principle.

In the second case, contracts that involved the wrongful behavior of one party were not enforced. The belief that one party has overreached in the contract process underlies the defenses of fraud, duress, concealment, misrepresentation and mistake. These contracts are voidable upon the proof of circumstances that indicate that one party did not willingly consent to the terms of the agreement. Modern contract law, as set forth in the Uniform Commercial Code and the Restatement (Second) of Contracts, includes an implied covenant of good faith and fair dealing in all commercial agreements. The modern principle of unconscionability assumes the inequality of the consumer in contract negotiations. While these modern expansions of contract rights are useful tools for lawyers who litigate contract disputes, they also erode the significance of a contract as a "vow" while reminding us of the significance of the seal as a cautionary impediment to the formation of bad contracts.

Modern contracts have become mere expressions of intent rather than the making of a vow. Formerly, contracts could be challenged when the voluntariness of consent was questionable. Now, contracts are challenged because the results were unexpected.

ILLEGAL CONTRACTS

Some contracts have always been unenforceable because of their nature and subject matter. Rules declaring certain types of contracts illegal were based upon the desire to protect the public at large. Illegal contracts were both statutory and judicially mandated. Contracts illegal under Common Law included restraints against competition and improper influence on public affairs. Usury statutes, aimed at excessive interest charges, and gambling statutes, which originally included most insurance contracts, date to the earliest criminal statutes and were also illegal under Common Law.

Antitrust laws and guidelines regarding the enforcement of restrictive covenants were rooted in the liberty right to engage in one's profession without interference by contract.

Bribery and corruption laws prevented an unequal benefit by appealing to government assistance for special treatment. These included lobbying activities engaged in with the intent to obtain special favors rather than educating the public official.

The law of private contracts needs to be understood to understand the relationship of the individual to government, because of the "social contract" expression of the relationship of the individual to government in American constitutional law. Coke's application of private legal theory to the king formed the basis of English constitutional law. The Puritans' understanding of private contract law formed the basis of American constitutional law.

Not all private contracts were enforceable. Contracts obtained without the consent of a party were not enforceable. Not all individuals were entitled to enter into contracts. The Nineteenth Century argument that each individual had an absolute right to enter into contracts, and be bound to all of the terms absolutely, as a matter of constitutional law, had no precedent under private contract law.

CONTRACT LAW AND THE CONSTITUTION

The idea that the right to contract, an element of the pursuit of happiness, should be a constitutionally protected inalienable right, lasted about 50 years. The right to contract was really a part of Locke's theory of the right to property. Locke wrote that the interest in property included the right to own, use and possess property. Entering into agreements pertaining to the use of property was a necessary part of the ownership of property, and therefore, an indispensable element in the concept of economic freedom.

Bentham's "expectations" theory of property requiring legal enforcement also applied to contract law. Marshall's holdings in Fletcher v. Peck and Dartmouth College v. Woodward both relied on an analysis of property law and contract law that upheld the inalienability of rights by the individual and the obligation of the government to bind itself to its own contracts.

THE REJECTION OF NATURAL LAW

The strong theological foundations of the Declaration of Independence were never fully accepted by the United States Supreme Court, even in the early days. The colonists resorted to natural law to support their claims of rights as individuals, notwithstanding their status as English citizens bound to English constitutional law. In the Declaration of Independence, natural law superseded constitutional law.

Almost immediately, natural law was rejected in favor of constitutional interpretation in Calder v. Bull (1792). Natural law, despite its acceptance under Common Law as a foundation for private contracts, was rejected as the basis for defining the government's contractual obligations in Ogden v. Saunders. Natural law was not only accepted, but vitally necessary, under both Common Law theory of contracts and the political philosophy of drafters of the Declaration of Independence to justify separation from England. In spite of the necessity and importance of natural law as a fundamental theory of adjudicating private rights and in political philosophy, natural law was never accepted as part of constitutional law by the United States Supreme Court despite the contract nature of constitutional law.

In Ogden, the Supreme Court upheld the right of a state to pass legislation that restricted the ability of parties to contracts to create certain obligations in contracts not yet in existence. The legislation did not affect contracts already made. The Court interpreted Article I, Section 10 of the Constitution, which denied to Congress the power to "pass any bill of attainder, ex post facto law, or law impairing the obligation of contracts," to permit

Congress, or the states, to pass legislation affecting contracts not yet in existence.

Chief Justice John Marshall dissented vigorously in <u>Ogden</u>, arguing that the right to contract was not dependent upon Article 1, Section 10 of the Constitution, but derived from Common Law. Marshall's application of Common Law rules of contract to constitutional law was in accordance with a tradition established by both Bracton and Coke. The Declaration of Independence acknowledged that rights are inherent as well as inalienable. By rejecting natural law, and looking only to the Constitution for the source of rights, the Court in <u>Calder</u> and <u>Ogden</u> separated the Constitution from the Declaration of Independence. Chief Justice Marshall, who first established under American law the principles of the inalienability of property and the inalienability of contracts, was the first to recognize this critical change in philosophy.

<u>Ogden</u> represents two major changes in the perception of the liberty of contract. One, liberty of contract could be restricted by legislation. Two, the secular social contract replaced the sacred social contract. Although the majority decision correctly interpreted the "contracts clause" as preventing the impairment of existing contracts, the dissenting opinion recognized that the language supporting the majority opinion allowed the legislatures to challenge the principles of existing contract law and restrict and limit the terms of entire future contracts. Marshall's attempt to prevent the use of police power to mandate the terms and conditions of prospective contracts was rooted in a theological understanding of contracts as a part of economic liberty. As a result of <u>Ogden</u>, future legislatures were granted a new power to add to the list of prohibited contract terms for whatever reason the legislature could justify. In the future, the Supreme Court would find itself in the middle of a conflict that pitted secular Darwinist liberty of contract against liberated police power.

THE "CONTRACT CLAUSE"

The basic purpose of Article 1, Section 10, which includes what is known as the "Contracts Clause," was to prevent the legislative branch from exercising judicial power. Bills of attainder and ex post facto laws had been employed by monarchs to incarcerate and execute their political opponents. They simply criminalized certain conduct and convicted persons of crimes for acts committed prior to the enactment of the criminal law. Their prohibition by the draftsmen in the Constitution, rather than in the Bill of Rights, signifies their importance.

At that time, exploitation of the money supply was equally important. The Northwest Ordinance of 1787 provided that no legislature could pass any law "that shall; in any manner whatsoever, interfere with or affect private contracts, or engagements, bona fide, and without fraud previously found." The purpose was to prevent Congress from changing the rules, and the economic status of individuals, by the issuance of paper money or other currency, or to affect debtor-creditor relationships to the disadvantage of either party. Contracts are impaired when governments change the money supply. Madison, in "Federalist Number 44," even advocated the prohibition of the printing of money as that would change the terms, by affecting the value, of contracts in existence.

Madison and Marshall believed that legislation that affected the obligation of future contracts was just as unconstitutional as legislation affecting contracts already made. Marshall's interpretation of the Contract Clause was that Congress could outlaw no bargain so long as the bargain was made without fraud and for a lawful purpose, which is consistent with Common Law. Marshall disagreed with the majority in Ogden v. Saunders that asserted that contracts were "the creature of society." Rather, according to Marshall, contract rights and obligations "exist anterior to, and independent of society" and the only purpose of civil government was to provide a remedy for breach of contract.

Marshall's refusal to support the legislation in Ogden v. Saunders was not because it violated the Constitution. Marshall opposed the legislation because it exceeded the jurisdiction of the government to interfere with the liberty of individuals, whose inalienable right to pursue happiness could not be violated if not inconsistent with the inalienable rights of others. The liberty to contract could not be restricted by the police power except in the proper exercise of the adjudication function, already acknowledged and functioning as Common Law, to settle conflicts according to established rules of contract law.

Ogden attempted to settle the issue of whether the Contract Clause could be applied retroactively or prospectively. It opened the door to a long conflict between the individual's freedom to contract, as an individual liberty right to pursue happiness, now made an alienable right, and the exercise of government police power to legislate for the public good. The liberty right and police power were balanced and secularized. After a long conflict, the liberty right disappeared.

POLICE POWER DEFEATS
LIBERTY TO CONTRACT THEORY

The significance of the departure from Marshall's traditional, historical and logically consistent understanding of constitutional contract law can be seen by observing the subsequent struggle to reconcile the conflict between liberty of contract theory and government's police power. The concept of police power had always been resident in the Court's refusal to enforce illegal contracts. A person who entered into a contract to do something immoral or to violate God's law could not use the courts to enforce remedies against the breaching party who, in effect, had decided to do the right thing. Similarly, courts would not enforce contracts where the breaching party entered into the agreement against his own will. Under Common Law, there was no liberty to violate the law. And, there was no liberty for the party who entered into a contract contrary to the other party's will under coercion. Individual liberty, relative to contracts, was viewed the same as individual liberty for all other matters of conduct.

The first change in the legal philosophy regarding contracts occurred in Ogden. Foreshadowing a favorite future technique for the Court, the majority in Ogden analyzed the words of the text of the Constitution without addressing the legal philosophy that was commonly understood at the time the original text was drafted. Marshall's dissent in Ogden clearly articulated the common understanding that the right to contract was an inherent and inalienable right as part of the "pursuit of happiness" that could only be regulated by traditional Common Law principles. In essence, the regulation of contracts was a traditional Common Law function of the courts and not a legislative function. The Contract Clause was an attempt to remove the legislative branch from contract law.

As could be seen in Stone v. Mississippi, when the legislature began to enter into contracts in an administrative capacity on a large scale, the ability of the legislatures to regulate those contracts also increased. But after the Civil War, the legal philosophy regarding contracts and economics would change again as would the basis for the protection of individual rights. Rather than looking to Common Law or the Declaration of Independence, individual rights would now have to be found in the newly enacted Fourteenth Amendment.

The origin of the constitutional discussion of the power to regulate the usage of property can be traced to Mugler v. Kansas (1872). In Mugler, the Supreme Court upheld state laws eliminating the production and distribution of alcoholic beverages as a response to the public safety dangers of alcohol.

211

<u>Mugler</u> more specifically related to the regulation of contracts. <u>Mugler</u> was an aberration in its time. In the era of an almost unrestrained liberty to contract, <u>Mugler</u> stood for the principle that a certain type of contract could be entirely prohibited, in the interest of public safety. In <u>Mugler</u>, a very subtle change in how the Court used the Fourteenth Amendment occurred.

<u>Mugler</u> is not inconsistent with a Christian influence on constitutional law. There was, until recently, no constitutional right to engage in destructive activities. The "right to pursue happiness" meant the right to define and pursue one's own concept of a Christian life. God-given inalienable rights did not include an absolute right to engage in sinful behavior or pursue destructive conduct. Special interest legislation would erode the <u>Mugler</u> rationale. Eventually, the Christian ideal in regulatory legislation would become irrelevant.

In <u>Powell v. Pennsylvania</u> (1888), the <u>Mugler</u> rationale that dangerous industries could be regulated was applied to the oleomargarine industry. Under Common Law, certain contracts were made illegal, over the centuries, rarely and with caution based on tradition and strict moral principles. In <u>Powell</u>, public safety regulations enacted to further public morality, as in <u>Mugler</u>, were subtly transferred into public safety regulations enacted to satisfy special private interests.

Then in <u>Holden v. Hardy</u> (1898), the Supreme Court openly balanced police power with private property rights. All that had been necessary to sustain regulation was that it be related to a valid public purpose. The balancing test later had to be replaced by the rational basis test, because there was no criterion or standard to judge the balance. Ownership and control of private property had become subject to the police power to confiscate and regulate for whatever public purpose the legislature could conjure. Regulations made after careful deliberation regarding moral considerations were first allowed to satisfy public safety concerns but then permitted to favor some companies over their competitors based upon dubious scientific arguments presented by special interests. This expanded list of industries that could be regulated was eventually opened wide to allow legislatures to regulate anything for any reason so long as legislatures purported to have a reason.

In the latter years of the Nineteenth Century, the sociology of Herbert Spencer and the philosophy of Charles Darwin had taken the economics of Adam Smith and modified it to create a new philosophy of freedom of contract. Nineteenth Century industrialists, symbolized and exemplified by the towering figure of John D. Rockefeller, combined a serious and sincere belief in Christianity with a Darwinist philosophy of "the survival of the fittest." Government-granted privileges became God given rights. The Court used the newly enacted Fourteenth Amendment protection of property and liberty as a guarantee of an almost unlimited freedom to contract. Existing Common Law principles regarding restraints of trade, fraud, undue influence and unfair competition were subordinate to the new political philosophies and constitutional philosophy of the Court.

For a time, the Court resisted the attempts of the legislature to both grant privileges and regulate the outcomes of the confusion it had created. The constitutionalization of laissez-faire economics began in <u>Allgeyer v. Louisiana</u>, in which the Supreme Court prevented the application of a Louisiana statute to a New York insurance company that insured property in Louisiana. In <u>Allgeyer</u>, the Court announced a newly defined Darwinist liberty interest in contract. The "right to contract in relation to persons or property or to do business...may be regulated and sometimes prohibited when the contracts or business conflict with the policy of the State as contained in its statutes." Acknowledging that the Court had expanded existing law, relative to constitutional liberty right to contract, the Court went on to say, "but...it is true that these remarks were made in regard to questions of monopoly, but they well describe the rights which are covered by the word 'liberty' as contained in the Fourteenth Amendment." In the words of a noted law professor, the Court had extracted substantive due process from its tie with anti-monopoly and "catapulted into an unchartered domain." <u>Allgeyer</u> had adopted the philosophy of the day.

The case of <u>Lochner v. New York</u> would symbolize the Court's constitutionalization of laissez-faire economics and the criticism of the Lochner Court would lead to a hasty retreat by the Court and a change in philosophy. In <u>Lochner</u>, the Court struck down maximum hours legislation in a case which now symbolizes the error of the Court in what is referred to as substantive due process policy-making by the Court in economic cases. Not unlike today's current conflict in the substantive due process right to privacy cases, the Court was unable to continue balancing the economic due process rights of one class of individuals versus the life, liberty and pursuit of happiness rights of everyone else.

Eventually, the Court would backtrack rapidly. In <u>Nebbia v. New York</u> (1934), the Supreme Court completely reversed direction and announced that due process only requires that legislation be reasonable to legitimate the exercise of police power. Police power equaled general welfare, and judicial power would only be *functus officio*.

In <u>United States v. Carolene Products</u> (1938), the Court continued its retreat from the confrontation with police power begun in <u>Powell v. Penn-</u>

sylvania when it sustained a federal statute that forbade the distribution in interstate commerce of filled milk made in semblance of milk or cream in any form. The Supreme Court had adopted what would be called an analysis of "minimal scrutiny in theory and virtually none in fact."

The retreat continued in Day-Brite Lighting, Inc. v. Missouri (1952), in a case in which the practical application of the statute on an individual made no sense at all. The Supreme Court denied a challenge to a state law that required employers to provide employees four hours of paid leave to vote. An employer refused to pay an employee who lived across the street from a polling place. The Court announced that it would only review legislation to determine if procedural due process rights were violated. The expropriation of private interests were no longer protected by substantive due process. An at-will employment relationship could be regulated even when the legislation made no sense in its actual application.

The eulogy for liberty to contract was provided by Justice Hugo Black in Ferguson v. Skrupa (1963), who declared that, "Whether the legislature takes for its textbook Adam Smith, Herbert Spencer, Lord Keynes, or some other is no concern of ours."

SECULAR INALIENABLE RIGHTS ARE NONEXISTENT

The liberty of contract, as a God-given inalienable right, was abandoned in Ogden v. Saunders. Attempts to create a right to contract under secular theory could not prevail when balanced against police power, defined as the public interest. The liberty of contract, as part of a right to pursue happiness, was no longer of concern to the United States Supreme Court by 1963.

The new secular fundamental law theory was weak and police power was growing. In Stone v. Mississippi, the Court permitted contracts to be altered by police power. In Holden v. Hardy (1898), the Court made the liberty of contract subject to police power.

By the end of the Nineteenth Century, theories of anti-expropriation and liberty of contract were only weak counter measures to the rising police power. Political conflict railed between societal pressures for economic reform and traditional values of individual property rights. The Populist movement, steeped in the values of rugged individualism from the rural West, held firm to the founding fathers' tradition of antimonopoly and individual rights. But the political battle for liberty of contract was fought by those whose views of liberty of contract were Darwinian and hostile to those who were antimonopolists. Populist and traditional principles of free trade had been suppressed in favor of a broader secular principle of freedom of contract.

On the other side were the advocates of increased police power that recognized no inalienable individual rights that were not subordinate to the public good. Advocates of free trade capitulated to proponents of big government in an alliance to oppose big business. They saw benign government regulation as less fearful than actual and destructive economic tyranny. Recognizing the lack of political and theoretical support for the constitutionalization of secular laissez-faire economics, the Court began in 1934 to separate constitutional law from laissez faire economics.

Today, the right to pursue happiness, to the extent that it is recognized as having any economic basis, is an *alienable* right. Economic rights are subject to utilitarian and majoritarian manipulations. The defender of individual liberty, the Supreme Court, has formally abandoned any role in defending individual liberty in economics.

The right to enter into agreements with another, for the purpose of improving life, according to each individual's judgment and choice, was once considered sacred. America's uniqueness is partly based upon each individual's right and duty to establish a relationship with God and work through God's plan for individual happiness and blessings. No individual could interfere with that sacred plan. Beginning in 1837, by either legislative or judicial fiat, personal decisions could be replaced by group choices. Individuals who can ally themselves with others and muster majority rule have combined to regulate any and all conduct, for almost any purpose, with the Supreme Court's consent.

That power to regulate eventually was tendered to individuals, or small groups. The Federal Reserve Board is the best example, by the extension of the rationale that led to the demise of the liberty of contract. The Fourteenth Amendment, viewed as a sword wielded on behalf of the people by the government, could interfere with any private contract. The Fourteenth Amendment, as a shield in the hands of private individuals, was taken away by the courts. Christian individual freedom, when mixed with Darwinism was untenable when offered as a theory by the industrialists. Christianity, when infused with principles of socialism advanced by people in general, was a useful tool to move the focus from the individual rights theory of the Declaration of Independence to a community rights theory adaptable to the new utilitarian constitutional model.

Robber Baron economics first led to the subordination of individual rights to majority rule. The Robber Barons in the Twentieth Century would counterattack, leading to an even greater heresy: the subordination of individual rights to a managed economy.

CHAPTER 13

THE ROBBER BARON HERESY - II
PRIVATE MONOPOLY AND ECONOMICS

"There is absolutely nothing to be said for government by a plutocracy, for government by men very powerful in certain lives and gifted with 'the money touch,' but with ideals which in their essence are merely those of so many glorified pawnbrokers."

President Theodore Roosevelt (1913)

"Although competition and justice may have little else in common, it is as much a commendation of competition as of justice that it is no respecter of persons."

F. A. Hayek, *Road to Serfdom* (1944)

"The great danger to the consumer is monopoly—whether private or governmental. His most effective protection is free competition at home and free trade throughout the world. The consumer is protected from being exploited by one seller by the existence of another seller from whom he can buy and who is eager to sell to him. Alternative sources of supply protect the consumer far more effectively than all the Ralph Naders of the world."

Milton Friedman,
Free to Choose (1979)

◆ ◆ ◆

Like the corrupt beneficiaries of the patronage of King John and the Sheriff of Nottingham, the Robber Barons arose as a new, privileged class during the period known as Reconstruction. Despite the enactment of the Fourteenth Amendment and the Civil Rights Act of 1871, which promised equality to all individuals, patronage became a common practice during the Post Civil War era, and did so without interference from the Supreme Court.

America's antimonopoly heritage, rooted in opposition to the king's prerogative and the antiquated feudalist land system, was behind the right to contest government-granted monopolies. That right was swept away by the Supreme Court in The Slaughter-House Cases, ruling that the privileges and immunities and equal protection of the law did not extend to the opposition to government granted monopolies.

By the turn of the century, Tom Johnson, the mayor of Cleveland, Ohio, who became wealthy as the owner of Cleveland's exclusive streetcar franchise, remarked, "no monopoly could exist, or continue to exist, without the assistance of the government."

Government-approved monopoly took two forms: direct grants and exclusive privileges for private individuals without interference by the courts, and by the court's reluctance to stop anticompetitive practices that were prohibited under Common Law.

The prohibition of private restraints on competition existed under Common Law and were routinely administered by the courts when adjudicating noncompetition clauses in contract disputes. These principles were used to attack the growth of monopolies in the Nineteenth Century. As a result, private antimonopoly principles are related, sometimes erroneously, to the late Nineteenth Century constitutional principles of liberty of contract. The issues are different and in conflict.

Constitutional liberty of contract issues from the Nineteenth Century pertain to the relationship of government interference with private contracts. Antimonopoly, or antitrust issues also pertain to interference with private contracts and free trade, but the interference and restrictions are imposed and maintained by private individuals or corporations, not governments. These restrictions are found in covenants not to compete between companies and key employees and are also seen in agreements to boycott competitors.

The basic principles of free trade, sometimes defined as the individual right to pursue the common callings, have survived through the rise and fall of liberty of contract as a constitutional issue. The continuance of antitrust laws, as a separate theory, is almost entirely due to the enactment of the Sherman Act in 1890. The freedom of an individual to pursue his own employment or trade, as an aspect of a pursuit of happiness, is, like the freedom to contract, rooted in Common Law and deep in English and American legal tradition. From the time of the Constitutional Convention until 1890, antimonopoly principles were analyzed with a view of liberty attributable to either a fundamental Common Law right or a Fourteenth Amendment substantive due process right.

ANTITRUST LAW 101

Antimonopoly, as a Common Law and substantive due process right, has two major thrusts. The first has always been the opposition to public monopoly, based on the principle of equality. The Puritans' understanding of equality led to opposition to the exercise of royal prerogative in England and in America. The second thrust opposed private monopoly and developed in court decisions predating opposition to the Stuart kings. Both aspects of antimonopoly were incorporated into the Sherman Act.

The antitrust laws, meanwhile, as interpreted by the Supreme Court subsequent to the enactment of the Sherman Act in 1890, contain three main protections. One, an individual cannot be denied the ability to compete by private agreements that restrict the right to engage in one's chosen profession. This line of cases restricts the suppression of competition in employment contracts. Two, contracts or conspiracies cannot be directed against the right of another person to engage in competition. These cases focus on the suppression of competition by competitors. Third, the concentration of power in the hands of one or more individuals or entities cannot be used to foreclose a market from competition. These cases focus on the evidence of market power by monopolists or oligopolists.

ANTITRUST LAW PRIOR TO THE SHERMAN ACT

The evil opposed by antimonopolists is the suppression of competition and free trade by government or private individuals. Early opposition to monopoly focused on, but was not limited to the grant of public monopolies by the king. This early opposition is evident in the first codification of law in America, published by the Massachusetts colony in 1641. This statute provided, "no monopolies shall be granted or allowed,..." even in the absence of a statute. In an 1836 Connecticut case, Norwich Gaslight Co. v. Norwich City Gas Co., the Court based its decision on antitrust law on Common Law stating that private restraints had always been repugnant.

The Common Law on monopolies had deep roots. In the Schoolmaster Case of 1410, two masters of a grammar school attempted to exclude a competitor by judicial process. The court denied relief. In Dyer's Case of 1415, individuals trained in the act of dyeing were required to be guaranteed by bond, that the trainee would not compete in the same territory for 1½ years. The Court voided the trainee's obligation. Eleven cases of the same type were decided between 1415 and 1685. Common Law principles and early political opposition to restraints on competition and the exercise of monopoly power were based on the protection of individual rights.

Today, the discussion and concern in antitrust law is based upon economic theory. This conflict and relationship between antitrust laws and economics was foreshadowed by the changes in the law regarding forestalling. Forestalling laws prohibited attempts to corner the market in foodstuffs to raise prices; England outlawed it in 1266. Most forestalling laws were repealed during the reign of George III, largely due to Adam Smith, who argued that the middleman played a constructive role in the expansion of the English economy; forestalling laws were antiquated.

Forestalling laws were regulations of private conduct based upon assumptions about economic theory. Adam Smith challenged the prevailing economic theory and the laws were changed. Considerations of economic theory were paramount. From the standpoint of the middleman, individual rights were protected, but individual rights were not the consideration. In England, utilitarian theory, applied into law by economists, was on the rise.

CORPORATIONS FOR ANY PURPOSE WITHOUT RESTRICTIONS

At the same time, but unrelated to pure economic theory, another major change in commercial practices was developing. Since the early 1600s, entrepreneurial activity had developed rapidly in England. A separate commercial middle class had developed by the time of America's separation from England. But a vestige of the royal prerogative remained in the form of government granted charters and franchises, for the purpose of financing large private ventures.

Government granted charters are the older versions of the modern corporation. Prior to the 1800s, corporate charters were limited in number and purpose in England and unpopular in America. However, early legislatures in America continued to grant corporate charters for the development of roads, canals and institutions of learning.

The changing view about corporations occurred in three separate steps. First, American ideas of equality and inalienable rights were ignored upon the issuance of new charters, because all persons had an equal right to incorporate. Accordingly, the number and authority of new corporations increased rapidly. The <u>Dartmouth College</u> case, legally significant because of Chief Justice Marshall's interpretation that the government must be bound to the terms of its own contracts, also clearly established the precedent that the corporation had a legal status, separate from the state that had granted the charter, that could not be revoked or arbitrarily conditioned. As a result, the number of corporations increased and the restrictions on the corporation's purpose and scope of activities was virtually unlimited.

In the second step, the central holding of <u>Dartmouth College</u>, that the state could not restrict the activities of a corporation once the charter was issued, would be distinguished in <u>Stone v. Mississippi</u>, then later forgotten. But the effect of the <u>Dartmouth College</u> decision, that corporate charters could be routinely issued for any purpose, opened the gates to legislative patronage and creative financing during the Reconstruction era. The scope and purpose of corporate charters broadened. The government interest in development also broadened. All business expansion became a government purpose. Political theory gave way to economic pragmatism as the post Civil War industrialization of America began.

Essential to the accumulation of capital sufficient to industrialize was the corporate form of organization, and the grant of privileges to the corporation in the form of land grants and exclusive franchises. Pragmatism triumphed.

The Robber Barons had the power and a dubious Darwinian liberty theory that reigned until the next century. The popular fear and hatred of monopoly, though, was not lost by the people. The populist movement began in the American Midwest. At the turn of the Twentieth Century, the political battle that pitted the rich elite against the populist poor and middle class overwhelmed all other issues.

Despite populist political victories, however, the third step in the development of the corporation presented new problems. When the Supreme Court held that corporations were entitled to all of the protections of the Constitution as a person under the Fourteenth Amendment, a new entity with a new constitutionally protected legal status had been created. Neither the people nor sympathetic legislators knew how to oppose the new entity, essentially a constitutionally protected "person" that could be comprised of and owned by any number of people and other businesses. Without the resources and power to negotiate or compete with the monopolists, who had obtained negotiating strength by eliminating competitors with the government's protection, the Robber Barons' opponents were forced to fight with neither power nor any clearly identified principle or theory. The Robber Barons' privilege and status, once achieved, could be maintained by bribery, kickbacks, incentives for those who cooperated and exclusion for those who did not.

THE FEDERAL ANTITRUST LAW

Just as the Nineteenth Century Robber Barons had confused Christianity with Darwinism and equated the Fourteenth Amendment with the right to contract, the Nineteenth Century industrialists also equated unlimited free enterprise with competition. This new philosophy regarding antitrust law ignored Common Law restrictions against unfair competition and unlawful restraints of trade that had governed contractual business relationships for almost 500 years. One side to the debate glossed over the fact that the development of the industrialist's wealth had occurred because of the cooperation of the legislatures in the first place.

Because of popular political pressure, several states passed antimonopoly legislation. Some states prohibited anticompetitive behavior; others prohibited monopolies; still others legislated specifically at the corporate form. But neither the people nor the legislature could convincingly address the problem presented by the increased number of corporate entities. Politics addressed only the symptoms, because the corporation had become a legal creature far changed from its original purpose. The cause of this new class of powerful elite, the creation of new legal entities that allowed persons to combine together as a single person, had evolved from entities created for a single purpose for a limited time, to a means to concentrate both power and wealth.

Ultimately, some of the new corporate giants became so large in scope that they were unaffected by the laws of a single state. Western Populists clamored for a federal law that would neutralize monopolists who engaged in business that crossed state lines. Congress responded by passing the Sherman Act of 1890. The Supreme Court has called the Sherman Act "the Magna Charta of Economic Freedom," as it established "overarching and fundamental policies" pertaining to the duties and rights toward each other among corporations and traders in a free economic system. The substantive portion of the Sherman Act is:

> § 1: Every contract, combination in the form of trust or otherwise, or conspiracy, in restraint of trade or commerce among the several States, or with foreign nations, is declared to be illegal...
>
> § 2: Every person who shall monopolize, or attempt to monopolize, or combine or conspire with any other person or persons, to monopolize any part of the trade or commerce among

the several States, or with foreign nations, shall be deemed guilty
of a misdemeanor.

Immediately after its enactment, corporate giants challenged the Sherman Act as unconstitutional. But in <u>United States v. Joint Traffic Association</u> (1898), the Supreme Court upheld the Sherman Act as a lawful exercise of the Commerce Clause, as within Congress' legitimate power to regulate interstate commerce. The Court narrowed the text of the Sherman Act and interpreted Congressional intent to uphold contract restrictions ancillary to business operations with non-ancillary restrictions designed to scuttle competition. The Court interpreted the Sherman Act as nothing more than the application of Common Law to interstate commerce.

In <u>Mitchel v. Reynolds,</u> a 1711 English case, Judge Macclefield divided contracts into two categories. The first was contracts in restraint of trade, ancillary to a lease, sale or employment agreement. If reasonable, such clauses were consistent with legitimate economic and social objectives. In the second category were contracts of overbreadth, that included non-ancillary restraint designed to fix prices, restrict production or apportion territory. These clauses were declared to be contracts in restraint of competition, and void. Private restraints were not voidable by authority of Magna Charta, but by the authority of the courts exercising their function under Common Law to refuse to enforce illegal contracts. The Supreme Court made the same distinction in <u>Joint Traffic Association</u> and found that Congress also has "the power to say that no contract or combination shall be legal which shall restrain trade in interstate commerce by shutting out the operation of the general law of competition."

The power to protect competitors was, in 1890, an economic and legal principle, based in the tradition of the English and American Common Law view of contracts and the Biblical view of equality. The English and American tradition rejected preferences and encouraged the diffusion of concentrated, economic power to prevent economic tyranny. But the principle of free trade, advocated to allow each individual an equal opportunity to compete in the common callings, would be attacked by larger competitors by a number of different theories and practices.

At the core of the new theories is the acceptance of utilitarian philosophy, that primary concern is focused upon what is the best result for the most people. This philosophy is in contrast with a Biblically-based rights theory, that protects the basic rights of each person. The new economic theory that emphasizes production, efficiency and consumer welfare was in conflict with a legal theory that focused on wrongful conduct, motive and damage to competitors. The significance of this modern position is that monopolists can now attempt to demonstrate that, despite monopolistic activity or conduct, public policy is served by such activity if it can be shown to be pro-competitive under the "rule of reason." The economic consideration of the effect on competition is now more important than the effect on an individual competitor.

Common Law focused on conduct rather than economic theory. Conduct and motive to exclude competitors, which violates another individual's economic liberty, can be understood by making an analogy with Locke's argument against permitting a conqueror in an unjust war to claim title to the conquered property:

> That the Aggressor, who puts himself into the state of War with another, and unjustly invades another Man's right, can, by such an unjust War, never come to have a right over the Conquered, will be easily argued by all Men, who will not think, that Robbers and Pyrates have a Right of Empire over whomsoever they have Force enough to master; or that Men are bound by promises, which unlawful Force extorts from them. Should a Robber break into my House, and with a Dagger at my Throat, make me seal Deed to convey my Estate to him, would this give him any Title? Just such a Title by his Sword, has an unjust Conquerour, who forces me into submission. The injury and the Crime is equal, whether committed by the wearer of a Crown, or some petty villain. The Title of the Offender, and the Number of his Followers make no difference in the Offense, unless it be to aggravate it. The only difference is, Great Robbers punish little ones, to keep them in their Obedience, but the great ones are rewarded with Laurels and Triumphs, because they are too big for the weak hands of Justice in this World, and have the power in their own possession, which should punish offenders. What is my Remedy against a Robber, that so broke into my House? Appeal to the Law for Justice.

Much of the criticism of the Nineteenth Century Robber Barons was directed at the practice of buying and then absorbing competitors into the large corporate structures owned by monopolists. A voluntary surrender of rights in exchange for benefits under principles of contract law is one thing, but an involuntary or coerced surrender of rights in exchange for benefits dictated by the aggressor violates basic principles of economic liberty.

Adam Smith is often misidentified as an advocate of a form of laissez faire economics in opposition to principles of antitrust law. But Adam Smith's warnings regarding inhibitions to competition support neither laissez faire economics nor the proposition that individual conduct always works toward the public good, as if guided by an "invisible hand." Smith's observations about merchants' behavior and motivation also includes a prophetic warning about lobbying activities and special interest legislation:

> The interest of the dealers, however, in any particular branch of trade or manufacture, is always in some respects different from, and even opposite to, that of the public. To widen the market and to narrow the competition, is always the interest of the dealers. To widen the market may frequently be agreeable enough to the interest of the public; but to narrow the competition must always be against it, and can serve only to enable the dealers, by raising their profits above what they naturally would be, to levy, for their own benefit, an absurd tax upon the rest of their fellow-citizens. The proposal of any new law or regulation of commerce which comes from this order, ought always to be listened to with great precaution, and ought never to be adopted till after having been long and carefully examined, not only with the most scrupulous, but with the most suspicious attention. It comes from an order of men, whose interest is never exactly the same with that of the public, who have generally an interest to deceive and even to oppress the public, and who accordingly have, upon many occasions, both deceived and oppressed it.

From Locke and Smith is a recognition that some individuals will attempt to restrain competition by eliminating competitors, and such conduct is both bad economics and bad law.

The view that the economy should be managed by the legislative branch pursuant to police power, and the judicial branch by emphasizing judicial economic policy making under the "rule of reason," focuses both branches on consumer protection. Consumer protection laws tend to be utilitarian in principle, distorting the traditional emphasis on competition, that protects individual rights. This modern change has obscured the first and primary objective of the Sherman Act. The inalienable right to liberty and the pursuit of happiness includes economic freedom for all persons, which means that industries cannot be foreclosed by either government or private action, regardless of the economic theory currently in fashion.

MUNN V. ILLINOIS - REGULATING COMPETITION

The loss of individual freedom to compete can be traced to and explained by reference to three unrelated United States Supreme Court decisions: Munn v. Illinois (1873), Standard Oil v. New Jersey (1913), and

Wickard v. Filburn (1941).

The first case, Munn, was brought by a group of grain elevator operators in Chicago who attacked price fixing legislation passed by the state of
Illinois. In that case, the Supreme Court held that in the event a "virtual
monopoly" existed affecting the source of goods in an industry of vital
importance to the public, the Fourteenth Amendment permitted the exercise
of the government's police power in support of the right to be free of monopoly. Furthermore, the Fourteenth Amendment could not be used to prevent
the regulation of a monopolist's private contract rights by the government.
In many respects, the decision was significant. Metaphorically, Munn was
an exception at that time to the use of the Fourteenth Amendment as a shield
against government power. The grain elevator operators were denied the use
of the shield. On the contrary, the case was the first to use the Fourteenth
Amendment as a sword in a positive attack on the problem of monopoly, but
the sword was wielded by the government and not individuals. The Fourteenth Amendment, enacted as a shield against government power, was
interpreted to uphold government power.

The newly discovered right to regulate industries that tended toward
monopoly because of high fixed startup costs—such industries as railroads,
or oil, where natural resources were limited and costly to extract—led to the
creation of a new bureaucracy. Congress established the Interstate Commerce Commission in 1889; other regulatory statutes and agencies followed.
In a short period of time after this, the Supreme Court would uphold industry regulation even in the absence of a "virtual monopoly" in Brass v. North
Dakota ex rel Stoeser (1894). All pretext at regulating in the interest of antimonopoly was replaced by management of industry on economic theory.

Eventually, Justice Brandeis would introduce a new economic theory by
using the term "destructive competition" in his dissent in New State Ice
(1932). The right of the legislature to regulate would be absolute and unre-
stricted after Nebbia and the legislature could experiment with new and
untested economic theories.

Brandeis' concept of "destructive competition" coincided with the popularity of Lord Maynard Keynes, the famous British economist. Keynes
believed that governments needed to manipulate their economies by fiscal
policy, by using the taxing and spending powers of the legislative branch.
Such Keynesian theories were essential to New Deal proposals. Classical
economics and its advocacy of competition and openness to entry of markets
were replaced by centralized planning. Industry and the supply of money
were not only regulated but openly manipulated. Except for the occasional
and limited enforcement of the Sherman Act, free trade was as misunder-

stood in theory, and consequently ignored, as freedom of contract theory.

STANDARD OIL V. NEW JERSEY
JUDICIAL ECONOMIC POLICY MAKING

The second case leading to the erosion of the law of free competition was Standard Oil of New Jersey, which introduced the concept of the "rule of reason." The principle arose from the Supreme Court's finding that the Sherman Act only prevented "unreasonable" restraints of trade. But rather than focusing on improper conduct and Judge Macclefield's analysis of reasonable versus unreasonable contracts, the Court substituted economic principle for Common Law contract principles, and reviewed the reasonableness of the contract's effect on competition rather than the reasonableness of the contract clause itself.

Free trade, as prohibited by antitrust laws, has survived in practice but has been eroded, modified and limited in enforcement by the substitution of modern economic theory in place of the freedom to pursue the common callings as part of the liberty to contract. Because the Constitution no longer provided protection for individuals to compete, the source of the individual's right to compete now rested in the private enforcement provisions of the Clayton Act of 1914, supplemental to the Sherman Act of 1890. The Sherman Act was originally upheld as constitutional under the power of Congress to regulate interstate commerce in United States v. Joint Traffic Association (1898), where the Supreme Court stated that Congress had the authority to apply the "law of competition" from Common Law to interstate commerce. Common Law principles prohibited conduct that prevented competition by protecting the competitor. The Clayton Act allowed competition to be enforced by competitors, which was a remedy nonexistent at the time of Munn. Competitors should have been given the remedy under the Fourteenth Amendment, but that right was not recognized in The Slaughter-House Cases. That right and remedy had to be provided by the Clayton Act.

Economic principles were required to be considered after Standard Oil of New Jersey. Some legal commentators have since suggested that the conduct sought to be restricted by the Sherman Act is now irrelevant under modern economic principles. The prevalent theory of many modern legal scholars limits the role of antitrust laws to the promotion of economic efficiency. Even when the individual is harmed by anticompetitive practices, an economic theory can be presented as evidence that the long-term economic effect is minimal. Justice Brandeis' "destructive competition," based on anecdotal evidence rather than pure theory, became a new tool to protect the

Robber Barons from legal challenges brought by smaller competitors. To the economists, the individual has no inalienable rights. Rather, the individual should simply reallocate his resources elsewhere.

The consideration of economic principles rather than the legal rights of competitors substitutes utilitarian principles for the Biblically-based right to pursue economic happiness set forth in the Declaration.

Competition, in economic theory, is important for its effect on the overall performance of the economy. It tends to minimize production costs and move resources out of declining markets into markets where there is a greater need for production. This is described in economics as productive efficiency.

Competition is favored and monopoly disfavored, in theory, because as long as prices cannot be controlled, production will be increased until increased production meets the demand. Price competition will cause the price to decline, or costs to decrease for companies that are more efficient. The inefficient companies will then leave the market as consumer prices decline. In most industrialized economies, these market forces guide economic activity, stimulate innovation, minimize resource waste, and satisfy consumer desires. This is the stated goal of economics. But pure competition is unwieldy, confusing and unmanageable. The desire of the government to control economics absorbs the prior contradictory assumption that monopolists should not also control the market.

The need by government and large corporations to prove the benefits of monopoly and market control has led economists to provide evidentiary, anecdotal theories to support control. The absolute understanding that control is anticompetitive is no longer accepted and disregarded as unimportant. In the mid-1900s, the courts moved from the practical intuition, from which Justice White inferred monopoly power in <u>Standard Oil</u> to an analysis of "theoretical mechanics" under economic principles. Market power had been defined as the power to control prices or exclude competition. Some economists believed that if the economic model was not definite enough to support a clear theory, as the Chicago School of Economists viewed oligopolistic markets, then no inferences of market power, collusion, or conspiracy could be inferred.

In <u>Eastman Kodak v. Image Technical Services</u> (1992), the majority and dissent debated the role of the effect of economic theory in a situation when the facts were clear that the monopolists' anticompetitive conduct had adversely affected a competitor's ability to compete. Judicial policy making employing the "rule of reason," accepted managing markets rather than protecting private rights, thus permitting the monopolists and oligopolists to restrict and/or obscure the evidence of anticompetitive activity by presenting counter evidence that "managed competition" can be preferable to free trade. The hypothetical example of a competitor who was not foreclosed from competition supported a theory used to argue that a competitor who was stopped from competing, as a factual truth, be denied relief under the Sherman Act, because, theoretically, the corporation could compete. The majority simply pointed out that the theory was interesting, but that the evidence was clear that the competitor was shut out of the market. To some judges and economists, theory is more important than fact, and economics supersedes individual rights.

WICKARD V. FILBURN
LEGISLATIVE ECONOMIC POLICY MAKING

The third significant case representing the loss of individual freedom to compete in favor of "managed competition" is Wickard v. Filburn (1941). Wickard represents the culmination of the extension of the two theories. One, the government may regulate all economic activity in the name of managed competition. Two, individual economic freedom is irrelevant.

Wickard was preceded by two cases, National Labor Relations Board v. Jones & Laughlin Steel Corporation (1937) and United States v. Darby (1936), which expansively interpreted the Commerce Clause to link federal regulatory power with the "general welfare" language in the preamble to the Constitution.

Wickard involved the case of an individual who grew wheat on his own land for personal consumption and to feed his livestock. The individual was charged with violating a federal law restricting the amount of wheat that could be grown pursuant to a federal program intended to manage the national supply of wheat. The Supreme Court found that the individual's minimal harvest would have an effect on commerce if all individuals acted similarly in the aggregate, and, therefore, prosecution was permissible under the Commerce Clause. Clearly, no individual conduct was so minor as to be beyond the scope of federal regulation.

In U.S. v. Lopez (1995), Justice Thomas challenged the other members of the Court to find any limitation of federal police power under Wickard's definition of commerce. No Justice answered his challenge. But Lopez only limited the definition of commerce as a grant of federal power. Within the scope of commerce, all activities can still be regulated.

The power to regulate commerce, as a part of the promotion of the general welfare, had led to the Court's sanctioning of federal police power over economics. Chief Justice Marshall used the commerce power to strike state legislation granting a monopoly in the shipping industry. <u>Wickard</u> used the Commerce Clause to regulate an individual's conduct in agriculture. Not only had the traditional distinction between commerce, agriculture, and manufacturing been lost, broadening the scope of the Commerce Clause, as Justice Thomas pointed out in <u>Lopez</u>, but individual rights had been sacrificed in favor of the imposition of utilitarian policies based on assumptions of aggregate behavior as analyzed by economists.

MANAGING "DESTRUCTIVE COMPETITION"

<u>Munn</u> granted state legislatures the power to regulate. <u>Standard Oil</u> led to the Supreme Court's role as economic policy makers rather than the adjudicators of private rights. <u>Wickard</u> sanctioned the centralization of economic policy making in the federal government. In <u>New State Ice</u>, Justice Brandeis adopted the philosophy of socialism and the economics of intervention of Lord Maynard Keynes by introducing the idea of "destructive competition" into the law of antimonopoly.

Antitrust had evolved from a private right to compete into a political issue for legislative consideration, focusing on the benefits to the consumer rather than the benefits of free trade. Since <u>Nebbia v. New York</u> (1934), the Court has deferred to the legislature's blanket authority to experiment, in the name of the public good, with untested and unproven economic theory, abandoning its judicial duty to protect the economic liberty rights of individuals. The result of the long run application of short run economics is our present circumstance. We currently operate under a utilitarian, socialistic economic system which acknowledges, but seldom enforces or protects, the legal rights of the individual when related to economic liberty.

The Robber Barons lost their battle in the Supreme Court for a Darwinist definition of liberty of contract under constitutional law, but they made a comeback in the legislature. When economic freedom was lost by the loss of liberty of contract as an inalienable right, the Supreme Court also abandoned any responsibility to stop economic privilege. To the extent that the Robber Barons can achieve any economic advantage legislatively or bureaucratically, the Supreme Court is not interested and the economists are silent.

Pragmatism is, by definition, not theoretical. The long term effects of America's shift to pragmatism from a principled individual rights political theory is evident everywhere. Pragmatism alone tends to create more problems than it solves. Pragmatism also tends to corruption and the pursuit of power over principle. Although the people still despise the new Robber

Barons, their animosity is based more on envy than principle.

Ethics have no place in a utilitarian economy. All that matters is to achieve enough significance to have an effect on the aggregate; the privilege that attaches to that significance will be enhanced and protected by the Court.

Pragmatism, as a philosophy, is distinctively American. Pragmatism favored individual rights in the Nineteenth Century, helping to create Robber Barons whose influence grew more powerful.

Pragmatism favored utilitarianism and managed competition in the Twentieth Century and the Robber Barons became partners with the government.

In this new government by Leviathan, individual rights are no longer important and the old concept of privilege, as antithetical to Biblical equality, is considered archaic by the elitists who manage the government and the government-run economy.

CHAPTER 14
LEVITICUS OR LEVIATHAN

"We have no government armed with power capable of contending with passions unbridled by morality and religion. Avarice, ambition, revenge, or gallantry, would break the strongest cords of our Constitution as a whale goes through a net. Our Constitution was made only for a moral and religious people. It is wholly inadequate for the government of any other."

President John Adams

"There are no great men without virtue; and there are no great nations, it may almost be added, there would be no society, - without respect for rights, for what is a union of rational and intelligent beings who are held together only by the bond of force?"

Alexis De Tocqueville (1835)

"The principle that the end justifies the means in individualist ethics is regarded as the denial of all morals. In collectivist ethics it becomes necessarily the supreme rule; there is literally nothing which the consistent collectivist must not be prepared to do if it serves 'the good of the whole,' because the 'good of the whole' is to him the only criterion of what ought to be done."

F. A. Hayek, *Road to Serfdom*

In 1995, I attended the Twenty-Fifth Annual International Bar Association Section of Business Law conference in Paris, France. The theme of the conference was "The Rule of Law."

I attended numerous sessions where prominent business lawyers from different countries were trying to figure out what the "Rule of Law" should be and where to find its roots; there was no question that this group meant to be part of the deciding group.

A couple of months later, I spoke at a completely different type of con-

ference at Catholic University in Lublin, Poland. This conference involved East and Central Europeans, not just westerners, and I was the only lawyer and one of two resident Americans. The participants were primarily academicians, politicians and clergymen. It was my first trip behind the Iron Curtain. This made me acutely aware of my rights as an American, rights which all Americans subconsciously take for granted. Yet, as a former criminal defense lawyer, I knew that those rights really meant nothing in Poland. My liberty and welfare depended solely on the grace of the Polish people and their government. This was my first practical experience with the inherent conflict between a person's natural inalienable rights versus the concept of fundamental, constitutional rights.

When I returned to America, I finished my lecture series at my church, where I had started using the term and teaching the concept that we needed to make a choice between Leviticus or Leviathan. Our choice is not just personal, but also practical and political. My preference is God-given liberty and the clarity that results from the Biblically based Reign and Rule of Law to the "Rule of Law" that originates in lawyer discussion groups.

A snapshot of modern American politics clearly shows that it centers entirely upon the promotion of economics while declaring religion to be only a private, personal matter. So, it is no coincidence that in just more than 50 years of the Supreme Court's 1947 reinterpretation of the separation of church and state, the most important issues in American politics and culture center on the question of ethics.

Political leaders regularly and with impunity commit ethical violations. Yet, when confronted with accusations of ethics violations, they respond by alleging that their ethical violations are not legal violations, i.e. "against the law."

Adding further confusion to the bewildered American voter is the contention that the problem in politics is not ethical transgressions that violate the law, but ethical conduct that is not illegal. And what is needed, so goes the popular perception, are more and different laws, and less enforcement of current law. This argument is not surprising when it is understood that in a secular culture, ethics apart from the law has no meaning.

In modern America, ethics, like religion, is subjective and relative. Therefore, ethics, as objective theory, is meaningless. Ethics is not a standard wielded by leaders but a weapon used against those who would contest the leaders' power.

To have meaning, ethics as a theory needs an objective standard. So what is ethics and what is the relationship between ethics and personal virtue; and ethics and the rule of law?

THE RELATIONSHIP OF ETHICS AND VIRTUE

In the American political environment, which generally reflects society at large, there appears to be no ethics. The only ethical standard appears to be to do whatever it takes to win. From both a theoretical and practical standpoint, the need for personal virtue becomes clear. If everyone misbehaved, we would have a societal meltdown. Perhaps the most difficult question faced today, both individually and collectively, is the role virtue should play in law and politics. Some virtue is needed. What virtue can be required? And should virtue always be required or should we only demand it from our political opponents?

Americans are familiar with the vague platitude that each person has rights because the nation was founded on principles of liberty and freedom, but they are not as familiar with the relationship of "rights" to individual responsibility. Because ethics, as a distinct subject matter, generally refers to what we "ought" to do rather than to what we are legally required to do, modern discourse about ethics usually degenerates into platitudes or psychobabble based on a wistful vision of unachievable goals. In truth, ethics, as a moral consensus decided by the majority, is meaningless unless enacted into law. Laws based on ungrounded ethics provide no moral compass and have no legitimacy.

Ethics, as a moral imperative practiced by individual Christians, is desperately needed but deemed unconstitutional when suggested as a collective imperative under modern constitutional law. The irony of modern America is that now that the practice of Christian virtue has been deemed to be personal and voluntary, more laws are needed to define and induce virtuous behavior from the secular masses. Yet, the practical result of a proliferation of ethical laws is not virtuous behavior; because of the volume and complexity of ethics laws, the emphasis is on either technical compliance or artful evasion. Virtue is defined as obedience to the law rather than ethical conduct. Because prosecutors are not as much concerned with virtue or morality as with political advantage, the practical result of enacting new ethics laws is the punishment of negligent behavior, not the establishment of a more virtuous culture.

Anyone who witnesses the obvious ethical failures of modern leaders might conclude that the founding fathers failed to consider the consequences of self-government by not dealing realistically with the issue of personal responsibility. Whether in politics, academia, or Christian circles, all leaders seem incapable of forming a substantive ethical position attractive to others. But the founding fathers understood the basis of self-government better than we do. From the historical record, it is clear that they understood Christian theology, classical philosophy and Common Law.

The founding fathers knew that understanding theology and law were prerequisite to leadership, but they saw it also as essential to self-government. And they believed that these principles must be commonly understood by the governed. They seemed to be unanimous in agreement that the Christian religion was a necessary prerequisite to a government based on liberty and equality for all people.

In Daniel Webster's statement, "to be a Christian is to be responsible for the nation, because this is a divine experiment in self-government," he offers more than a platitude or a goal as to the role of ethics in self-government. He expressed an understanding that America's radical new form of politics was not only completely different but also entirely Christian. Christianity in belief and in practice were both essential to the success of self-government.

CHRISTIANITY AS GOVERNMENT'S ETHICAL FOUNDATION

Self-government is failing in America today because the ethical foundation upon which the government was established is deteriorating. To a large extent, inertia and tradition can sustain an institution that has forgotten its purpose and vision, so the illusion of liberty still persists.

Our American purpose and vision has been forgotten because it was changed gradually. The purpose and vision of a nation must be defined in revolutionary times, as witnessed in our American Revolution and in the modern fall of Communism, both to gain support for the revolution, and to establish the new government and its institutions after the revolution. That purpose and vision can be forgotten over time in the absence of a crisis that forces people to think seriously about first principles.

America's revolution was so long ago that we forgot that her radical new form of politics was not only completely different from Old World governments, but also was entirely Christian. Yet, the problems of governing then were the same then as they are now. America's founding fathers faced issues and decisions from the same perspective of leaders and citizens in the former communist countries of eastern and central Europe of recent times. Most of the former communist countries share a common culture and heritage with the rest of central and western Europe. The Roman Catholic

Church is as strong in Poland as it is anywhere in western Europe. The Reformation was as strong in East Germany, Czechoslovakia and Hungary as in western Europe. Because of the fall of Soviet-controlled communist governments, these nations needed to re-establish new governments and political institutions. In addition, their leaders also needed to establish rights of private property ownership and codes of personal conduct; then erect legal institutions to support these rights and enforce the complimentary responsibilities. These nations had the same opportunity as America's founding fathers had 200 years ago—either to establish government on Christian principles or to install a new government based on the old principles. They had no recent precedents or traditions to guide them. They were free to establish new precedents and traditions. They needed a political philosophy to guide them. Which philosophy should they have chosen?

DEMOCRACY IN AMERICA IS A HABIT

As Americans, we support the establishment of new democracies patterned after America's model, but we have forgotten how the model was made. Europeans often understand America's history and traditions better than we do; they are puzzled that our leaders are teaching principles different from America's original principles. Americans most likely still believe the principles in the Declaration of Independence without realizing that the Supreme Court has declared most of these principles to be unconstitutional.

America's continued existence relies more on tradition than theory. When considering matters of law, justice and theology within the confines of the Declaration of Independence and the political confines of the United States of America, the law's boundaries as they relate to individual freedom are generally accepted. This is because of the relative security America has enjoyed for an extremely long time, as nations are judged by history. Americans feel secure because they have confidence in the traditions of their institutions.

When considering matters of law, justice and theology in relation to our dealings with other countries, both as to our rights as individuals and our national policies, the application of law becomes uncertain; the security of individuals traveling to foreign lands and the security of the nation as a whole become much more uncertain. The reign and rule of law, though it is often disregarded by our courts and ignored and not understood by Americans, still provides a foundation for the principles and precedents that have followed. In international matters, these foundational principles are not the same.

An American traveling to or transacting business with a foreign nation will immediately become aware of the conflict between law and ethics. Our laws have little validity or effect in other lands. Each nation has its own view of sovereignty, but it is clear that America's view of its sovereignty and the importance of individual rights has no relevance when an individual travels outside of the limits of America's jurisdiction. Our laws have no effect and cannot assist in resolving disputes between Americans and foreigners, unless the other country has agreed by treaty with the United States as to the law and rules to be applied. With no force of law and/or uncertainty as to the application of laws to protect individual rights and enforce agreements, the gap between law and ethics becomes clearer. With the absence of any clear authority or rule of law for protection based on a clear grant of rights, the ability to travel and engage in commerce is limited by the grace and virtue of the host country. Without any understanding of the ethics and civic virtue practiced by the host country, existence and communication, much less commerce, is a struggle. We may ignore Christian virtue as irrelevant in America, but we pray for the existence of Christian virtue in foreign lands.

Americans take their government and their freedoms for granted. But the modern image of government and freedom is different than it was at the beginning, and it is changing. Our government and freedom have become an image that reflects inaccurately an ideal from the past, because the true nature behind the image is no longer understood. The modern understanding of the institutions of American government and the concepts of liberty, freedom, rights and justice are no longer based on a reasoned understanding of legal and political principles as they were at America's founding. Partly because of lack of interest, but mostly because Americans no longer begin at the beginning, which is the existence and sovereignty of God, Americans' modern understanding of political and legal philosophy is shallow and rootless.

CHRISTIANITY AND AN UNCHANGING RULE OF LAW

Because theology cannot be considered in American law and politics, either because God is presumed by too many to not exist or simply because the Supreme Court has declared that God must be ignored, modern American law and politics has become a confusing mix of utilitarian and libertarian philosophy. The secular view announced by the Supreme Court establishes fundamental rights originating from an unidentified source. This secular philosophy of fundamental rights is both libertarian and pantheistic.

The source of modern fundamental rights can no longer be identified objectively, but can only exist subjectively. Fundamental rights, therefore, exist only as decreed by the Court as the final product of the judicial opinion process. But all fundamental rights decreed by the courts are also limited.

In most cases, fundamental rights are balanced by the opposing standard of the compelling government interest, also defined by the court. At the root of the compelling government interest test lays utilitarianism philosophy. Utilitarian philosophy can be Christian or secular. Laws enacted to require adherence to a moral law for the good of the culture, are utilitarian. National accountability to God's law, as taught by Webster and Lincoln, is also utilitarian. Secular utilitarianism is pure collectivism. Collectivism and libertarianism must always be in conflict, as the philosophic principles are irreconcilable. The collectivist ethic sacrifices the individual for the welfare of the community. The libertarian ethic sacrifices nothing to exist independently of the political community.

For both collectivists and libertarians, the rule of law always changes. Under collectivism, the rules must change constantly as the political sovereign maximizes public welfare. Libertarians must define their own existence and the means and rules to make their decisions and choices.

The true nature of the rule of law is far different from that held by collectivists and utilitarians. The modern rule of law bears little resemblance to the former rule of law. In place of the former "reign and rule of law," where the courts administered justice in accordance with established centuries old principles and rules, is a modern court that mediates and arbitrates in accordance with the judge's own set of beliefs and rules. The authority of the judge is limited only by the individual's right to appeal to another tribunal which does the same thing. The inevitable result is a system that has created chaos and confusion in its law, cynicism and gamesmanship among litigants, and an overworked judiciary.

The most important question, therefore, is if the Rule of Law remains, then whose rules and what laws will control? A second question is, what standards will control correct behavior? If ethical conduct and virtuous behavior are necessary, what law governs and from where do the rules come?

When the Biblical moral standards that formed the foundations of American government are removed, new arbitrary ethical standards will become law. "Political correctness" is the most recent attempt to formulate a code of correct behavior. Do these new rules even work, and do they have any legitimacy?

THE RELATIONSHIP OF ETHICS TO LAW

Ethics is the study of correct behavior necessary to preserve civilization. "Ethics" derives from the Greek *ethikos*, meaning custom. The American view of ethics is based partly on old customs that are now being replaced by new customs. That is why there is so much confusion.

The study of ethics involves the relationship of conduct, moral values, and duties. Ethics has also been defined as the science of moral duty, or more broadly, as the science of ideal human character. But these considerations are not much about science but a lot about cultural values.

Ethics is related to virtue and to law but not in the same way. Ethics and virtue has a Christian ideal. Augustine wrote of ethics and virtue when stating, "God orders what we cannot do, that we may know what we ought to ask of Him." Few Christians would want Augustine's standard enacted into law. Augustine refers to a perfected ideal not attainable by human will. Ethics, as related to virtue, refers to a goal based on ideal character.

Law, in contrast to virtue, refers to a minimum acceptable standard of conduct. According to the United States Supreme Court, "[I]t is the province of ethics to consider of actions in their relation to motives, but jurisprudence deals with actions in their relation to law, and for the most part independently of the motive." Adler v. Fenten (1861).

Historically, the law dealt only with the consequences of actions rather than the molding of correct thoughts. Casey failed to draw a line between personal beliefs and conduct based on erroneous belief, allowing all conduct if based on personal belief. In comparison, political correctness will not allow beliefs that do not conform to the political sovereign's standard. Though the root of Casey is libertarian philosophy while the root of political correctness is collectivist, both blur the historical distinction between the standard of the ethical ideal and the standard of conduct sanctionable under the law.

Law, in contrast to ethics, is the practical enforcement of rules of conduct. Political law is also the result of the efficacy of command of the political sovereign. Creation is an example of the efficacy of God's command, as are the announcement of the Ten Commandments and the continuous existence of Divine Providence in the affairs of human activity.

Hobbes rejected the efficacy of divine command in *The Leviathan*. To Hobbes, any appeal to custom or natural law, without reference to the authority of the political sovereign to make them binding, was without legitimacy. To Hobbes, custom could only be derived "from the will of the commonwealth, that is to say, from the will of the representative."

Despite Hobbes' apparent belief in Christianity, he separated religious truth from political will. Hobbes ascribes no credit to the possibility that the will of the political sovereign is no more legitimate than the expressed written will of the ultimate sovereign.

Hobbes rejected both general and special revelation. He has been linked to Marshall as the forerunner of the requirement that all law be written. Unlike Marshall, however, Hobbes rejected unwritten law as a source of fundamental law. To Hobbes, no law could originate outside of the enactments of the political sovereign. Marshall, in contrast, never rejected Common Law and the use of custom and tradition, often obtained from written and oral Scriptural tradition. In effect, Hobbes was forced to reject special revelation because of his opposition to law based on general revelation. The result is Hobbes' stark image of Leviathan, the symbol of political sovereignty, as the only efficacy behind the law.

Modernists use ethics in an attempt to soften the troublesome vision of Leviathan as the efficacy behind the law. They believe that an appeal to ethics is an appeal to virtue.

Law, on the other hand, finds its power in the fear of punishment. The distinction is illusory. Modern ethics has been united with law.

Oliver Wendell Holmes is probably the best-known apologist for the modern theory of ethics. In *The Path of the Law*, Holmes proposed a new theory of ethics that radically differed from the classical view that virtue implied something more than acting to avoid punishment by the law. The new theory also clearly and firmly placed the foundation of standards of virtue into the hands of man, rather than God. Holmes stated, "A legal duty so called is nothing but a prediction that if a man does or omits certain things he will be made to suffer in this or that way by judgment of the court; and so of a legal right." To Holmes, ethics and law are essentially the same thing, and virtue is reinforced by fear of Leviathan.

The dilemma created by disharmony between law and ethics profoundly affects contemporary Americans, given that the current view is that law and ethics are the same. Virtue, not enforced by legal sanction, is irrelevant. All discussions about ethics must result in new laws or be based on old laws. This viewpoint is inconsistent with the classical and historical view of philosophers who wrote about ethics. But the modern view necessarily resulted from the separation of law from Biblical truth, and the separation of modern law from principles of Biblically-based natural law.

Modern ethics raises many questions that cannot be satisfactorily answered. What if there is a law but the law is never enforced? What if enforcement of the law is dependent upon the decision or discretion of administrative agencies or executive officials? What if the decision to enforce is based upon the receipt of bribes or kickbacks? What if the law was not enacted properly or exceeds the bounds of legitimate government authority? How does an individual respond to those situations when the decision may require a violation of conscience or Biblical mandate? These questions all arise from the conflict between law and ethics and the subordination of ethics to law under Holmes' view. What recourse does anyone have if Leviathan is a tyrant or simply is mistaken? To Hobbes and Holmes there is no appeal.

RECONCILING LAW AND VIRTUE UNDER CHRISTIANITY

American courts are vested only with the authority to uphold and enforce written law. American courts had not historically been given the responsibility or the jurisdiction to distinguish between what conduct "ought" to be, the object to which the study of ethics relates, and what the law "is," the reality of the effect of law that has been enacted politically. Ethics and law are different.

Christians believe in personal virtue not sanctioned under the law. As evident from the Sermon on the Mount, Christians are called to act more righteous than the law requires and more righteous than we are capable.

The profound experiment tried in America is to allow personal freedom without the overarching fear and control of an all-encompassing political sovereign. The founding fathers clearly understood that a civilization based on freedom must have personal virtue apart from law.

SUBMISSION TO A SOVEREIGN

Holmes' theory of law and ethics is akin to Hobbes' theory of law and politics. The symbol of Leviathan represents raw political power exercised absolutely by whomever is in power at a particular point in time. Virtue is irrelevant and a waste of time. Modern judges and legal scholars who advance theories of fundamental law, without rooting the fundamental law in Biblical theology, either assume the role of Leviathan, decreeing fundamental precepts by their own act of will, or struggle to find support for natural law theories derived from fuzzy natural law philosophy based on tradition or generalized ethical goals gleaned from history. Rousseau's "general will" and Kant's "phenomenal realm" were followed quickly by the brutal realism of the French Revolution and the despair-driven irrationality of modern existentialism. A weak and discredited philosophical theory cannot be supported without government force and an apathetic ignorance of the citizens. The enforcement of ethics becomes as arbitrary as the personal expression of the opinion of the political ruler.

Christians need to understand a simple point about the relationship of theology to ethics and law. If the Garden of Eden was a myth, then the forbidden fruit of the tree of good and evil was also a myth. Either natural law is based upon Genesis or all law is positivist, a product of the command of whoever holds the practical political power in any political subdivision. Ethics can come from no other source. If Genesis is true, then so is Exodus, Leviticus, Numbers and Deuteronomy.

The Old Testament law is, therefore, a written expression of the absolute command of the Divine Sovereign, that cannot be countermanded by man. This is the root of law as it had been practiced from medieval times to recent days. This view of natural law was also the view of Reformation theologians expressed as political theory in Locke's *Two Treatises of Government* and Rutherford's *Lex Rex*, first laid down as a foundational principle of government in the Declaration of Independence. There is natural law, but only based on divine command, either in creation or in the written text. Early legal encyclopedias, compiled by Bracton, Coke and Blackstone, had no reservation about expressing that religious truth, clearly established throughout Christendom and accepted as known and discoverable by all, was to be considered the law.

For Christians, ethics and law are not the same thing. Under American law, historically, rights protected by law and conduct sanctioned by law are different. The individual right to pursue virtue is established in the Declaration of Independence by the use of the term "happiness." To the individual, ethics refers to virtue. The pursuit of virtue is an individual right and is not the government's responsibility.

From the standpoint of theology and law, rights and justice, both derived from the Hebrew term *mishpat*, are the same. They appear in the same place in the Bible but are used in different contexts. Rights are also defined as virtue. The pursuit of happiness defines identically the pursuit of blessings as expressed in the beatitudes. Happiness is the English equivalent of the Latin *beatis*. The beatitudes are an expression of Biblical virtue, or what Bonhoeffer called a "better righteousness." A "better righteousness," however, is not a goal of government but a goal of each individual.

The Virginia Statute of Religious Freedom, expressing the same principles as contained in other simultaneous writings of Jefferson and Madison, separated the coercive threat of government sanction for matters of personal beliefs. Personal virtue, like religious belief, is a matter of government coercion only when manifested in conduct affecting others. Virtue may equal perfect justice, but it is a level of justice not achievable by coercion or human understanding. Thus, the definition of religion used by Jefferson restricts the jurisdiction of the government in matters of religion and personal virtue. Jefferson's definition is consistent with Reformation theology and its emphasis on an individual's responsibility to God. Personal virtue and religious belief were choices left to individuals.

As a result, the American form of government is, essentially, a government of lower goals than theocracies or governments based upon Marxist or socialist goals. Calvin, from the standpoint of theology, and Hobbes, from the standpoint of political philosophy, did not choose as a better form of government among the three possibilities: (1) monarchy, (2) aristocracy, (3) democracy. The success of government depended upon the righteousness of the political leader.

In America, representative democracy was established by the Constitution. The principle of equality was established by the Declaration of Independence. The equality principle mandates a democratic or republican form of government in America because no single ruler or group of elites could claim a greater entitlement to rule than any other individual.

The coexistence of democracy and equality, resulting in a government by consent, is a foundational principle of American government. The Declaration of Independence established this foundational concept of consent and equated it with freedom. Hobbes placed all sovereignty in the hands of the holder of political power, whether a monarchy, aristocracy or a democracy. But in America, political power was limited to only those powers that were the proper function of government. The people had not consented to an absolute sovereign. Rather, powers not delegated to government remained with the individual, and that formed the basis of the American concepts of freedom and liberty.

A Christian government does not force its citizens to be Christians. Reformation theology and the New Testament taught that wisdom and salvation were between God and each individual. Wisdom and salvation are matters of choice and not coercion. Wisdom and salvation are not matters for the government under the American theory of government. Even though Americans may view this as a Christian nation, and historically America has been a Christian nation, jurisdiction of the government still would not extend to insuring that each individual achieved ultimate wisdom and personal salvation.

"DUTY" AND THE BOSTON TEA PARTY

The relationship of ethics and law is symbolically and linguistically represented by the Boston Tea Party. The word "duty," describing a legal obligation, can often be in conflict with "duty" as a moral obligation to obey the law. The colonists, by tossing 1700 chests of tea off the Dartmouth into Boston Harbor, had resolutely defined their moral duty to resist an unlawfully imposed duty on tea in an unambiguous assertion of their rights and duties as Christians, while defying an unlawful act of Parliament.

The Boston Tea Party example clearly shows how law and ethics can be in conflict. Jean Calvin, like the Apostle Paul, had attempted to reconcile ethical and legal duties by determination of whether an individual's loyalty should, in the questioned circumstance, be to God or Caesar. Calvin, like Hobbes, recognized that favoring a moral duty over a legal duty could have legal consequences. Locke, like the founding fathers in the Declaration of Independence, appealed to the Supreme Judge, and argued that the appeal by Jeptha to God to choose between the sons of Israel or the sons of Ammon was the only possible appeal left when the civil magistrates, to whom Calvin identified as the only viable option to appeal, refused to properly apply Biblical law.

Matters of ethics are personal, but they have validity apart from the political law only if Biblically rooted. Each individual is subject to the absolute command of the Divine Sovereign and the command of a political sovereign. We are subject to Caesar in some instances and God in other instances, but always to one or the other. Like Leviathan, the will of the political sovereign is subject to the will of God. We are all, like the centurion in the New Testament, subject to authority. Liberty is only as granted by the sovereign.

THE EVOLUTION OF SOVEREIGNTY

The tyranny of Hobbes and Holmes, in contrast to the liberty of Rutherford and Locke, results from the relationship of the rule of law to ethically correct behavior as decreed by the sovereign, who must be both infallible and, accordingly, without limitation.

Because of the Court's view of its own infallibility, it felt compelled to follow its groundless decision in Roe with an equally groundless decision in Casey. The Court, in Casey, acknowledged that Roe was without support in law or tradition. Roe was upheld so that the integrity of the Court be upheld. The evolution of the Court, from Marshall to Casey, is as dramatically different as the comparison of the authority of Saul, King of Israel, limited by Samuel, to Darius, King of Persia, an absolute monarch. The modern Court's remorse in <u>Casey</u> is reminiscent of the remorse of King Darius, forced to sentence his friend and trusted advisor Daniel to the lion's den because of Daniel's refusal to obey an order that Darius had unwittingly signed, decreeing that all must worship Darius as the sovereign. Daniel submitted to Darius' authority, but not Darius' sovereignty. By Persian law, an order of the sovereign could not be rescinded or ignored. Such is the nature of the secular "Rule of Law."

CONSTITUTIONAL SOVEREIGNTY LIMITED BY THE LAW

Christian ethics cannot simply mirror the culture. Nor can Christians submit to written law that conflicts with ultimate religious truth. Christians must take the responsibility to make the effort necessary to discover the law and resist the temptation to be misled by and/or acquiesce to custom or man-made law that is not based on general revelation discovered through reason, and special revelation discovered by a diligent study of Scripture. What Chief Justice Holt said in the *Case Against Monopolies*, "Now, my Lord, I do think, that practice and usage is a great evidence of the law," can be helpful but also misleading.

Law exists, under natural law theory, and is discovered, rather than commanded. What Christians mean by natural law, or fundamental law, is neither evolving nor mystical. Our basic understanding of fundamental law has been discovered through reason and practiced for centuries as evidenced by many of our customs and traditions. When fundamental law is suddenly discovered, and is in conflict with centuries of Christian tradition and custom, Christians should be skeptical.

Justice Douglas discovered natural law in a "penumbra" of "rights of privacy" in <u>Griswold</u> in 1965. The Court found a right to an abortion in <u>Roe</u>, in 1973, because of "modern realities."

Unlike the custom of slavery that had been in conflict with principles since ancient times, America's newest fundamental rights have never been accepted in American culture or under its law. In America, tradition has given way to principle many times. The Alien and Sedition Acts were repealed even though such laws had existed in England for centuries. Racial and many gender restrictions that were traditionally upheld under the law were later found to be without support or precedent in Scripture. Early Americans rejected the sovereign prerogative as a violation of the equality mandate. Americans introduced the idea of inalienable rights. Legal precedent, whether legislatively or judicially enacted, has been overruled in America when it conflicted with fundamental law as determined through reason or study of Biblical truth.

Modern courts and legislatures scoff at the assertion that natural law is subject to divine law and that positive law is limited. But in so doing, evidence and tradition that supported the old definitions of law and ethics must also be denigrated and rejected. A new tradition, only recently announced without support from either evidence or tradition, then must be substituted to support America's new principles of fundamental law.

The source of tradition and custom that reflects law and ultimate truth must be identified. To do so, the first principles of law, the first questions, must be addressed. Who started the practices and usage that became the customs and traditions that reflect the law? Who made the government that made the laws? If only the political sovereign can make the government, then who made the sovereign?

Hobbes, Rousseau and Locke had different definitions of a social compact and different ideas about political sovereignty. Jean Calvin and the Apostle Paul were unequivocal as to who made the government and the political sovereign. By the Declaration of Independence, the sovereign American people formed their government. But they also understood that the government was subject to the will of Divine Providence and subject to the law of the Supreme Judge.

THE IDENTITY OF THE SOVEREIGN

The discussion of ethics and law cannot be separated from the subject of sovereignty. Without law, we simply exist in the state of nature, which is, as a practical matter, the state described by Hobbes as a constant state of war. The commonwealth was established to keep the peace and administer justice. The government can only keep the peace and administer justice if it is legitimately vested with the authority to govern; or it maintains power through coercion subjecting the people to its authority against their will. In the state of nature, mankind either submits to the most powerful ruler, according to Hobbes, or voluntarily consents to the establishment of a political community, according to Locke. Hobbes and Locke were ultimately both pragmatists. Neither Locke nor Hobbes ever completely acknowledged the answer to the first philosophical questions.

While Locke and Hobbes discussed who had the authority to govern, neither answered how that political authority related to the political principle of divine authority. What are the limits of the legislative authority of the

247

government? What binds the members of the political community? Those answers had been previously provided by Jean Calvin and built upon by Samuel Rutherford. Locke was trained in Calvinist theology and well acquainted with Rutherford's teaching. The drafters of the Declaration of Independence, who rested their right to establish a new government on the "law of nature and of nature's God," were also Calvinists. They concluded that all man-made law is subject to divine law and all political sovereignty is subject to divine sovereignty.

Americans must once again choose as their rulers either Leviticus or Leviathan.

Leviticus establishes a system of law and government based on divine sovereignty and it is a symbol of the special revelation of Scripture that traditionally formed the basis of Common Law and America's constitutional law.

Leviathan, in contrast, establishes a system of law and government dependent on the will of a small group of flawed humans, whose right to rule springs from power, position and wealth, and that answers only to the few. Leviathan's laws can, by the will of the powerful, ignore or embrace human rights; and the powerful can choose the definition of which kinds of humans to protect. Leviathan offers an unpredictable, unstable and unjust form of government with absolute sovereignty in the hands of the humans who control it.

For Leviticus to succeed, citizens and government must submit to the absolute sovereignty of the omnipotent God. For Leviathan to succeed, citizens must submit to the absolute sovereignty of all-powerful humans. Under Leviathan, human rights are alienable, deriving their status from the government, and they can be stripped away at its whim. Under Leviticus, inalienable human rights derive from the Hand of God, and no government can strip them away.

Thomas Aquinas, in describing the sovereign, said it is "exempt from the law, as to its coercive power, since, properly speaking, no man is coerced by himself, and law has no coercive power save from the authority of the sovereign." While acknowledging fundamental rights, Hobbes vested absolute sovereignty in the monarch, aristocracy, or people and analogized the sovereign power to Leviathan in Job 41. But the Leviathan of Job and from Hobbes was subject to divine law. By rejecting divine law, fundamental rights and limits on sovereignty are voided and made null. Political power then becomes absolute and limitless, a philosophical necessity under the Hobbes and Holmes view.

DIVINE LAW TRUMPS MANDMADE VERSIONS

Without question, America was founded on the understanding that natural law was subject to divine law and superior to any written law, whether enacted legislatively, judicially, or by the executive. The events leading to the American Revolution began with an attempt to secure constitutional rights and ended with an appeal to natural rights. These natural rights, existing pursuant to the law of nature and the God who created all nature, were antecedent and superior to any rights conferred by courts, legislatures, or in written constitutions. Without such an appeal to the supremacy of natural rights over constitutional rights, no revolution could have been justified, and the Declaration of Independence, enacted in violation of English constitutional law, would have been a nullity.

America's rejection of the sovereignty of God was neither recent nor sudden. It has been incremental and encouraged by all branches of government.

Even though natural law was necessary to the legitimacy of the Declaration of Independence in 1776, the Supreme Court rejected the use of natural law in Calder v. Bull in 1792.

When the use of natural law that formed the Common Law of contracts conflicted with the legislative prerogative, the legislature prevailed in Ogden v. Saunders in 1827.

Although Lincoln revived natural law to prevent the southern states from seceding over the slavery issue, and natural law was incorporated into the Constitution by ratification of the Fourteenth Amendment, the Supreme Court again rejected natural rights arguments in The Slaughter-House Cases (1873) and the Civil Rights Cases (1883).

In the Twentieth Century, individual rights became subordinate to economic policymaking by judges in Standard Oil of New Jersey v. United States (1913) and the legislature, Nebbia v. New York (1934) and federal power became centralized and paramount. Wickard v. Filburn (1941).

Ultimately the Supreme Court decreed that fundamental law would be determined by the court, in Cooper v. Aaron (1958), and would be gleaned from an evolving Constitution, Griswold v. Connecticut (1965).

The Supreme Court's declarations of fundamental law would be final even when in conflict with tradition rooted in Christian principle, Roe v. Wade (1973). It ignored the expressed will of the majority of the people who had enacted abortion-related legislation based on the standards of Christian morality.

The Court condemned the people's position on morality as bigotry.

Romer v. Evans (1996). The judicial power to refuse to enforce legislation enacted in violation of the Constitution by Marshall in Marbury had evolved to subvert the Constitution and the rule of law and, ultimately, ridicule the people who still maintained allegiance to the sovereignty of God.

CROSSING OVER TO TYRANNY

In America, the provisions for religious freedom and limited government politically and legally limited the sovereign's power. Thomas Jefferson wrote to Francis W. Gilmer on June 7, 1816. Jefferson, a student of Locke, Coke and Roger Williams, wrote of his opposition to the theory of the "social compact" as expressed by Jean Jacques Rousseau. Rousseau's theory had formed the philosophical basis for the French Revolution.

> Our legislators are not sufficiently apprised of the rightful limits of their power; that their office is to declare and enforce only our natural rights and duties, and to take none of them from us. No man has a natural right to commit aggression on the equal rights of another; and this is all from which the laws ought to restrain him; every man is under the natural duty of contributing to the necessities of society; and this is all the law should enforce on him; and no man having a natural right to be the judge between himself and another, it is his natural duty to submit to the umpirage of an impartial third. When the laws have declared and enforced all this, they have fulfilled their functions; and the idea is quite unfounded, that on entering into society we give up any natural right. The trial of every law by one of these texts, would lessen much the labors of our legislators, and lighten equally our municipal codes.

Not only has our government violated these principles by the expansive use of police power, but courts and legal philosophers have blurred the distinction between law and ethics by failing to recognize these distinctions. Modern courts refer to positive law, which is the absolute will of the sovereign expressed in command, and natural law, which is an overriding set of principles based on tradition with no identifiable source. Modern courts no longer refer to Divine Law.

THE CHRISTIAN RESPONSE TO TYRANNY

Medieval theologians and political philosophers equated the moral duty to resist a tyrant who violated what the conscience perceived as the law of

God as a precept of true religion. In America, the precept was written into law in the Declaration of Independence. The moral duty of what "ought to be" became a political right by stating that "whenever any form of government becomes destructive of these ends, it is the right of the people to alter or abolish it."

As Americans, we cannot accept the proposition that, as a matter of morals, every command of the sovereign ought to be obeyed. We ultimately must choose whether to submit to Leviticus or Leviathan. As Americans, our history shows that we chose between the nobles at Runnymede and King John, in effect supporting resistance to a tyrant, by our adherence to the Magna Charta. We also chose to support Sir Edward Coke over King James when we agreed to submit to a fundamental rule of law that is greater than the king. We established the American nation on these choices by following George Washington over George III. By resisting the magistrates in his battle for religious freedom, William Penn established, and Americans agreed, that religious freedom takes precedence over judicial authority. By opposing the sheriffs and supporting the people who gave refuge to the fugitive slaves, we chose our political theory and exalted ethics over legislatively enacted law. Absolute obedience to a political sovereign was the main defense at the Nuremberg trials, and the defense was rejected. Bonhoeffer warned against "false obedience" to authority. History exalted Bonhoeffer and condemned the Nuremberg defendants. Absolute obedience to illegitimate law, or to Leviathan, although often presented as doctrine in modern churches and by modern leaders, has never ultimately been accepted when used as a defense by individuals in their attempt to defend their own unethical actions.

The question of where modern courts and legislatures derive their authority and why they reject divine law must be answered before Christians submit to that alleged authority. The Declaration of Independence stated that rebellions are not justified by "light and transient causes." It has been well said, "In politics, as in every other episode in the adventure of life, the price of moral freedom is the responsibility of acting at one's peril." That Christians are generally remembered as martyrs rather than victors should not overshadow the importance of the Declaration of Independence, the American experience and tradition or distort its true meaning.

The sovereignty of God means more than that Christians are authorized to resist tyrants. The acceptance of the sovereignty of God also means that Christians understand and obey God's moral law and its established righteousness. American Christians have the further privilege and responsibility of restoring America's government and institutions to their proper place, subject to the sovereignty of God as acknowledged and established in the principles of the Declaration of Independence. To Dietrich Bonhoeffer, who was subject to Nazi authority, submission was not to be equated with a "false obedience" to tyranny, but that the "better righteousness" exemplified by Christian ethics was neither limited nor illegal under secular government. Morality and Christian ethics must be maintained under a secular ruler regardless of the legitimacy of its political laws, until legitimate government can be restored.

AMERICA'S HISTORICAL RESPONSE TO TYRANNY

When America was founded by the signers of the Declaration of Independence, God's moral law had already been ingrained into Common Law and accepted as a necessary ingredient in the institutions of government. The political institutions, the legislative and executive branches, could be sustained only so long as the people remained virtuous. The tyranny of the legislative branch had been experienced with Parliament and was deemed intolerable when tolerance for the inalienable rights of man were absent. At that time, God's moral law was more visible in the decisions and actions of the judicial branch. The historical tradition of the Common Law, with its roots in the deliberations of Teutonic tribesmen in the first millennium, and modified and enlarged by the medieval Catholic Church and the Protestant Reformation, was the basis for judicial decisions and the limitation on judicial power until the Twentieth Century. Because God's moral law is no longer the basis for judicial decisions, it is also no longer a limitation on judicial power.

The opinion and caution of the founding fathers remains clear. Upon leaving Independence Hall in Philadelphia after the vote approving the adoption of the new constitution was completed, Benjamin Franklin was asked what form of government America would have. The proceedings had been secret and rumors ran rampant; one such rumor claimed that George Washington would be installed as America's first king. Franklin's answer was simple and insightful: "A republic, madame, if you can keep it."

The drafters of the Constitution understood that a government of the people could only support the fundamental principles of liberty and equality if the political sovereign, the people, supported and defended those principles. And those principles would be supported and defended by the people only if the people understood them and exercised their freedom and their sovereign power to choose good over evil. The people would choose good over evil only if they were virtuous and moral. Morality, to the founders, could only be supported by a religious people instructed in good government and willing to exercise their own freedom and liberty consistent with the same exercise of freedom and liberty by all others. Only in America, with political sovereignty residing with the people and the power of government limited, was personal virtue an exercise of authority rather than an example of obedience to an appointed sovereign.

The founding fathers were similarly unambiguous and straightforward in their belief that it was the Christian religion, and not religion generally, that was necessary to support America's political institutions. Patrick Henry emphatically claimed that references to religion were not generally directed at religion but specifically directed at Christianity declaring:

> It cannot be emphasized too strongly or too often that this great nation was founded, not by religionists, but by Christians; not on religion, but on the Gospel of Jesus Christ. For this very reason peoples of other faiths have been afforded asylum, prosperity, and freedom of worship here.

In his farewell address, George Washington laid the framework for understanding the importance of religion under self-government. His statement, which used to be mandatory reading in public schools, addressed the futility of attempting self-government without religion and personal virtue:

> Of all the dispositions and habits which lead to political prosperity, religion and morality are indispensable supports. In vain would that man claim the tribute of patriotism who should labor to subvert these great pillars of human happiness, these firmest props of the duties of men and citizens. The mere politician, equally with the pious man, ought to respect and to cherish them. A volume could not trace all their connections with private and public felicity. Let it simply be asked: Where is the security for property, for reputation, for life, if the sense of religious obligation desert the oaths which are the instruments of investigation in courts of justice? And let us with caution indulge the supposition that morality can be maintained without religion. Whatever may be conceded to the influence of refined education on minds of peculiar structure, reason and experience both forbid us to expect that national morality can prevail in exclusion of religious principle.

Our nation's present inability to understand the distinction between good and evil is derived from our attempt to maintain self-government without understanding and applying the doctrinal truth learned from Christian teaching.

The American form of government is based upon a choice made by our founding fathers. It is the same choice faced by any new government. Do we consent to be subject to the reign and rule of law that is constant and unchanging, derived from the divine sovereignty of God or to the ever changing rule of the law of Leviathan? Modern legal scholars and statesmen attempt to distinguish between the rule of law and the law of the jungle. But there is little difference in liberty when Leviathan rules the jungle. Only God ultimately rules Leviathan. The American choice was to reject the political Leviathan of the Old World and to substitute a new form of government based upon the New Covenant theology of the Reformers' interpretation of the New Testament.

Each individual is, first and foremost, subject to God. Not only is the government limited by the Constitution, but the political sovereignty of the people is also limited. Virtue, being the same thing as justice, is not simply a right; it is a necessary responsibility of each individual. No Supreme Court justice or legal philosopher can inhibit an individual Christian's right to do justice or be virtuous. On the contrary, even secular philosophers recognize the need to have Christian ethics practiced to sustain a civilized culture. It is the civility and virtue practiced by individuals, without the threat of law or expectation of compensation, that permits the existence of communication upon which commerce and individual freedom can thrive.

The signers of the Declaration of Independence made a decision that would affect the lives of everyone in the New World. They had either to submit to tyranny or reject the political philosophy of the Old World. In 1776, America made the right choice. In the Declaration of Independence, the signers not only established America upon Christian principles but also rested its fortunes on the continued guidance and assistance of Divine Providence. After connecting the central holding of the case for independence to the laws of nature and of Nature's God and principles established by the Creator, and then making the case for independence, the authors of the Declaration of Independence unambiguously submitted the fortunes of this country to the sovereignty of God:

> And for the support of this Declaration, with a firm reliance on the protection of DIVINE PROVIDENCE, we mutually pledge to each other our lives, our fortunes, and our sacred honour.

The decision to choose to submit to the sovereignty of God rather than the tyranny of Leviathan was bold and unique only in that it had been done collectively. The reference to "divine providence" was not a mystical projection by secular men. The delegates to the Continental Congress were led by Anglicans from the southern colonies, direct descendants from the English royalists, and the descendants of Puritans from New England. Divine providence had one meaning and it referred to a specific God. The truly pious man will, as Augustine said, "refer everything to Divine Providence." Divine providence refers to an active God.

The New England Puritans understood the teachings of William Ames, that; "the providence of God is that efficiency whereby He provides for existing creatures in all things in accordance with the counsel of His will." The Anglicans understood and adhered to the Westminster Confession (1646) in which,"God, the great Creator of all things, doth uphold, direct, dispose, and govern all creatures, actions, and things from the greatest even to the least, by His most wise and holy providence."

This reliance upon and call to Divine Providence is natural for those who equate Divine Providence with the God who acts upon and intervenes in human affairs. To Jean Calvin, "providence consists in action" and "as it is taught in Scripture, is opposed to fortune and fortuitous happenings."

AMERICA'S MOST IMPORTANT CHOICE: LEVITICUS OR LEVIATHAN

Americans today have the same choice to make: to be ruled by Leviticus or by Leviathan. If Christians really believe in God's existence, then submission to His sovereignty is a philosophical and theological necessity. To do otherwise is rebellion. Leviticus symbolizes God's moral law. God's moral law, established in creation, has never changed and will always be supreme to any governmental decree. To refuse to acknowledge and enforce God's moral law is to submit to Leviathan.

Leviathan has assumed many different forms over the centuries. Any political sovereign that rejects the sovereignty of God, by establishing rules of conduct and behavior inconsistent with God's moral law, has assumed the role of Leviathan.

In early America, the political sovereign was limited, but today's new political Leviathan acts without limits. The founding fathers limited political sovereignty by deliberately enumerating specific powers granted to the federal government in the Constitution; it placed specific limitations on federal authority in deference to the states with the Tenth Amendment. Those limitations were later rejected by the Supreme Court. But political sovereignty had also been limited by the Ninth Amendment, which reserved rights to individuals, and by the Fourteenth Amendment, which acknowledged the existence of fundamental, natural rights and then restricted the powers of states to deny fundamental rights; hard lessons learned because of the slavery experience and the Civil War. Those Constitutional provisions were never acknowledged in court decisions. For Americans also to reject God's sovereignty, and to submit to an absolute political authority in the legislative and judicial branches that ignore God's moral law, is to also reject the terms and conditions upon which the institutions of American government were established in 1776, 1787 and 1865. Americans, in rejecting God as the sovereign and the foundation for our government, which is our political community, are also rejecting America's past and its whole basis for existence, and substituting in God's place an ancient idol from the Old World.

In the Declaration of Independence, the colonists appealed to the "Supreme Judge" for the rectitude of their actions and to "Divine Providence" to guide, direct and assist America in its unique acceptance of divine sovereignty as to God's judgment and beneficial intervention. Many Americans still uphold this original view that God will both judge and bless us, individually and collectively, if His divine sovereignty is acknowledged and respected. Many more American Christians are unaware of the historical tradition that formed the basis for this country's existence, and blindly submit to secular authority. The need to choose between Leviticus and Leviathan is becoming more apparent. The extent to which each individual consents to a political sovereign, subject to God's ultimate sovereignty, should be an informed consent. We need to remember that our reason for continued existence is linked to the reason for our formation.

In America, we have built a new government on a new constitution based on the First Amendment. The First Amendment, the successor to the freedom to dissent politically, first found in the English Bill of Rights, has been changed. A subtle change in terminology from free "speech" to free "expression" has misled modern Americans into thinking that American freedom is about libertarianism and that traditional, Christian-based morality must be separated from law. But what comes first: the First Amendment or the First Commandment? Christians have closed their eyes to the obvious command to keep God first. The First Commandment is supreme. The First Amendment cannot replace the Declaration of Independence, although in practice, the First Amendment is now America's first principle. Leviticus, as symbolic of God's law, must replace Leviathan, the positivist result of America's illegitimate regime.

CHAPTER 15

THE CITY ON A HILL
AMERICA'S NATIONAL IDENTITY

"And the life of man, solitary, poorer, nasty, brutish and short."

Thomas Hobbes, *The Leviathan*

"For we must consider that we shall be a city upon the hill. The eyes of all people are upon us, so that if we shall deal falsely with our God in this work we have undertaken, and so cause Him to withdraw His present help from us, we shall be made a story and a byword through the world."

John Winthrop (1630)

It seems to me that many Americans are ashamed of themselves when comparing this country with Europe. I have never felt that way, even during political or business discussions with my European friends. My travels have made me more aware of our uniqueness. Although Americans seem to represent an oversimplified view of morality and a reckless, blind faith in the future, a "tree is know by it fruit." Europeans cannot share in our optimism because of their history.

My personal view is that America's most important role in the world is evangelical, and not military or economic. I realized this halfway through my 1995 speech in Poland. I gave that speech ad lib because of comments made by previous speakers. It became almost a "city on a hill" speech and I knew when I was giving it that, paradoxically, I couldn't have given it in America.

I know for certain that American lawyers would have rolled their collective eyes and college students would have shouted me down. My sense, while giving my speech in Poland explaining the importance of the Decla-

257

ration of Independence, is that they didn't believe that Americans really agreed with me either; still they wanted to hear it. You see, their hope is in our principles—not in our actions. When America's actions back our principles, there is hope for the billions of people who still live under tyranny. These emerging democracies are proud to think of the day when their own country will be free to follow American principles; they are saddened when we don't do the same.

◆ ◆ ◆

T he hope and promise in the New World contrasted dramatically with that of Europe. Life was bleak in the Old World. For the individual without privilege, life was solitary, nasty, brutish and short. Hobbes described life in the state of nature as consisting of individuals in a constant "state of warre" needing intervention from a civil authority, to whom was given absolute sovereignty to keep the peace. The rulers maintained peace at the expense of individual equality and individual rights. Individual opportunities were limited. Peace was, however, regularly sacrificed for the maintenance and accumulation of power and glory of the monarch.

The existing order was challenged, in theory, by the Reformers and then, in practice, by the English Puritans. England in the 1600s experienced almost 100 years of conflict and civil war on its way to constitutional government. The end of the Seventeenth Century was marked by Locke's *Two Treatises of Government*, and the English Bill of Rights submitted in support of the limited monarchy of the Restoration of 1688. These documents formed the basis of the Declaration of Independence and the American Bill of Rights. Locke's *Treatises* provided the theory and the English Bill of Rights provided the precedent for religious freedom and limited government in America. These ideas had never been incorporated into any nation's formal documents. But both ideas had been tried and proven successful in the New World by colonial governments.

A NEW BEGINNING

The planting of the cross at Cape Henry, Virginia on April 29, 1607 marked a new beginning in world history and political philosophy. Each colony in the New World published a charter declaring its purposes and its principles. John Winthrop's "City on a Hill" statement is both a declaration and a symbol. "For we must consider that we shall be a city upon the hill. The eyes of all people are upon us, so that if we shall deal falsely with our

God in this work we have undertaken, and so cause Him to withdraw His present help from us, we shall be made a story and a byword through the world." Winthrop's declaration is also a promise. In Puritan theology and English fundamental law, it is an offer to enter into a covenant with an unchanging God. If the colonists kept their promise and were faithful, they believed that God would keep His promise and be faithful in return. The colonists hoped for security and for the blessings of liberty consistent with God's promise to Israel under the old covenant.

History affirms the wisdom of the colonists' covenant. In *The Wealth of Nations*, written in 1776, based upon a lecture series given by Adam Smith in Edinburgh, Scotland, Smith made numerous references to the wealth and prosperity of the colonists in the New World as he described the changing nature of economics in the Old World. To Adam Smith, the colonists provided a perfect example of the character and structure of a prosperous economic system. The economic success of the colonies was not limited, however, to textbook study. The New World prosperity contrasted sharply with little economic prosperity enjoyed by Europeans. Because of the trade and commerce between the colonies and the Old World, the New World's success had dramatic and positive effects on the economies of all nations that did business with the colonies. Many factors contributed to the colonists' prosperity, in Smith's view, such as the absence of arbitrary and self-absorbed governments and the absence of ancient land laws that inhibited growth and innovation. Yet, the overall picture created by Adam Smith's description is of a shining "city on a hill," inhabited by bold, hard-working, but peaceful, inhabitants. The contrast between Smith's description of life in the Old World, archaic and warlike, and life in the New World, industrious and peaceful, is striking.

Smith's ideal of an economic system was based on individual freedom and initiative and the diffusion of wealth and economic power. This was a dramatic contrast with the concentration of wealth and power in the control of European rulers, their monopolist manufacturer friends, and Europe's ancient landed aristocracy. Democratic principles arose naturally from America's democratic capitalist economic system. England's attempt to regain control of America's wealth and to reassert political control in the 1760s was met by immediate and popular resistance.

THE POLITICAL SEPARATION FROM THE OLD WORLD

Independence had been only a remote and radical option in 1760. America did not seek independence but was driven to it. America's walk to independence was slow and gradual. The path chosen by our founding fathers was directed by the options presented to the colonists by Parliament.

From the beginning of America's settlement, the colonists had been allowed a meaningful political independence and significant economic freedom because of the distance to the New World and the wild, uncivilized land that was settled. As America became more prosperous, the colonies became more valuable to the British Empire. At the same time, the colonists were developing a distinct personality and culture. The ancestors of the Virginia cavaliers and the New England Puritans had fought in England, but their descendants were more American than British. Common cultural ties and economic interests had developed among the colonies. The British could sense that the colonies were becoming independent, even though political independence had not yet been considered.

The British needed to develop interdependence with the American colonies. Rather than cultivate a better and more flexible relationship with them, Parliament decided to try to legislate more control. Between 1760 and 1765, Parliament attempted to restrict trade between the colonies and other nations. The colonists were ready to compete economically in world markets. Britain wanted the colonists to trade only with Britain or other colonies under British control.

At the same time, Parliament attempted to regain control of the colonial legislatures. By charter, the colonies had operated independently from the time of the first settlements. Especially in New England, the colonists had legislated democratically, without interference, under valid constitutions and charters that had been issued by the kings of England during the Seventeenth Century. Parliament's attempt to veto colonial legislation was not authorized in those charters and constitutions.

The intensity of colonial resistance escalated when Parliament passed the Stamp Act and the Quartering Act in 1765. The Stamp Act was a tax on all printed matter. The Quartering Act required the colonists to house and pay for British soldiers that remained in America after the French and Indian War. The British complained about the colonists' ingratitude. From the British view, they were defending the Americans but the Americans refused to pay for their own defense.

The colonists had a different point of view. Another war between England and France, this time spread across the Atlantic to the New World, was finally over. The colonists felt that the soldiers were kept in America to spy on them and to maintain control. The fact that the colonists were asked to pay for the intrusion, without their consent, was not only an insult, but also illegal.

Tracts and pamphlets began to appear in the colonies, especially New England, dissenting from the Stamp Act and the Quartering Act. The colonists were not complaining about the insult nor were the colonists discussing independence. The colonists were becoming very interested in English constitutional law. The constitutional authority of Parliament was being questioned.

The political response to the Stamp Act and the Quartering Act was a colonial boycott of all British goods. Parliament's economic policy had backfired. British merchants appealed to Parliament to repeal the Stamp Act, which they did.

Most Americans believe that the American war for independence was only about economics. In 1765, Parliament made the same mistake. In the same session that repealed the Stamp Act, Parliament passed the Declaratory Act. The Declaratory Act was not about economics, but about who wielded political power in the colonies. Disregarding colonial charters and constitutions, Parliament declared that it had the authority to pass any law in the colonies that it wanted. The political issue was no longer simply economics. Parliament had claimed unlimited jurisdiction over the colonies. The colonists considered the Declaratory Act unconstitutional and a usurpation of authority.

Parliament had created a constitutional crisis. The Stuart kings had used the authority to establish the colonies by charter during the early 1600s. The contractual relationship was between the king and the people living within the colonies. Parliament became the political sovereign in England in 1689. In 1765, the political sovereign, Parliament, attempted to govern colonies though it had no agreement with them.

Rather than negotiate this constitutional dilemma, Parliament simply tried to seize control and force its will on the colonies. In 1767, Lord Townshend, the Chancellor of the Exchequer, levied a series of direct taxes. Enforcement of the taxes was carried out in the Customs House of Boston. The intellectual discourse carried on by political activists and lawyers had become reality to the merchants and people of Boston. Tax collectors levied taxes, seized property and convicted merchants without trials. Appeals were ignored by the local magistrates appointed by the king.

What began as a constitutional discussion about authority had expanded to a constitutional discussion about criminal procedure. The colonists had been seeking to preserve their rights as Englishmen. Parliament was not interested in justice nor concerned with English constitutional law and its application to Bostonians. Parliament was only interested in punishing Boston and demonstrating its imperial authority throughout the empire.

The Bostonians refused to submit. The Massachusetts legislature responded by distributing the Circular Letter throughout the colonies. The Circular Letter was both an appeal for solidarity among the colonists and a discussion of "rights." The era of civil disobedience was at hand.

Parliament dissolved the Massachusetts legislature and sent troops to Boston. In March 1770, a demonstration in north Boston was interrupted by gunfire. Reports that citizens of Boston had been killed spread quickly through the colonies. The Boston Massacre galvanized the colonists, from north to south, and gave them a new goal—complete independence.

Parliament repealed the Townshend Acts because, like the Stamp Act, they were a failure. Still, it continued its attempt to control the colonies by economic policies. The tea tax was not repealed, and it was not particularly economically devastating. The tea tax was, however, unconstitutional. The colonists and Parliament both understood the significance of the tea tax. The purpose of the tea tax was to maintain control.

In 1773, 1700 chests of tea were shipped to the colonies. The tea tax would be effective when the tea was unloaded. The first ships were turned away, but the governor of Massachusetts would not allow one ship to leave. On December 16, a band of colonists threw the tea into the harbor.

Parliament was incensed by the Boston Tea Party and retaliated against the insurrection in Boston. The Intolerable Acts, which included the Boston Port Act, was punitive legislation enacted to punish the people of Boston for their civil disobedience. The city of Boston was under siege. The rest of the colonies, which were never completely sympathetic to the stubbornness and legalistic arguments of the Puritans in New England, were suddenly supportive. They began sending financial aid and encouragement to the New Englanders.

Parliament's actions had united the colonies in their opposition to injustice and in support of the natural rights of men. The colonists met together for the first time at the First Continental Congress in Philadelphia in 1774. Congress had condemned the acts of the British since 1763, promoted a boycott of all British goods, and issued a declaration establishing their rights on the natural rights of men; not just their rights as Englishmen. The Massachusetts delegation had won the political battle. Each individual's God-given rights were recognized as superior to the privileges granted by Parliament.

The British declared martial law. British troops marched to Lexington and Concord and the fighting began in April 1775. In May 1775, the Second Continental Congress was convened in Philadelphia and George Washington was put in charge of a continental army. The British attacked with full force. The war was going badly for the colonists. Resistance appeared futile and foolhardy.

The colonists did not believe they could win the war. One more attempt was made for reconciliation. The Olive Branch Petition was drafted and delivered to London personally by a delegation led by Benjamin Franklin; the king refused to see him. At the same time, the colonists drafted the "Declaration of Causes and Necessity of Taking Up Arms."

England had not only attacked the colonies, they had also isolated the colonies from the rest of the world. While reaching out to England, the colonists were also reaching out for support under international law.

Parliament delivered its answer to the "Olive Branch Petition" on December 22, 1775. It passed the Prohibitary Act declaring the colonies in rebellion and an alien nation. If any nation gave aid or even traded with America, that nation was at war with Britain. On January 1, 1776, the British attacked and burned Norfolk, Virginia to the ground.

The American colonists were forced to either surrender or set up new governments. They could choose to submit to illegitimate authority or declare independence and convince the world that the establishment of a new nation was their only just alternative to submission to an unjust, illegitimate tyrant. In May 1776, Congress advised the colonists to set up new governments. Virginia went first, on June 12, 1776. On June 7, 1776, Richard Henry Lee of Virginia had introduced a resolution in Congress calling for a declaration of independence, which would allow other nations, under international law, to extend formal recognition and military support. Congress formed a committee to draft the Declaration of Independence. The last paragraph of the Declaration is as follows:

> We, therefore, the representatives of the United States of America, in General Congress assembled, appealing to the Supreme Judge of the world for the rectitude of our intentions, do, in the name, and by authority of the good people of these colonies, solemnly publish and declare, that these United Colonies are, and of right ought to be, FREE and INDEPEN-DENT STATES, that they are absolved from all allegiance, to the British crown, and that all political connexion between them and the state of Great Britain is, and ought to be totally dissolved.

The charters and constitutions of the colonies, which had established the terms and conditions of the relations between the colonies and England, had been breached. Accordingly, all agreements were declared terminated by America, and the new nation of the United States of America had begun.

More significant than the legal maneuver used by the delegates to the Second Continental Congress to justify independence was the ultimate authority invoked by the drafters of the Declaration of Independence to judge the legality of their argument. The reference to the Supreme Judge, by appeal, rather than to the judgment of the nations, is profoundly significant. The theory, as was much of the theory of the Declaration of Independence, can be directly traced to John Locke.

Locke's conclusion and major point in his second treatise was his justification for revolution by people who are subject to a tyrannical ruler. Locke said that a tyrannical ruler, defined as authority refusing to be bound by the rule of law, is also not capable of dispensing justice. The dilemma for such people is whether to submit to slavery or to refuse to be bound by the tyrant. To Locke, the Scriptural answer could not be known for sure.

Locke based his choice between two Scriptural options. He saw two primary Biblical references to God as the Supreme Judge. In Genesis 18:25, Abraham said to the Lord, "Shall not the Judge of all the earth deal justly?" In Judges 11:27, Jeptha appealed to God, stating, "May the Lord, the Judge, judge today between the sons of Israel and the sons of Ammon."

Locke concluded his discussion of political theory in Book Two of the *Two Treatises of Government* by basing the need and justification for revolution on the account of Jeptha, specifically discussing the Biblical text as the sole basis for resolving the dilemma of people who are subject to a tyrannical ruler. God's ultimate judgment would be revealed through history.

Locke's conclusion and terminology provided the philosophical and legal basis for the appeal to the Supreme Judge in the Declaration of Independence. The delegates were troubled by the prospect of war based on their refusal to submit to the illegitimate authority of the king and of Parliament. The dilemma of the delegates was the same faced by Locke and that we face today. Does Romans 13:1 require that an unjust ruler be obeyed? Or does Galatians 5 mandate that a tyrant be disobeyed? The discussion of these Scriptural texts was extensive in Philadelphia in 1776. The view of Samuel Adams and like-minded Christian delegates prevailed. Appealing to the Supreme Judge, knowing that only history would verify their decision, the delegates unanimously voted for independence.

By all historical accounts, America's first 200 years were the most prosperous and blessed of any nation in all of history.

RESTORATION OF THE SOVEREIGN

On July 2, 1776, the vote was taken for independence and it was unan-

imously approved to declare independence from England, the most powerful nation in the world. In the room at Independence Hall in Philadelphia,
56 delegates signed the Declaration of Independence. The British captured
five signers and charged them as traitors, torturing them before they died.
Nine others fought and died from wounds or handicaps of war. Others lost
their homes and families. They had been successful, educated men who
pledged their lives, fortunes and sacred honor for principles and a cause that
is neither understood nor contemplated by today's cynical recipients of the
benefits of their sacrifice.

Samuel Adams, the leader of the Massachusetts delegation, expressed
the significance of the Declaration of Independence. He was the son of a
brewer, who had been converted to Christianity by George Whitefeld when
revival came to Harvard College in the 1730s. Sam Adams was not motivated by economics or business. His Massachusetts neighbors had already
suffered because of the conflict. He had been unyielding when confronted
with encroachments by the British upon the jurisdiction of the Massachusetts legislature and that of the Congregational Church.

The Puritans had left England because of conflicts with the Anglican
Church and had prospered in New England. They could have tolerated the
imposition of small taxes economically. But they refused to compromise on
the greater principle that affected their freedom to organize their community around the teachings of Puritan clergymen. It was New England's resistance, centered in Boston, led by Sam Adams, that caused the events culminating in the vote for independence. To the British, Sam Adams had almost
single-handedly driven the colonies to independence.

It was symbolic, then, that after the vote for independence, Sam Adams
would speak for the new nation. At a time when the colonists had declared
independence from the most powerful nation on earth and had, in all proba-
bility, agreed to their own execution for treason, he said, "On this day we
have restored the Sovereign, to whom alone men ought to be obedient. He
reigns in heaven and...from the rising to the setting sun, may His Kingdom
come."

Our nation's capitol is filled with monuments and inscriptions which
declare and symbolize the testimony of the faith of our founding fathers. On
June 27, 1962, in response to the Supreme Court decision of Engle v. Vitale
which declared school prayer unconstitutional, Robert C. Byrd, Democratic
Senator from West Virginia delivered the following message to Congress:

> Inasmuch as our greatest leaders have shown no doubt
> about God's proper place in the American birthright, can we, in

our day, dare do less?

In no other place in the United States are there so many, and such varied official evidences of deep and abiding faith in God on the part of Government as there are in Washington.

Every session of the House and the Senate begins with prayer. Each house has its own chaplain.

The Eighty-third Congress set aside a small room in the Capitol, just off the rotunda, for the private prayer and meditation of members of Congress. The room is always open when Congress is in session, but it is not open to the public. The room's focal point is a stained glass window showing George Washington kneeling in prayer. Behind him is etched these words from Psalm 16:1: "Preserve me, O God, for in Thee do I put my trust."

Inside the rotunda is a picture of the Pilgrims about to embark from Holland on the sister ship of the Mayflower, the Speedwell. The ship's revered chaplain, Brewster, who later joined the Mayflower, has open on his lap the Bible. Very clear are the words, "the New Testament according to our Lord and Savior, Jesus Christ." On the sail is the motto of the Pilgrims, "In God We Trust, God With Us."

The phrase, "In God We Trust," appears opposite the President of the Senate, who is the Vice-President of the United States. The same phrase, in large words inscribed in the marble, backdrops the Speaker of the House of Representatives.

Above the head of the Chief Justice of the Supreme Court are the Ten Commandments, with the great American eagle protecting them. Moses is included among the great law givers in Herman A. MacNeil's marble sculpture group on the east front. The crier who opens each session closes with the words, "God save the United States and this Honorable Court."

Engraved on the metal on the top of the Washington Monument are the words: "Praise be to God." Lining the walls of the stairwell are such biblical phrases as "Search the Scriptures," "Holiness to the Lord," "Train up a child in the way he should go, and when he is old he will not depart from it."

Numerous quotations from Scripture can be found within its [the Library of Congress] walls. One reminds each American of his responsibility to his Maker: "What doth the Lord require of thee, but to do justly and love mercy and walk humbly with thy God" (Micah 6:8).

Another in the lawmaker's library preserves the Psalmist's acknowledgment that all nature reflects the order and beauty of the Creator, "The heavens declare the glory of God, and the firmament showeth His handiwork" (Psalm 19:1). And still another reference: "The light shineth in darkness, and the darkness comprehendeth it not" (John 1:5).

Millions have stood in the Lincoln Memorial and gazed up at the statue of the great Abraham Lincoln. The sculptor who chiseled the features of Lincoln in granite all but seems to make Lincoln speak his own words inscribed into the walls.

"...That this Nation, under God, shall have a new birth of freedom, and that government of the people, by the people, for the people, shall not perish from the earth."

At the opposite end, on the north wall, his Second Inaugural Address alludes to "God," the "Bible," "providence," "the Almighty," and "divine attributes."

It then continues:

As was said 3000 years ago, so it still must be said, "The judgments of the Lord are true and righteous altogether."

On the south banks of Washington's Tidal Basin, Thomas Jefferson still speaks:

"God who gave us life gave us liberty. Can the liberties of a nation be secure when we have removed a conviction that these liberties are the gift of God? Indeed I tremble for my country when I reflect that God is just, that his justice cannot sleep forever."

[These words of Jefferson are] a forceful and explicit warning that to remove God from this country will destroy it.

America's historical link to Biblical Christianity is beyond challenge.

AMERICA AS A SYMBOL

The declarations and symbols that testify to the faith of the nation are no less significant than the declarations and symbols which individual believers employ to testify to our own faith in God. Monuments, inscriptions and symbols testify to our purpose. They are part of and incorporated into the demonstration of who we are by our example. We continue to demonstrate our example as individuals and as a nation. It is America's uniqueness as a nation that makes this demonstration of standards of truth, standards of justice, standards of virtue, the blessings of liberty, and devotion to God, by individuals important. Just as an economic system that promotes competition and entrepreneurship is more productive than one based on slavery or feudalism, a political system that promotes liberty and freedom over coercion and centralized command results in a stronger and more vibrant people. Liberty and freedom also allow a people to increase in their commitment and devotion to God because of their own free will. Genuine spiritual revival, whether experienced individually or on a mass scale, is beyond centralized, institutional command.

America is the political demonstration of the New Covenant theology of the Reformation. We relinquish our vision of our unique heritage when we consider ourselves one of many democratic or constitutional nations. We are, rather, in the words of G. K. Chesterton, the "only nation founded on a creed."

The Declaration of Independence is not just a legal document establishing a new nation. The Declaration of Independence is also a theological document, and is perhaps the best statement of natural law, based on Biblical truth, ever written. As a nation, America is unique in its history and in its founding principles of law, as it is the only nation founded on the principles of religious freedom and limited government, gleaned by Locke and Jefferson from the theology of Luther and Calvin.

The uniqueness of America makes America a symbol. And it makes each American a demonstration of the founding principles. America's leadership in the world cannot be inconsistent with the character of the nation and its people. America is not a symbol of police power, Robber Baron individualism, or of individuals exercising their autonomy to define their own existence. America is not a symbol of economic power nor is it a symbol of political or military power. America, and its people, are symbols of the "blessings of liberty" resulting from a commitment to each individual's vertical relationship with God and each individual's horizontal respect for the rights of others. The nature and source of our blessings are not always recognized. But America is still the "city upon a hill" to the rest of the world.

AMERICA AS A STANDARD

America is more than a symbol of the blessings of liberty. America is the standard around which opponents of tyranny have rallied and continue to honor as the symbol of hope for peoples still oppressed throughout the world.

At the core of God's covenant with Israel and the new covenant of the Gospel is to trust God and be faithful to His principles and instructions. Individual Christians have a duty to seek the truth and to demonstrate that truth in their lives. Because of the unique nature of America established by the Declaration of Independence, our national character and will are shaped by the individual choices of the people. Legally, political sovereignty in America resides with the people. America's mandate and purpose cannot conflict with the promises of our founding fathers.

We hold these truths to be self-evident. That all men are

created equal, and are endowed by their Creator with certain inalienable rights, that among these are life, liberty and the pursuit of happiness.

The right to liberty formed the core of the Declaration of Independence and the war for independence with England. It was for liberty that they pledged their lives, fortunes and sacred honor. The historical symbol of liberty was the Liberty Bell, upon which is inscribed the words from Leviticus 25:10, "Proclaim liberty throughout the land."

In Massachusetts, where the resistance began by opposition to the Stamp Act, the members of the Boston Tea Party carried the Liberty Tree Flag of the Sons of Liberty upon which was written "Liberty Tree" and "Appeal to God."

The written text upon which the founding fathers' definition of liberty rested was Galatians 5:1: "It was for freedom that Christ set us free, therefore, keep standing firm and do not be subject again to a yoke of slavery."

As a nation, America has been guided by the words of Isaiah 61. "The Spirit of the Lord God is upon me...to proclaim liberty to the captives and the opening of the prison to them that are bound." As recently as the inauguration of President Kennedy, we were exhorted to, "undo the heavy burdens and let the oppressed go free."

Liberty is a right as between each other but, more so, liberty is a gift from God. Like the colonists, when liberty is threatened, we must, in accordance with the principles of Calvin, Rutherford and Locke, appeal to the law for justice. If tyranny reigns, rather than the rule of law, we must appeal to God for justice. The signers of the Declaration affirmed that "for the support of this Declaration, with a firm reliance on the protection of DIVINE PROVIDENCE," and appealed "to the SUPREME JUDGE of the world for the rectitude of our intentions." Samuel Adams sealed the vote for independence with his words, "On this day we have restored the Sovereign, to whom alone men ought to be obedient."

Defense of liberty and opposition to tyranny are different perspectives of the same principle. America not only symbolizes the fruit of a nation blessed with liberty, it is also a symbol of the continuous defense of liberty and opposition to tyranny. Twice in the Twentieth Century, America rescued humanity from tyranny. Winston Churchill once declared to Adolf Hitler, "We will not truce or parlay with you or your gristly gang who work your wicked will. You may do your worst and we will do our best."

America came to the assistance of England and western Europe, liberating them from Hitler's tyranny and restoring liberty to most of Europe.

The rest of Europe was later liberated, in part, by the insistence of President Ronald Reagan that the Soviet Union was an "evil empire," and not simply a political movement and rival that could be appeased by appealing to the better intentions of its leaders. To Lech Walesa, and to others who stood firm against the "evil empire" from the other side of the Iron Curtain, America had to remain steadfast and free because America is the world's last hope for freedom. To millions of others who endured life behind the Iron Curtain, it was President Reagan's steadfast opposition to the "evil empire" that stayed the Soviet military when the people of Poland confronted tyranny.

America must be clear and unambiguous in its opposition to tyranny. As the main proponent of self-government in the world, America must send a clear message to the people of the world that we will not support or do business with tyrants. While Americans need to do a better job of teaching and demonstrating self-government to its own people, so must Christians worldwide teach self-government and the Christian principles that form its basis to others. Each nation, and the people of each nation, must take responsibility and be accountable for its own choices when exercising self-government.

America's defense of liberty and opposition to tyranny must return to its evangelistic roots. To "proclaim liberty" and "set the captives free" requires an action beyond symbolism. America's "shining city on a hill" may be inspirational to oppressed peoples throughout the world, but it will remain an unreachable dream if America supports the tyrants who oppress or looks the other way when people who rally to America's standard of liberty are put down.

When the colonists first came to the "New World," they were seeking opportunities unavailable in the Old World. But they also sought to fulfill the Great Commission. The colonies flourished and were blessed for 150 years until independence was achieved. For the next 150 years, America continued to flourish and be blessed until it became the most powerful nation in the world. The symbol of liberty and the shining city on the hill had become the most powerful nation in the world. To what ends were these blessings granted?

America has not remained faithful to its original promise. America has forgotten its Sovereign. Americans have not vigilantly defended self-government from the encroaching Leviathan state. Americans have forgotten that the principles of liberty were built on the principles of Christianity. Americans weakly decline to oppose heresy, both religious and political, in the false hope that tolerance of evil can coexist with continued prosperity and blessings. American Christians' apathy at home is reflected in her reluctance to offend abroad. America will vigorously defend its national interests and expand its markets economically, but the Great Commission is no longer acceptable politically in a multi-cultural world.

America must return to faithfulness to God and fulfill its original promise. The restoration of America depends on nothing else. The principles upon which this nation was founded have not been legally changed.

Liberty is still a right between individuals and a gift from God. The promises made by the founding fathers in establishing a new government have never been rescinded by the people, and the people still hold political sovereignty, able to change the nature and form of their government. Divine law has not changed. God is still sovereign. And America is still the symbol of liberty and the city on a hill to the rest of the world.

The original mandate, to proclaim liberty to the captives and throughout the land, is not finished. Americans must recognize and confront the tyranny they have tolerated because of the lack of attention by Christians. Christians are responsible for the support and the continued existence of self-government. If Christians are vigilant in challenging the heresies and the tyrants that will always be present, the tyrants need not be victorious.

◆ ◆ ◆

"Observe good faith and justice toward all nations. Cultivate peace and harmony with all. Religion and morality enjoin this conduct; and can it be that good policy does not equally enjoin it? It will be worthy of a free, enlightened, and at no distant period, a great nation, to give to mankind the magnanimous and too novel example of a people always guided by an exalted justice and benevolence. Who can doubt that in the course of time and things the fruits of such a plan would richly repay any temporary advantages which might be lost by a steady adherence to it? Can it be that Providence has not connected the permanent felicity of a nation with its virtues? The experiment, at least, is recommended by every sentiment which ennobles human nature. Alas! is it rendered impossible by its vices?"

President George Washington,
Farewell Address (1796)

TABLE OF CASES

Civil Rights Cases, 109 U.S. 3 (1883)

Cooper v. Aaron, 358 U.S. 1 (1958)

Dartmouth College v. Woodward, 17 U.S. (4 Wheat.) 518 (1819)

Day-Brite Lighting, Inc. v. Missouri, 342 U.S. 421 (1952)

Dred Scott v. Sandford, 60 U.S. (How.) 393 (1857)

Eastman Kodak Co. v. Image Technical Services, Inc., 504 U.S. 451 (1992)

Eisenstadt v. Baird, 405 U.S. 438 (1972)

Employment Division, Dept. of Human Res. v. Smith, 494 U.S. 872 (1990)

Engel v. Vitale, 370 U.S. 421 (1962)

Epperson v. Arkansas, 393 U.S. 97 (1988)

Everson v. Board of Education, 330 U.S. 1 (1947)

Ferguson v. Skrupa, 372 U.S. 726 (1963)

Flast v. Cohen, 392 U.S. 83, 88 (1968)

Fletcher v. Peck, 10 U.S. (6 Cranch.) 87 (1810)

Frontiero v. Richardson, 411 U.S. 677 (1973)

Gibbons v. Ogden, 22 U.S. (9 Wheat.) 1 (1824)

Gillette v. United States, 401 U.S. 437 (1971)

Griswold v. Connecticut, 381 U.S. 479 (1965)

Grutter v. Bollinger, 123 S. Ct. 2325 (2003)

Helvering v. Davis, 301 U.S. 619 (1937)

Holden v. Hardy, 169 U.S. 366 (1898)

Hoyt v. Florida, 368 U.S. 57 (1961)

Jones v. Alfred H. Mayer Co., 392 U.S. 409 (1968)

King v. John Hampden, 1 Hargrave's State Trails 506 (1638)

Lee v. Weisman, 505 U.S. 577 (1992)

LeVake v. Independent School District No. 656, et al., 625 N.W.2d 502 (Minn. Ct. App. 2001), rev. denied, (Minn. 2001)

Lochner v. New York, 198 U.S. 45 (1905)

Mapp v. Ohio, 367 U.S. 643 (1961)

Marbury v. Madison, 5 U.S. (1 Cranch.) 137 (1803)

McCollum v. Board of Education, 330 U.S. 205 (1948)

McCulloch v. Maryland, 17 U.S. (4 Wheat.) 316 (1819)

Meyer v. Nebraska, 262 U.S. 390 (1923)

Michael M. v. Superior Court of Sonoma County, 450 U.S. 464 (1981)

Mitchell v. Reynolds, 24 Eng. Rep. 347 (Ch. 1711)

Mugler v. Kansas, 123 U.S. 623 (1887)

Muller v. Oregon, 208 U.S. 412 (1908)

Munn v. Illinois, 94 U.S. 113 (1877)

National Labor Relations Board v. Jones & Laughlin Steel Corporation, 301 U.S. 1 (1937)

Nebbia v. New York, 291 U.S. 502 (1934)

New State Ice Co. v. Liebmann, 285 U.S. 251 (1932)

Norwich Gaslight Co. v. Norwich City Gas Co., 25 Conn. 19 (1836)

Ogden v. Saunders, 25 U.S. (12 Wheat.) 213 (1827)

Osborn v. Bank of the United States, 22 U.S. (9 Wheat.) 738 (1824)

Pierce v. Society of Sisters, 268 U.S. 510 (1925)

Planned Parenthood of Central Mo. v. Danforth, 428 U.S. 52 (1976)

Plessy v. Ferguson, 163 U.S. 537 (1896)

Poe v. Ullman, 367 U.S. 497 (1961)

Powell v. Pennsylvania, 127 U.S. 678 (1888)

Reed v. Reed, 404 U.S. 71 (1971)

Regents of Univ. of Cal. v. Bakke, 438 U.S. 265 (1978)

Roe v. Wade, 410 U.S. 113 (1973)

Romer v. Evans, 517 U.S. 620 (1996)

Ross v. Bernhard, 396 U.S. 531 (1970)

Rostker v. Goldberg, 453 U.S. 57 (1981)

Skinner v. Oklahoma, 316 U.S. 535 (1942)

Standard Oil Co. of New Jersey v. United States, 221 U.S. 1 (1911)

Steward Machine Co. v. Davis, 301 U.S. 548 (1937)

Stone v. Mississippi, 101 U.S. 814 (1880)

Terret v. Taylor, 13 U.S. (9 Cr.) 43 (1814)

The Antelope, 23 U.S. (10 Wheat.) 66 (1825)

The Rector, etc. of Holy Trinity Church v. United States, 143 U.S. 457 (1892)

The Ship Money Case (1638)

The Slaughter-House Cases, 83 U.S. (16 Wall.) 36 (1873)

Torcaso v. Watkins, 367 U.S. 488 (1961)

Tull v. United States, 481 U.S. 412 (1987)

United States v. Butler, 297 U.S. 1 (1936)

United States v. Carolene Products, Co., 304 U.S. 144 (1938)

United States v. Darby, 312 U.S. 100 (1941)

United States v. Dege, 364 U.S. 51 (1960)

United States v. Joint Traffic Association, 171 U.S. 505 (1898)

United States v. Lopez, 514 U.S. 549 (1995)

United States v. Seeger, 380 U.S. 163 (1965)

United States v. Virginia, 518 U.S. 515 (1996)

Valley Forge Christian College v. Americans United for Separation of Church and State, Inc., 454 U.S. 464 (1982)

West Coast Hotel Co. v. Parrish, 300 U.S. 379 (1937)

West Virginia State Board of Education v. Barnette, 319 U.S. 624 (1943)

Wickard v. Filburn, 317 U.S. 111 (1942)

Wolman v. Walter, 433 U.S. 279 (1977)

Wong Sun v. United States, 371 U.S. 471 (1968)

Yick Wo v. Hopkins, 118 U.S. 356 (1886)

Zorach v. Clausen, 343 U.S. 306 (1952)

SELECTED BIBLIOGRAPHY

The Philosophy of Locke, In Extracts from The Essay Concerning Human Understanding, (Henry Holt and Company 1891)

Eastern & Western History, Thought & Culture 1600 - 1815, by Walter W. Davis, (University Press of America, Inc. 1993)

Defending the Declaration, by Gary T. Amos, Ph.D. (Wolgemuth & Hyatt, Publishers, Inc. 1989)

The Light and the Glory, by Peter Marshall and David Manuel, (Baker Book House Co. 1977)

The Great Legal Philosophies, Edited by Clarence Morris, (University of Pennsylvania Press 1959)

Understanding the Times, by David A. Noebel, Ph.D. (Summit Press 1991)

From Sea to Shining Sea, by Peter Marshall and David Manuel, (Fleming H. Revell Company 1986)

Bulwark of the Republic, by Burton J. Hendrick, (Little Brown and Company 1937)

The Leviathan, by Thomas Hobbes, (Prometheus Books 1988)

Lincoln at Gettysburg, by Garry Wills, (Simon & Schuster 1992)

The Road to Serfdom, by F. H. Hayek, (The University of Chicago Press 1994 edition)

Confusion Twice Confounded, by Joseph H. Brady, (Seaton Hall University Press 1955)

Fundamental Law of American Constitutions, by Fred Baker, (1966)

The Philosophy of Law and Freedom, by M. H. Schuster, (The Christopher Publishing House 1948)

Leviathan and Natural Law, by F. Lyman Windolph, (Princeton University Press 1951)

Midwestern Progressive Politics, by Russell B. Nye, (Michigan State College Press 1951)

The Birth of the Bill of Rights 1776-1791, by Robert Allen Rutland, (The University of North Carolina Press 1955)

Substantive Due Process of Law - A Dichotomy of Sense and Nonsense, by Frank R. Strong, (Carolina Academic Press 1986)

Journal of Christian Jurisprudence, (Regent University 1990)

The Cost of Discipleship, by Dietrich Bonhoeffer, (1937, MacMillan Publishing Company Edition 1963)

The City of God, Saint Augustine, (The Modern Library 1993)

The Wealth of Nations, Adam Smith, (The Modern Library 1994)

"The Federalist Papers," by Alexander Hamilton, John Jay and James Madison, (Washington Square Press 1964)

Democracy in America, Alexis de Tocqueville, (Penguin Group 1956)

Sources of Our Liberties, edited by Richard L. Perry, (William S. Hein & Co., Inc. 1990)

Christianity and the Constitution, by John Eidsmoe, Ph.D. (Baker Book House 1987)

The Oxford Dictionary of American Legal Quotations, by Fred R. Shapiro, (Oxford University Press 1993)

Handbook on Constitutional Law, by John E. Nowak, Ronald D. Rotunda, Jay Nelson Young, (West Publishing Co. 1978)

Handbook of the Law of Antitrust, by Lawrence Anthony Sullivan, (West Publishing Co. 1977)

The Illustrative Cases on Constitutional Law, by James Parker Hall, (West Publishing Co. 1927)

Two Treatises of Government, by John Locke (Cambridge University Press 1960)

Contacting Wayne Holstad

Mr. Holstad frequently speaks on issues concerning the law and liberty. As well, he is qualified to speak on legal issues concerning contract and title law.

To contact Mr. Holstad about questions concerning this book, speaking to your group, participating in a debate or panel, or making a media appearance, please write to Alethos Press LLC at:

Alethos Press LLC
PO Box 600160
St. Paul, MN 55106

For an email inquiry, you may go to http://www.alethospress.com and send a request via email.

On all inquiries for an appearance, be sure to indicate the date, time, location and any honorarium considerations. Please describe the group to which Mr. Holstad would be speaking in terms of type and expected size. As well, if others are to appear on the same program before, during or after Mr. Holstad, please include a roster of confirmed and invited speakers.

Please, no inquiries by telephone.